Step by Step Courseware

MICROSOFT OFFICE USER SPECIALIST

Microsoft® OFFICE

APPROVED COURSEWARE

Microsoft® Access2000

Microsoft Office Application

Expert Skills Student Guide

ActiveEducation™

PUBLISHED BY
Microsoft Press
A Division of Microsoft Corporation
One Microsoft Way
Redmond, Washington 98052-6399

Library of Congress Cataloging-in-Publication Data
Microsoft Access 2000 Step by Step Courseware Expert Skills Student Guide / ActiveEducation.
      p. cm.
   Includes index.
   ISBN 0-7356-0707-9 (4 color) -- ISBN 0-7356-0979-9 (1 color)
   1. Microsoft Access. 2. Database management. I. ActiveEducation (Firm)
QA76.9.D3 M55696 2000
005.75'65--dc21   99-057429

Printed and bound in the United States of America.

1 2 3 4 5 6 7 8 9   WCWC   5 4 3 2 1 0

Distributed in Canada by Penguin Books Canada Limited.

A CIP catalogue record for this book is available from the British Library.

Microsoft Press books are available through booksellers and distributors worldwide. For further information about international editions, contact your local Microsoft Corporation office or contact Microsoft Press International directly at fax (425) 936-7329. Visit our Web site at mspress.microsoft.com.

For ActiveEducation:

Managing Editor: Ron Pronk
Series Editor: Kate Dawson
Project Editor: Sandra L. Knauke
Writer: Curtis Frye
Production/Layout: Craig Wise, Lawrence Coles, Tracey Varnell, Linda Savell
Technical Editors: Nicole French, Jennifer Jordan
Proofreaders: Nicole French, Tracey Varnell, Neal Hyde
Indexer: Craig Wise

For Microsoft Press:

Acquisitions Editor: Susanne M. Forderer
Project Editor: Jenny Moss Benson

Contents

Course Overview

Welcome to the *Step by Step Courseware* series for Microsoft Office 2000 and Microsoft Windows 2000 Professional. This series facilitates classroom learning, letting you develop competence and confidence in using an Office application or operating system software. In completing courses taught with *Step by Step Courseware*, you learn to use the software productively and discover how to make the software work for you. This series addresses core-level and expert-level skills in Microsoft Word 2000, Microsoft Excel 2000, Microsoft Access 2000, Microsoft Outlook 2000, Microsoft FrontPage 2000, and Microsoft Windows 2000 Professional.

The *Step by Step Courseware* series provides:

- A time-tested, integrated approach to learning.
- Task-based, results-oriented learning strategies.
- Exercises based on business scenarios.
- Complete preparation for Microsoft Office User Specialist (MOUS) certification.
- Attractive student guides with full-featured lessons.
- Lessons with accurate, logical, and sequential instructions.
- Comprehensive coverage of skills from the basic to the expert level.
- Review of core-level skills provided in expert-level guides.
- A CD-ROM with practice files.

A Task-Based Approach Using Business Scenarios

The *Step by Step Courseware* series builds on the strengths of the time-tested approach that Microsoft developed and refined for its Step by Step series. Even though the Step by Step series was created for self-paced training, instructors have long used it in the classroom. For the first time, this popular series has been adapted specifically for the classroom environment. By studying with a task-based approach, you learn more than just the features of the software. You learn how to accomplish real-world tasks so that you can immediately increase your productivity using the software application.

The lessons are based on tasks that you might encounter in the everyday work world. This approach allows you to quickly see the relevance of the training. The task-based focus is woven throughout the series, including lesson organization within each unit, lesson titles, and scenarios chosen for practice files.

An Integrated Approach to Training

The *Step by Step Courseware* series distinguishes itself from other series on the market with its consistent delivery and completely integrated approach to learning across a variety of print and online training media. With the addition of the *Step by Step Courseware* series, which supports classroom instruction, the *Step by Step* training suite now provides a flexible and unified training solution.

Print-Based Self-Training in the Step by Step Training Suite

The proven print-based series of stand-alone *Step by Step* books has consistently been the resource that customers choose for developing software skills on their own.

Online Training in the Step by Step Training Suite

For those who prefer online training, the *Step by Step Interactive* products offer highly interactive online training in a simulated work environment, complete with graphics, sound, video, and animation delivered to a single station (self-contained installation), local area network (LAN), or intranet. *Step by Step Interactive* has a network administration module that allows a training manager to track the progress and quiz results for students using the training. For more information, see *mspress.microsoft.com*.

Preparation for Microsoft Office User Specialist (MOUS) Certification

This series has been certified as approved courseware for the Microsoft Office User Specialist certification program. Students who have completed this training are prepared to take the related MOUS exam. By passing the exam for a particular Office application, students demonstrate proficiency in that application to their employers or prospective employers. Exams are offered at participating test centers. For more information, see *www.mous.net*.

A Sound Instructional Foundation

All products in the *Step by Step Courseware* series apply the same instructional strategies, closely adhering to adult instructional techniques and reliable adult learning principles. Lessons in the *Step by Step Courseware* series are presented in a logical, easy-to-follow format, helping you find information quickly and learn as efficiently as possible. To facilitate the learning process, each lesson follows a consistent structure.

Designed for Optimal Learning

The following "Lesson Features" section shows how the colorful and highly visual series design makes it easy for you to see what to read and what to do when practicing new skills.

Lessons break training into easily assimilated sessions. Each lesson is self-contained, and lessons can be completed in sequences other than the one presented in the table of contents. Sample files for the lessons don't depend on completion of other lessons. Sample files within a lesson assume only that you are working sequentially through a complete lesson.

The *Step by Step Courseware* series features:

- **Lesson objectives.** Objectives clearly state the instructional goals for each lesson so that you understand what skills you will master. Each lesson objective is covered in its own section, and each section or topic in the lesson is covered in a consistent way. Lesson objectives preview the lesson structure, helping you grasp key information and prepare for learning skills.

- **Informational text for each topic.** For each objective, the lesson provides easy-to-read, technique-focused information.

- **Hands-on practice.** Numbered steps give detailed, step-by-step instructions to help you learn skills. The steps also show results and screen images to match what you should see on your computer screen. The accompanying CD contains sample files used for each lesson.

- **Full-color illustrations in color student guides.** Illustrated screen images give visual feedback as you work through exercises. The images reinforce key concepts, provide visual clues about the steps, and give you something to check your progress against.

- **MOUS icon.** Each section or sidebar that covers a MOUS certification objective has a MOUS icon in the margin at the beginning of the section. The number of the certification objective is also listed.

- **Tips.** Helpful hints and alternate ways to accomplish tasks are located throughout the lesson text.

- **Important.** If there is something to watch out for or something to avoid, this information is added to the lesson and indicated with this heading.

- **Sidebars.** Sidebars contain parenthetical topics or additional information that you might find interesting.

- **Margin notes** Margin notes provide additional related or background information that adds value to the lesson.

- **Button images in the margin.** When the text instructs you to click a particular button, an image of the button and its label appear in the margin.

- **Lesson Glossary.** Terms with which you might not be familiar are defined in the glossary. Terms in the glossary appear in boldface type within the lesson and are defined upon their first use within lessons.

- **Quick Quiz.** You can use the short-answer Quick Quiz questions to test or reinforce your understanding of key topics within the lesson.

Lesson Features

Lesson objectives clearly state the instructional goals for each lesson so that you under-stand what skills you will master.

Lesson introduction lists the sample files for the lesson and explains any necessary file preparation.

Each topic begins with explanatory information that teaches concepts and techniques.

Important notes state warnings or cautions.

The Microsoft Office User Specialist (MOUS) logo indicates that the section covers a task that will be tested on the certification exam.

Tips provide helpful hints and alternative ways to complete tasks.

Numbered steps provide detailed instructions to guide you through practicing new skills.

Illustrations give you visual feedback as you work through the lesson.

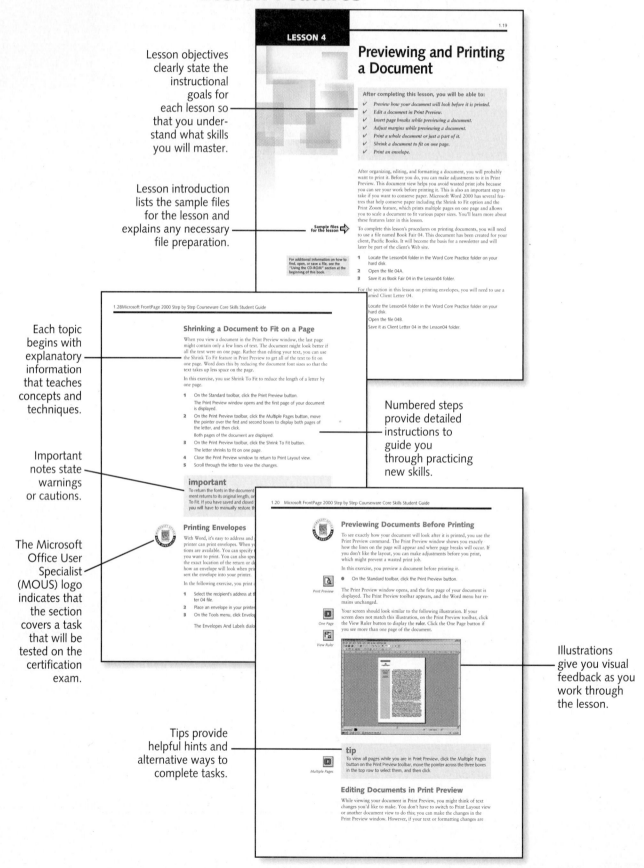

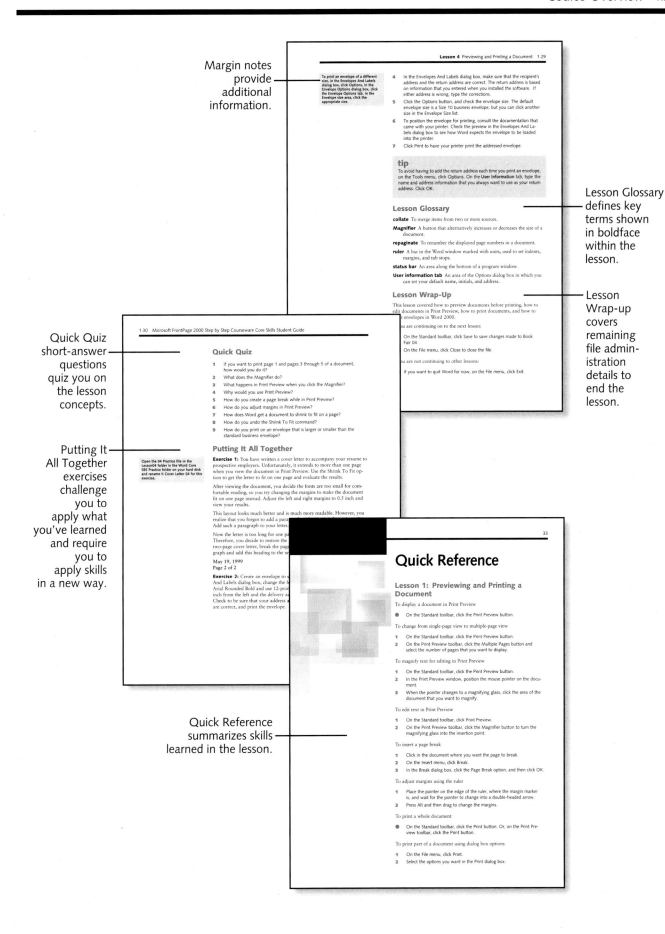

Margin notes provide additional information.

Lesson 4 Previewing and Printing a Document   1.29

To print an envelope of a different size, in the Envelopes And Labels dialog box, click Options. In the Envelope Options dialog box, click the Envelope Options tab. In the Envelope size area, click the appropriate size.

4   In the Envelopes And Labels dialog box, make sure that the recipient's address and the return address are correct. The return address is based on information that you entered when you installed the software. If either address is wrong, type the corrections.

5   Click the Options button, and check the envelope size. The default envelope size is a Size 10 business envelope, but you can click another size in the Envelope Size list.

6   To position the envelope for printing, consult the documentation that came with your printer. Check the preview in the Envelopes And Labels dialog box to see how Word expects the envelope to be loaded into the printer.

7   Click Print to have your printer print the addressed envelope.

tip
To avoid having to add the return address each time you print an envelope, on the Tools menu, click Options. On the **User Information** tab, type the name and address information that you always want to use as your return address. Click OK.

Lesson Glossary

collate   To merge items from two or more sources.

Magnifier   A button that alternatively increases or decreases the size of a document.

repaginate   To renumber the displayed page numbers in a document.

ruler   A bar in the Word window marked with units, used to set indents, margins, and tab stops.

status bar   An area along the bottom of a program window.

User information tab   An area of the Options dialog box in which you can set your default name, initials, and address.

Lesson Wrap-Up

This lesson covered how to preview documents before printing, how to edit documents in Print Preview, how to print documents, and how to t envelopes in Word 2000.

u are continuing on to the next lesson:

■   On the Standard toolbar, click Save to save changes made to Book Fair 04.

■   On the File menu, click Close to close the file.

u are not continuing to other lessons:

■   If you want to quit Word for now, on the File menu, click Exit.

Lesson Glossary defines key terms shown in boldface within the lesson.

Lesson Wrap-up covers remaining file admin-istration details to end the lesson.

1.30   Microsoft FrontPage 2000 Step by Step Courseware Core Skills Student Guide

Quick Quiz short-answer questions quiz you on the lesson concepts.

Quick Quiz

1   If you want to print page 1 and pages 3 through 5 of a document, how would you do it?

2   What does the Magnifier do?

3   What happens in Print Preview when you click the Magnifier?

4   Why would you use Print Preview?

5   How do you create a page break while in Print Preview?

6   How do you adjust margins in Print Preview?

7   How does Word get a document to shrink to fit on a page?

8   How do you undo the Shrink To Fit command?

9   How do you print on an envelope that is larger or smaller than the standard business envelope?

Putting It All Together exercises challenge you to apply what you've learned and require you to apply skills in a new way.

Open the 04 Practice file in the Lesson04 folder in the Word Core SBS Practice folder on your hard disk and rename it Cover Letter 04 for this exercise.

Putting It All Together

Exercise 1: You have written a cover letter to accompany your resume to prospective employers. Unfortunately, it extends to more than one page when you view the document in Print Preview. Use the Shrink To Fit option to get the letter to fit on one page and evaluate the results.

After viewing the document, you decide the fonts are too small for comfortable reading, so you try changing the margins to make the document fit on one page instead. Adjust the left and right margins to 0.5 inch and view your results.

This layout looks much better and is much more readable. However, you realize that you forgot to add a para... Add such a paragraph to your letter.

Now the letter is too long for one pa... Therefore, you decide to restore the... two-page cover letter, break the page... graph and add this heading to the se...

May 19, 1999
Page 2 of 2

Exercise 2: Create an envelope to s... And Labels dialog box, change the f... Arial Rounded Bold and use 12-poin... inch from the left and the delivery a... Check to be sure that your address a... are correct, and print the envelope.

33

Quick Reference summarizes skills learned in the lesson.

Quick Reference

Lesson 1: Previewing and Printing a Document

To display a document in Print Preview

●   On the Standard toolbar, click the Print Preview button.

To change from single-page view to multiple-page view

1   On the Standard toolbar, click the Print Preview button.

2   On the Print Preview toolbar, click the Multiple Pages button and select the number of pages that you want to display.

To magnify text for editing in Print Preview

1   On the Standard toolbar, click the Print Preview button.

2   In the Print Preview window, position the mouse pointer on the document.

3   When the pointer changes to a magnifying glass, click the area of the document that you want to magnify.

To edit text in Print Preview

1   On the Standard toolbar, click Print Preview.

2   On the Print Preview toolbar, click the Magnifier button to turn the magnifying glass into the insertion point.

To insert a page break

1   Click in the document where you want the page to break.

2   On the Insert menu, click Break.

3   In the Break dialog box, click the Page Break option, and then click OK.

To adjust margins using the ruler

1   Place the pointer on the edge of the ruler, where the margin marker is, and wait for the pointer to change into a double-headed arrow.

2   Press Alt and then drag to change the margins.

To print a whole document

●   On the Standard toolbar, click the Print button. Or, on the Print Preview toolbar, click the Print button.

To print part of a document using dialog box options

1   On the File menu, click Print.

2   Select the options you want in the Print dialog box.

■ **Putting It All Together exercises.** These exercises give you another opportunity to practice skills that you learned in the lesson. Completing these exercises helps you to verify whether you understand the lesson, to reinforce your learning, and to retain what you have learned by applying what you have learned in a different way.

■ **Quick Reference.** A complete summary of steps for tasks taught in each lesson is available in the back of the guide. This is often the feature that people find most useful when they return to their workplaces. The expert-level guides include the references from the core-level guides so that you can review or refresh basic and advanced skills on your own whenever necessary.

■ **Index.** Student guides are completely indexed. All glossary terms and application features appear in the index.

Suggestions for Improvements

Microsoft welcomes your feedback on the *Step by Step Courseware* series. Your comments and suggestions will help us to improve future versions of this product. Please send your feedback to SBSCfdbk@microsoft.com.

Support requests for Microsoft products should not be directed to this alias. Please see "Using the CD-ROM" for information on support contacts.

Conventions and Features Used in This Book

This book uses special fonts, symbols, and heading conventions to highlight important information or to call your attention to special steps. For more information about the features available in each lesson, refer to the "Course Overview" section on page vii.

Convention	Meaning
 **Sample files for the lesson**	This icon identifies the section that lists the files that the lesson will use and explains any file preparation that you need to take care of before starting the lesson.
You can switch to the Database window from any other window in Access by pressing F11.	Notes in the margin area are pointers to information provided elsewhere in the workbook or provide brief notes related to the text or procedures.
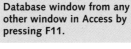	This icon indicates a new or greatly improved feature in this version of the software product and includes a short description of what is new.
AC2000E.2.1	This icon indicates that the section where this icon appears covers a Microsoft Office User Specialist (MOUS) exam objective. The number below the icon is the MOUS objective number. For a complete list of the MOUS objectives, see the "MOUS Objectives" section on page xix.
tip	Tips provide helpful hints or alternative procedures related to particular tasks.
important	Importants provide warnings or cautions that are critical to exercises.
Save	When a toolbar button is referenced in the lesson, the button's picture and label are shown in the margin.
Alt+Tab	A plus sign (+) between two key names means that you must press those keys at the same time. For example, "Press Alt+Tab" means that you hold down the Alt key while you press Tab.
Boldface type	This formatting indicates text that you need to type Or It indicates a glossary entry that is defined at the end of the lesson.

Using the CD-ROM

The CD-ROM included with this student guide contains the practice files that you'll use as you perform the exercises in the book. By using the practice files, you won't waste time creating the samples used in the lessons, and you can concentrate on learning how to use Microsoft Access 2000. With the files and the step-by-step instructions in the lessons, you'll also learn by doing, which is an easy and effective way to acquire and remember new skills.

The CD-ROM also includes a Microsoft Word file called Testbank.doc, which provides multiple-choice and true/false questions that you can use to test your knowledge following the completion of each lesson or the completion of the *Microsoft Access 2000 Step by Step Courseware Expert Skills* course.

System Requirements

Your computer system must meet the following minimum requirements for you to install the practice files from the CD-ROM and to run Microsoft Access 2000.

important

The Access 2000 software is not provided on the companion CD-ROM at the back of this book. This course assumes that you have already purchased and installed Access 2000.

- A personal computer running Microsoft Access 2000 on a Pentium 75-megahertz (MHz) or higher processor with the Microsoft Windows 95 or later operating system with 24 MB of RAM, or the Microsoft Windows NT Workstation version 4.0 operating system with Service Pack 3 and 40 MB of RAM.

- Internet Explorer 4 or later (Lesson 5 only).

- Microsoft Excel 95 or later (Lesson 2 and Lesson 8 only).

- At least 50 MB of available disk space (after installing Access 2000 or Microsoft Office 2000).

- A CD-ROM drive.

- A monitor with VGA or higher resolution (Super VGA recommended; 15-inch monitor or larger recommended).

- A Microsoft mouse, a Microsoft IntelliMouse, or other compatible pointing device.

If You Need to Install or Uninstall the Practice Files

Your instructor might already have installed the practice files before you arrive in class. However, your instructor might ask you to install the practice files on your own at the start of class. Also, if you want to work through any of the exercises in this book on your own at home or at your place of business after class, you will need to first install the practice files.

To install the practice files:

1   Insert the CD-ROM in the CD-ROM drive of your computer.

A menu screen appears.

important

If the menu screen does not appear, start Windows Explorer. In the left pane, locate the icon for your CD-ROM, and click this icon. In the right pane, double-click the file StartCD.

2   Click Install Practice Files, and follow the instructions on the screen.

The recommended options are preselected for you.

3   After the files have been installed, click Exit.

A folder called Access Expert Practice has been created on your hard disk, the practice files have been placed in that folder, and a shortcut to the Microsoft Press Web site has been added to your desktop.

4   Remove the CD-ROM from the CD-ROM drive.

Use the following steps when you want to delete the lesson practice files from your hard disk. Your instructor might ask you to perform these steps at the end of class. Also, you should perform these steps if you have worked through the exercises at home or at your place of business and want to work through the exercises again. Deleting the practice files and then reinstalling them ensures that all files and folders are in their original condition if you decide to work through the exercises again.

To uninstall the practice files:

1   On the Windows taskbar, click the Start button, point to Settings, and then click Control Panel.

2   Double-click the Add/Remove icon.

3   Click Access Expert Practice in the list, and click Add/Remove. (If your computer has Windows 2000 Professional installed, click the Remove or the Change/Remove button.)

4   Click Yes when the confirmation dialog box appears.

Using the Practice Files

Each lesson in this book explains when and how to use any practice files for that lesson. The lessons are built around scenarios that simulate a real work environment, so you can easily apply the skills you learn to your own work. The scenarios in the lessons use the context of the fictitious Lakewood Mountains Resort, a hotel and convention center located in the mountains of California.

The lessons in this book assume that your computer's operating system is set to display two-digit years (00) instead of four-digit years (2000). If your operating system is set to display four-digit years, all Microsoft Office applications will display four-digit years.

Some of the exercises in this book might not work if your operating system is set to display four-digit years. To change the default date format:

1   On the Windows taskbar, click the Start button, point to Settings, and then click Control Panel.

2   Double-click Regional Settings (or Regional Options if you're using Microsoft Windows 2000), and click the Date tab.

3   In the Short Date Style box, modify the format so that it uses two digits for the year ("yy"). (To change the format to four-digit years, modify the format so that it uses four digits ("yyyy").)

4   Click OK to save your changes.

The following is a list of all files and folders used in the lessons.

File Name	Description
Lesson 1	
Lakewood Mountains 01	Database used in Lesson 1.
Lesson 2	
Lakewood Mountains 02	Database used in Lesson 2.
Lesson 3	
Lakewood Mountains 03	Database used in Lesson 3.
LMRsmall.tif	Graphic used in Lesson 3.
Lesson 4	
Lakewood Mountains 04	Database used in Lesson 4.
Lesson 5	
Lakewood Mountains 05	Database used in Lesson 5.
Lesson 6	
Lakewood Mountains 06	Database used in Lesson 6.
Lesson 7	
Lakewood Mountains 07	Database used in Lesson 7.
Lakewood Mountains 07a	Database used in Lesson 7.
Lakewood Mountains 07b	Database used in Lesson 7.
Lakewood Mountains 07c	Database used in Lesson 7.
Lesson 8	
Lakewood Mountains 08	Database used in Lesson 8.
Lakewood Links	Database used in Lesson 8.

Replying to Install Messages

When you work through some lessons, you might see a message indicating that the feature that you are trying to use is not installed. If you see this message, insert the Microsoft Access 2000 CD or Microsoft Office 2000 CD 1 in your CD-ROM drive, and click Yes to install the feature.

Locating and Opening Files

After you (or your instructor) have installed the practice files, all the files you need for this course will be stored in a folder named Access Expert Practice located on your hard disk. To navigate to this folder from within Access and open a database file:

Open

1   On the Database toolbar, click the Open button.

2   In the Open dialog box, click the Look In down arrow, and click the icon for your hard disk.

3   Double-click the Access Expert Practice folder.

4   Double-click the file that you want to open.

All the files for the lessons appear within the Access Expert Practice folder.

On the first page of each lesson, look for the margin icon *Sample files for the lesson*. This icon points to the paragraph that explains which files you will need to work through the lesson exercises.

If You Need Help with the Practice Files

If you have any problems regarding the use of this book's CD-ROM, you should first consult your instructor. If you are using the CD-ROM at home or at your place of business and need additional help with the practice files, see the Microsoft Press Support Web site at *mspress.microsoft.com/support*.

important

Please note that support for the Access 2000 software product itself is not offered through the above Web site. For help using Access 2000, rather than this Microsoft Press book, you can visit *www.microsoft.com/support* or call Access 2000 Technical Support at (425) 635-7070 on weekdays between 6 A.M. and 6 P.M. Pacific Standard Time. Microsoft Product Support does not provide support for this course.

MOUS Objectives

Core Skills

Objective	Activity
AC2000.1.1	Determine appropriate data inputs for your database
AC2000.1.2	Determine appropriate data outputs for your database
AC2000.1.3	Create table structure
AC2000.1.4	Establish table relationships
AC2000.2.1	Use the Office Assistant
AC2000.2.2	Select an object using the Objects bar
AC2000.2.3	Print database objects (tables, forms, reports, queries)
AC2000.2.4	Navigate through records in a table, query, or form
AC2000.2.5	Create a database (using a wizard or in Design view)
AC2000.3.1	Create tables by using the Table Wizard
AC2000.3.2	Set primary keys
AC2000.3.3	Modify field properties
AC2000.3.4	Use multiple data types
AC2000.3.5	Modify tables using Design view
AC2000.3.6	Use the Lookup Wizard
AC2000.3.7	Use the Input Mask Wizard
AC2000.4.1	Create a form with the Form Wizard
AC2000.4.2	Use the control toolbox to add controls
AC2000.4.3	Modify format properties (font, style, font size, color, caption, and so on) of controls
AC2000.4.4	Use form sections (headers, footers, detail)
AC2000.4.5	Use a calculated control on a form
AC2000.5.1	Use the Office Clipboard
AC2000.5.2	Switch between object views
AC2000.5.3	Enter records using a datasheet
AC2000.5.4	Enter records using a form
AC2000.5.5	Delete records from a table
AC2000.5.6	Find a record
AC2000.5.7	Sort records
AC2000.5.8	Apply and remove filters (filter by form and filter by selection)
AC2000.5.9	Specify criteria in a query
AC2000.5.10	Display related records in a subdatasheet
AC2000.5.11	Create a calculated field
AC2000.5.12	Create and modify a multitable select query

Objective	Activity
AC2000.6.1	Establish relationships
AC2000.6.2	Enforce referential integrity
AC2000.7.1	Create a report with the Report Wizard
AC2000.7.2	Preview and print a report
AC2000.7.3	Move and resize a control
AC2000.7.4	Modify format properties (font, style, font size, color, caption, and so on)
AC2000.7.5	Use the control toolbox to add controls
AC2000.7.6	Use report sections (headers, footers, detail)
AC2000.7.7	Use a calculated control in a report
AC2000.8.1	Import data to a new table
AC2000.8.2	Save a table, query, form as a Web page
AC2000.8.3	Add hyperlinks
AC2000.9.1	Print database relationships
AC2000.9.2	Back up and restore a database
AC2000.9.3	Compact and repair a database

Expert Skills

Objective	Activity	Page
AC2000E.1.1	Set validation text	1.12
AC2000E.1.2	Define data validation criteria	1.12
AC2000E.1.3	Modify an input mask	1.8
AC2000E.1.4	Create and modify Lookup fields	1.14
AC2000E.1.5	Optimize data type usage (double, long, int, byte, and so on)	2.28
AC2000E.2.1	Create a form in Design view	3.2
AC2000E.2.2	Insert a graphic on a form	3.14
AC2000E.2.3	Modify control properties	3.16
AC2000E.2.4	Customize form sections (headers, footers, detail)	3.12
AC2000E.2.5	Modify form properties	3.17
AC2000E.2.6	Use the subform control and synchronize forms	3.18
AC2000E.2.7	Create a switchboard	3.23
AC2000E.3.1	Apply filters (filter by form and filter by selection) in a query's recordset	2.6
AC2000E.3.2	Create a totals query	2.7
AC2000E.3.3	Create a parameter query	2.14
AC2000E.3.4	Specify criteria in multiple fields (And vs. Or)	2.2
AC2000E.3.5	Modify query properties (field formats, caption, input masks, and so on)	2.4

Objective	Activity	Page
AC2000E.3.6	Create an action query (update, delete, insert)	2.10
AC2000E.3.7	Optimize queries using indexes	2.28
AC2000E.3.8	Specify join properties for relationships	2.25
AC2000E.4.1	Insert a graphic on a report	4.12
AC2000E.4.2	Modify report properties	4.10
AC2000E.4.3	Create and modify a report in Design view	4.2
AC2000E.4.4	Modify control properties	4.12
AC2000E.4.5	Set section properties	4.4
AC2000E.4.6	Use the subreport control and synchronize reports	4.14, 4.17
AC2000E.5.1	Establish one-to-one relationships	1.17
AC2000E.5.2	Establish many-to-many relationships	2.29
AC2000E.5.3	Set Cascade Update and Cascade Delete options	1.17
AC2000E.6.1	Create hyperlinks	5.2
AC2000E.6.2	Use the group and sort features of data access pages	5.12
AC2000E.6.3	Create a data access page	5.7, 5.8
AC2000E.6.3	Create a data access page	5.7, 5.8
AC2000E.7.1	Set and modify a database password	7.2, 7.4
AC2000E.7.2	Set startup options	7.15
AC2000E.7.3	Use add-ins (Database Splitter, Analyzer, Link Table Manager)	1.4, 7.12, 8.11
AC2000E.7.4	Encrypt and decrypt a database	7.5
AC2000E.7.5	Use simple replication (copy for a mobile user)	7.8
AC2000E.7.6	Run macros using controls	6.6
AC2000E.7.7	Create a macro using the Macro Builder	6.2
AC2000E.7.8	Convert database to a previous version	7.14
AC2000E.8.1	Export database records to Excel	8.7
AC2000E.8.2	Drag tables and queries to Excel	8.9
AC2000E.8.3	Present information as a chart (Microsoft Graph)	8.2
AC2000E.8.4	Link to existing data	8.11

Taking a Microsoft Office User Specialist Certification Test

The Microsoft Office User Specialist (MOUS) program is the only Microsoft-approved certification program designed to measure and validate your skills with the Microsoft Office suite of desktop productivity applications: Microsoft Word, Microsoft Excel, Microsoft PowerPoint, Microsoft Access, and Microsoft Outlook.

By becoming certified, you demonstrate to employers that you have achieved a predictable level of skills in the use of a particular Office application. Certification is often required by employers either as a condition of employment or as a condition of advancement within the company or other organization. The certification examinations are sponsored by Microsoft but administered through Nivo International.

For each Microsoft Office 2000 application, two levels of MOUS tests are currently or will soon be available: core and expert. For a core-level test, you demonstrate your ability to use an application knowledgeably and without assistance in a day-to-day work environment. For an expert-level test, you demonstrate that you have a thorough knowledge of the application and can effectively apply all or most of the features of the application to solve problems and complete tasks found in business.

Preparing to Take an Exam

Unless you're a very experienced user, you'll need to use a test preparation course to prepare to complete the test correctly and within the time allowed. The *Step by Step Courseware* training program is designed to prepare you for either core-level or expert-level knowledge of a particular Microsoft Office application. By the end of this course, you should have a strong knowledge of all exam topics, and with some additional review and practice on your own, you should feel confident in your ability to pass the appropriate exam.

After you decide which exam to take, review the list of objectives for the exam. This list can be found in the "MOUS Objectives" section at the front of the appropriate *Step by Step Courseware* student guide; the list of MOUS objectives for this book begins on page xix. You can also easily identify tasks that are included in the objective list by locating the MOUS logo in the margin of the lessons in this book.

For an expert-level test, you'll need to be able to demonstrate any of the skills from the core-level objective list, too. Expect some of these core-level tasks to appear on the expert-level test. In the *Step by Step Courseware Expert Skills Student Guide*, you'll find the core skills included in the "Quick Reference" section at the back of the book.

You can also familiarize yourself with a live MOUS certification test by downloading and installing a practice MOUS certification test from *www.mous.net*.

To take the MOUS test, first see *www.mous.net* to locate your nearest testing center. Then call the testing center directly to schedule your test. The amount of advance notice you should provide will vary for different testing centers, and it typically depends on the number of computers available at the testing center, the number of other testers who have already been scheduled for the day on which you want to take the test, and the number of times per week that the testing center offers MOUS testing. In general, you should call to schedule your test at least two weeks prior to the date on which you want to take the test.

When you arrive at the testing center, you might be asked for proof of identity. A driver's license or passport is an acceptable form of identification. If you do not have either of these items of documentation, call your testing center and ask what alternative forms of identification will be accepted. If you are retaking a test, bring your MOUS identification number, which will have been given to you when you previously took the test. If you have not prepaid or if your organization has not already arranged to make payment for you, you will need to pay the test-taking fee when you arrive. The current test-taking fee is $50 (U.S.).

Test Format

All MOUS certification tests are live, performance-based tests. There are no multiple-choice, true/false, or short answer questions. Instructions are general: you are told the basic tasks to perform on the computer, but you aren't given any help in figuring out how to perform them. You are not permitted to use reference material other than the application's Help system.

As you complete the tasks stated in a particular test question, the testing software monitors your actions. An example question might be:

> Create a new table named PhoneList that contains fields named FirstName, LastName, Title, DepartmentName, and Extension. Set the Extension field as the primary key. Set the DepartmentName field to display *Marketing* in each new record. Save the table.

The sample tests available from *www.mous.net* give you a clear idea of the type of questions that you will be asked on the actual test.

When the test administrator seats you at a computer, you'll see an online form that you use to enter information about yourself (name, address, and other information required to process your exam results). While you complete the form, the software will generate the test from a master test bank and then prompt you to continue. The first test question will appear in a window. Read the question carefully, and then perform all the tasks stated in the test question. When you have finished completing all tasks for a question, click the Next Question button.

You have 45 to 60 minutes to complete all questions, depending on the test that you are taking. The testing software assesses your results as soon as you complete the test, and the results of the test can be printed by the test administrator so that you will have a record of any tasks that you performed incorrectly. A passing grade is 75 percent or higher. If you pass, you will receive a certificate in the mail within two to four weeks. If you do not pass, you can study and practice the skills that you missed and then schedule to retake the test at a later date.

Tips for Successfully Completing the Test

The following tips and suggestions are the result of feedback received by many individuals who have taken one or more MOUS tests:

- Make sure that you are thoroughly prepared. If you have extensively used the application for which you are being tested, you might feel confident that you are prepared for the test. However, the test might include questions that involve tasks that you rarely or never perform when you use the application at your place of business, at school, or at home. You must be knowledgeable in *all* the MOUS objectives for the test that you will take.

- Read each exam question carefully. An exam question might include several tasks that you are to perform. A partially correct response to a test question is counted as an incorrect response. In the example question on the previous page, you might create the table, set the primary key field, and set the default value, but neglect to save the table. This would count as an incorrect response and would result in a lower test score.

- You are allowed to use the application's Help system, but relying on the Help system too much will slow you down and possibly prevent you from completing the test within the allotted time. Use the Help system only when necessary.

- Keep track of your time. The test does not display the amount of time that you have left, so you need to keep track of the time yourself by monitoring your start time and the required end time on your watch or a clock in the testing center (if there is one). The test program displays the number of items that you have completed along with the total number of test items (for example, "35 of 40 items have been completed"). Use this information to gauge your pace.

- If you skip a question, you cannot return to it later. You should skip a question only if you are certain that you cannot complete the tasks correctly.

- Don't worry if the testing software crashes while you are taking the exam. The test software is set up to handle this situation. Find your test administrator and tell him or her what happened. The administrator will work through the steps required to restart the test. When the test restarts, it will allow you to continue where you left off. You will have the same amount of time remaining to complete the test as you did when the software crashed.

■ As soon as you are finished reading a question and you click in the application window, a condensed version of the instruction is displayed in a corner of the screen. If you are unsure whether you have completed all tasks stated in the test question, click the Instructions button on the test information bar at the bottom of the screen and then reread the question. Close the instruction window when you are finished. Do this as often as necessary to ensure you have read the question correctly and that you have completed all the tasks stated in the question.

If You Do Not Pass the Test

If you do not pass, you can use the assessment printout as a guide to practice the items that you missed. There is no limit to the number of times that you can retake a test; however, you must pay the fee each time that you take the test. When you retake the test, expect to see some of the same test items on the subsequent test; the test software randomly generates the test items from a master test bank before you begin the test. Also expect to see several questions that did not appear on the previous test.

LESSON 1

Customizing Tables

After completing this lesson, you will be able to:

✔ *Create an index.*

✔ *Normalize a table.*

✔ *Set a default data entry value.*

✔ *Create and modify an input mask.*

✔ *Define a data validation rule.*

✔ *Create and modify a Lookup field.*

✔ *Create a relationship.*

A Microsoft Access database is made up of objects that allow you to store, view, and search for data. The most basic object in a database is the **table**, which holds the data in the database and makes it available for viewing or manipulation. After you create tables to store data, you'll often want to customize them to simplify data entry, improve performance, and cut down on data entry mistakes. Access 2000 has a number of features that you can use to enhance tables.

One way to improve the speed with which Access uses a table is to create an **index** of the frequently used fields in that table. When you search or sort the records in a table, Access uses the shorter index instead of examining all the records individually. Although using an index might not result in a noticeable difference with small databases (such as the one used for the exercises in this lesson), an index can save a significant amount of time when you work with large databases.

You can also improve tables by using the Table Analyzer Wizard. This wizard looks at the structure of a table, compares it to the rest of the tables in the database, and makes suggestions about how to improve it. In particular, the Table Analyzer Wizard looks for information that is stored in more than one table. The wizard looks for ways to store that redundant information in a separate table, improving the database's performance.

Access has a variety of ways to make data entry faster and more reliable. Input masks and data validation rules ensure that data entered in a field meet certain criteria, while default values fill in the field with a predetermined value unless a user specifies a different one. For example, you might set a data validation rule that requires a product code to begin with a letter. If a user accidentally enters a product code without a letter at the beginning, Access identifies the error and allows the user to re-enter the data. A **Lookup field** takes these concepts a step further by limiting the user's choices to a value from a predefined list.

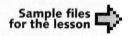

Sample files for the lesson

For additional information about opening the practice file for this lesson, see the "Using the CD-ROM" section at the beginning of this book.

To complete the procedures in this lesson, you will need to use a file named Lakewood Mountains 01 in the Access Expert Practice folder that is located on your hard disk. This database tracks employee orders, names and addresses of vendors, and names of employees at Lakewood Mountains Resort who are authorized to place orders.

Creating an Index

You use queries to extract certain records and fields from tables or to perform actions on the extracted data. Indexing can be used to make queries on large databases run faster. You can create an index at any time after you create the table containing the field that you want to index. Access tabulates information in indexed fields whenever you save tables, add records, or edit records. After these fields are indexed, Access uses the stored information to perform queries or to **sort** query results based on the contents of those fields. A sort reorganizes the contents of fields into a specific order, such as alphabetical or numerical. Indexes should be created only for fields that are frequently queried or sorted. If used inappropriately, indexes can slow data entry and editing.

Access offers three indexing options that you can specify for each field:

Option	Description
No	The field is not indexed. You should only index fields that are used in queries or sorts. Don't index fields that contain only a few different values. If you no longer need a field to be indexed, use the No option to change the Indexed field property.
Yes (Duplicates OK)	The field is indexed, and the same data can be entered in the field for more than one record. For example, an index for a product ID in a table of orders for the month of January would allow multiple entries of the same product ID (so you can order the same product more than once a month).
Yes (No Duplicates)	The field is indexed, and the same data cannot be entered in a field for more than one record. For example, an index for an OrderNumber field would not allow multiple entries of the same order number.

This book uses the Leszynski naming convention, which means that each object name is preceded by a three letter tag such as *tbl, frm, qry,* or *rpt*. The tag is always lowercase, the rest of the words in the name have the initial letter capitalized, and there are no spaces in the object name.

In this exercise, you open the Lakewood Mountains 01 database and set the Indexed property for the EmployeeID field of tblMarketingDepartment to Yes (No Duplicates) so that no two employees can have the same employee ID number.

1   On the Windows taskbar, click the Start button, point to Programs, and then click Microsoft Access.

Access starts, and a Microsoft Access dialog box appears.

2   Verify that the Open An Existing File option is selected, and click OK.

The Open dialog box appears.

3 Click the Look In down arrow, click the icon for your hard disk, and then double-click the Access Expert Practice folder.

The Open dialog box displays a list of files stored in the Access Expert Practice folder.

4 Click Lakewood Mountains 01, and click Open.

The Database window for the Lakewood Mountains 01 database appears.

5 On the Objects bar, click Tables, if necessary.

6 Click tblMarketingDepartment, and click Design on the Database window toolbar.

> You can also double-click the table name to open the table in Design view.

The table appears in Design view. The text *EmployeeID* is selected, meaning that the properties for the EmployeeID field appear in the Field Properties section.

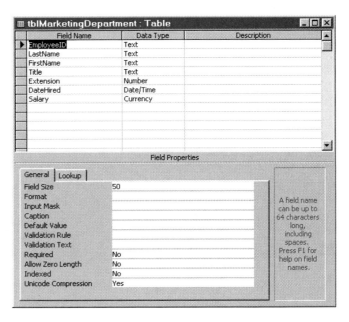

7 In the Field Properties section, click in the Indexed box, click the down arrow that appears, and then click Yes (No Duplicates).

> The Indexed box is set to No by default.

An index that does not allow duplicate employee ID numbers is created for the EmployeeID field.

Close

8 Click the Close button in the top-right corner of tblMarketingDepartment.

An alert box appears, asking if you would like to save changes.

9 Click Yes.

Access saves the changes, and the table closes.

Indexes

tip

You can create and edit multiple-field indexes by using the Indexes button on the Table Design toolbar. In the Indexes dialog box, you can select the fields to be indexed using the down arrow in the blank Field Name cells.

AC2000E.7.3

Normalizing a Table

The most efficient databases do not store the same data in more than one place. For example, consider a database that tracks customers, products, orders, and vendors for a sporting goods store. The most efficient design for the database would be to create four tables: one to list customers, one to list the available products, another to list the vendors supplying the products, and a final table containing individual orders. A less efficient design would be to create three tables: one listing customers, one listing orders, and a third table listing products and the contact information of each product's supplier.

The second design is less efficient because it stores the same vendor contact information in more than one record. The first design allows you to save disk space by referencing the vendor contact information table instead of re-entering the vendor's name and address for every product from that vendor.

Analyzing the tables in a database to eliminate redundant data storage is called **normalization,** and it is a task of the Table Analyzer Wizard. This wizard examines the design of a table and suggests a method to break the data into separate tables. The Table Analyzer Wizard also allows you to design the two new tables yourself.

> You can also tell the wizard that you want to set the primary key yourself.

During the normalization process, the Table Analyzer Wizard selects a **primary key** for each new table. The primary key is a field that contains a unique value for each record. For example, in a table of orders for February, each order would have a unique order number that could be used as the primary key because there would be no duplicate numbers. Another option, using the OrderDate as the primary key, would not work because more than one order could have been placed on the same day.

The Table Analyzer Wizard also gives you the option to create a query, which will look like your original table and will allow forms and reports based on your original table to continue to work. The query extracts information from the tables created during the normalization process. This query will keep the name of the original table but will be stored in the list of queries in the Database window. Queries created during normalization often contain a Lookup field, which the Table Analyzer Wizard inserts to maintain a connection between the tables created by the wizard.

After examining the tables in the Lakewood Mountains 01 database, you decide that tblProducts contains vendor contact information that could be stored more efficiently in a table by itself. In this exercise, you normalize tblProducts.

1   On the Tools menu, point to Analyze, and click Table.

The Table Analyzer Wizard appears.

2   Read the text of the first Table Analyzer Wizard dialog box, and click Next.

The next Table Analyzer Wizard dialog box appears.

You don't have to view the two introductory dialog boxes of the Table Analyzer Wizard. To go straight to the dialog box where you pick the tables to normalize, clear the Show Introductory Pages check box in the third Table Analyzer Wizard dialog box.

3   Read the text of the second Table Analyzer Wizard dialog box, and click Next.

The next Table Analyzer Wizard dialog box appears.

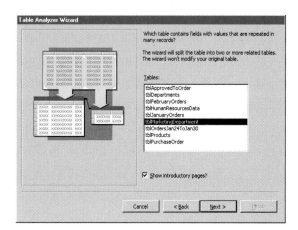

4   Click tblProducts, and click Next.

The Table Analyzer Wizard will normalize tblProducts. The next Table Analyzer Wizard dialog box appears.

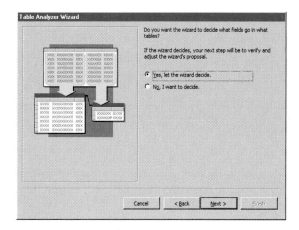

5   Click Next to let the wizard decide how to break up the table.

The next Table Analyzer Wizard dialog box appears, displaying the new tables that the wizard proposes to create based on the information in tblProducts.

The field lists for each table can be resized so that you can see all the field names. Point to the border of the box. When the mouse pointer changes into a double-headed arrow, drag the border to resize the box.

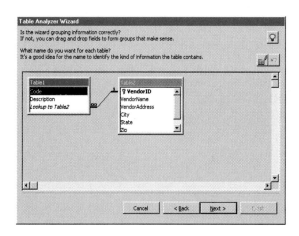

Rename Table

Another way to specify a new name is to double-click the title bar of the table that you want to rename and type the new name.

6 Verify that Table1 is selected, and click the Rename Table button.

The Table Analyzer Wizard dialog box appears with the current name of the table, Table1, already in the Table Name box.

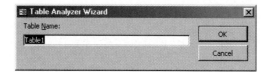

7 Type **tblProductsList**, and click OK.

8 Repeat steps 6 and 7 for Table2, naming it **tblVendors**, and then click Next.

The next Table Analyzer Wizard dialog box appears.

This dialog box looks very similar to the previous dialog box. Check that the dialog box contains the Primary Key button instead of the Rename Table button.

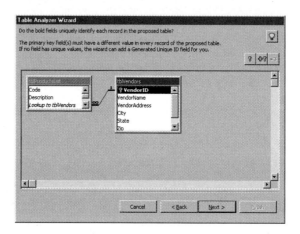

Primary Key

9 In the field list for tblProductsList, click Code, and click the Primary Key button.

A key icon appears in front of *Code* to indicate that the Code field has been selected as the primary key field for tblProductsList.

10 Click Next.

The next Table Analyzer Wizard dialog box appears.

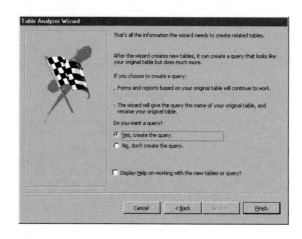

If you leave the Yes, Create The Query option selected, Access creates a query that duplicates the contents of the original table.

11   Click Finish.

The query runs, and an alert box appears, telling you that the query simulates your original table.

12   Click OK.

tblProducts appears as a query that pulls data from both of the new tables and displays it in one datasheet.

The Lookup field extracts data from tblVendors.

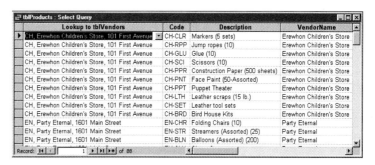

13   Close Access Help, and close the query.

The list of tables in the Database window now includes tblVendors, tblProductsList, and tblProducts_OLD, a copy of the original tblProducts.

Display the list of queries in the Database window, and note that tblProducts is listed as a query, instead of a table, in the Database window.

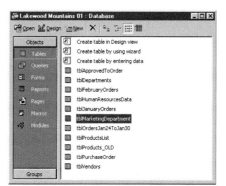

Setting a Default Data Entry Value

Data entry—typing information into database tables—is a time-consuming process, but Access can make it easier to enter data and minimize data entry errors. One way to simplify data entry is by setting a **default value** for a field.

A default value instructs Access to use a designated value in a field unless another value is specified. For example, if the majority of employees hired by your marketing department will be marketing reps, you can enter *Marketing Rep* as the default value for a field that keeps track of your employees' job titles. Once the default value is set, *Marketing Rep* will appear in the job title field each time a new record is created. The default value reduces data entry time because you need to type the job title only for employees who are not marketing reps.

In this exercise, you set *Marketing Rep* as the default value for the Title field of tblMarketingDepartment.

1   Open tblMarketingDepartment in Design view.

2   In the Field Name column, click in the Title cell.

The properties for the Title field appear in the Field Properties section of the Table Design view window.

> **You cannot set a default value for fields with an AutoNumber or OLE Object data type.**

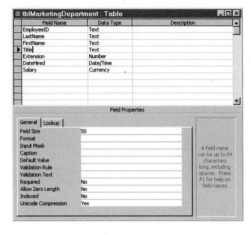

> **Entering a default value will not change the existing values in your table.**

3   In the Field Properties section, click in the Default Value box, and type **Marketing Rep**.

4   Save the table.

5   Display tblMarketingDepartment in Datasheet view.

Note that *Marketing Rep* appears in the Title field for the blank record.

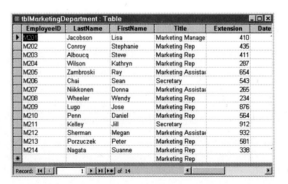

6   Close the table.

Creating and Modifying an Input Mask

AC2000E.1.3

When you enter data in a table, it's cumbersome to have to continually type dollar signs and decimal points for monetary values ($249.99, for example), or parentheses and hyphens for phone numbers. You can use an **input mask** to streamline data entry so that you don't have to type symbols or characters that appear in every entry. Input masks provide a template or "mask" for data entry input, ensuring that all data is formatted correctly when it's entered into the table.

You'll probably want to use the Input Mask Wizard the first few times you create an input mask. As you become more familiar with the input mask symbols, you'll probably find it easier to create an input mask directly in the Input Mask Property box.

Input masks can be created either by using the Input Mask Wizard or by typing the symbols for the mask directly into the Input Mask Property while the table is in Design view. When you create an input mask, you use a special set of symbols to specify how you want the input mask to appear. For example, if you type > in an input mask, the letters typed in the field will appear in the table and will be stored in all uppercase letters. Some input mask symbols require that data be entered in part of the field (for example, the first five digits in a Zip code), while others indicate that data entry is optional (such as the last four digits in a long Zip code).

Symbol	Displays the characters as	Data entry required
0	Digits (0 to 9). Blank spaces are displayed as zeroes.	Yes
9	Digits (0 to 9). Blank spaces are displayed as spaces.	No
#	Digits, plus signs (+), or minus signs (-). Blank spaces are displayed as spaces.	No
L	Letters.	Yes
?	Letters.	No
A	Letters or digits.	Yes
a	Letters or digits.	No
&	Letters, digits, spaces, or other characters.	Yes
C	Letters, digits, spaces, or other characters.	No
>	Uppercase letters.	n/a
<	Lowercase letters.	n/a
\	Characters instead of an Access command. For example, to use the backslash (\) in an input mask, you would type \\. The first backslash tells Access to treat the second backslash as a backslash, not as a command.	n/a

The characters in the Input Mask box define the way the masked field will appear and whether data entry is required or optional for different spaces in the field. For example, here's a typical input mask for a phone number:

!(999) 000-0000;;_

- The exclamation point requires the user to type data into the input mask from left to right without skipping any spaces.

- The 999 digits indicate that these are optional characters (the area code can be filled in by the user, but it's not required).

- The 000-0000 digits indicate that these characters must be typed during data entry (that is, a complete phone number is required to complete data entry for the record).

The first section of the input mask contains the mask itself.

■   The first semicolon separates the first section of the input mask from the second section, and the second semicolon separates the second section from the third section. There is nothing between the two semicolons, which indicates that the second section of the input mask is blank. When this section is blank, Access does not display placeholder characters in the field containing the input mask; instead the field is left blank until the user enters a value.

■   The underscore defines the placeholder character that will be used for all positions in the field. In this case, Access will display the input mask with an underscore to indicate that the user can "fill in the blanks."

As you look over the table that tracks sales representatives' performance in relation to quotas, you decide to include each rep's phone number in the table. In this exercise, you add a field to tblVendors for phone numbers and create an input mask for that field. The input mask will ensure that the phone numbers are stored in the following format: (###) ###-####.

1   Open tblVendors in Design view.

2   In the Field Name column, click in the first blank cell, type **Phone**, and then press Tab.

Text is selected as the default data type, and a down arrow appears in the Data Type cell.

Field Name	Data Type	Description
⚷ VendorID	Text	
VendorName	Text	
VendorAddress	Text	
City	Text	
State	Text	
Zip	Text	
▶ Phone	Text ▼	

3   In the Field Properties section, click in the Input Mask box.

The Build button appears next to the Input Mask box.

Build

4   Click the Build button. When you are prompted to save the table, click Yes.

The Input Mask Wizard appears with the Phone Number input mask selected, as shown on the following page.

If you know which symbols to use, you can type an input mask directly into the Input Mask box in the Field Properties section of the Table Design view window.

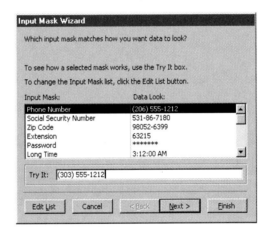

The Try It box lets you see how the input mask will format the data in the field.

If you do not click at the left end of the Try It box, the insertion point appears in the middle of the mask instead of at the beginning.

5   In the Try It box, click at the left end, and type **3035551212**.

The phone number is formatted correctly with parentheses and a hyphen.

6   Click Finish.

The input mask appears in the Input Mask box in the Field Properties section of the Table Design view window.

7   Save and close the table.

To change or make corrections to a mask, click in the Input Mask box and edit the input mask manually (if you know the symbols for the changes that you want to make) or click the Build button next to the box to edit the input mask by using the Input Mask Wizard.

AC2000E.1.1
AC2000E.1.2

Defining a Data Validation Rule

It's nice to have clearly formatted data, but it's even more important to have data that is correct. Access provides a simple way to check data at the data entry stage, before it ever gets into the database; you can create **data validation rules** that allow only certain values to be entered in a field. If someone tries to enter a value that breaks a data validation rule, Access prevents the value from being entered and displays an error message called **validation text**. For example, you would receive an error message if you tried to enter alphabetic characters into a field that was set to accept only numbers.

You create data validation rules by using a set of symbols that represent familiar concepts: equal to, greater than, less than, and so forth. The following table lists common symbols used in data validation rules.

> You can use more than one of these symbols in a data validation rule. For example, the rule >=#01/01/1990# will prevent entry of dates before 1990.

Symbol	Example	Meaning
<>	<>100	Value must not be 100.
Like	Like "Smith"	Value must be "Smith".
	Or Like "Joe" Or Like "Jill"	Value must be "Joe" or "Jill".
And	>10 And <20	Value must be greater than 10 and less than 20.
Not	Not "Frebbit"	Value must not be "Frebbit".
*	Like A*	Value must begin with A.
?	Like Fre??it	Value must begin with Fre, end with it, and have two characters in the middle.
=	=10	Value must equal 10.
>=, <=, >, <	>=10, <=10, >10, <10	Values must be greater than or equal to 10, less than or equal to 10, greater than 10, or less than 10 (the familiar algebraic meaning of the symbols), respectively.
#	#01/01/2000#	Marks the start and end of date values in rules.

important

Data validation rules are similar to input masks, but there are important differences in how Access interprets the symbols that you use. For example, using > in an input mask causes the contents of that field to be stored in uppercase letters, while using > in a data validation rule requires a user to enter a value that is greater than the value following the >. Make sure that you use the correct symbols for the item that you're creating.

In this exercise, you limit tblApprovedToOrder to employees from house-keeping (H), sports and recreation (S), or the restaurant (R) by setting a data validation rule for the EmployeeID field.

1 Open tblApprovedToOrder in Design view.

EmployeeID is selected, meaning that the properties for the EmployeeID field appear in the Field Properties section.

2 In the Field Properties section, click in the Validation Rule box.

3 Type **Like H* or R* or S***, and press the Down arrow key.

The insertion point moves to the Validation Text box, and the data validation rule changes slightly to *Like "H*" Or Like "R*" Or Like "S*"*.

When you move the insertion point to another cell, the word *Like* and pairs of quotation marks appear in the cell with the validation rule. The word *Like* is inserted before any rule that uses a wildcard, and the quotation marks are placed around the string of characters that Access will use to restrict data.

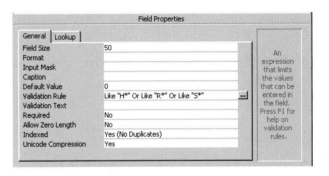

You do not have to set validation text for the validation rule to work.

4 In the Validation Text box, type **Employee ID must begin with H, S, or R**.

This message will appear if the user tries to enter a value that does not meet the data validation rule that you set in step 3.

Save

5 On the Table Design toolbar, click the Save button.

An alert box appears, asking if you would like to test the existing data with the new rules.

6 Click Yes.

Access saves the table.

7 Display the table in Datasheet view.

8 Click in the EmployeeID field for employee S607.

9 Delete the existing text, type **M101**, and then press Tab.

An alert box containing the message that you typed in step 4 appears.

10 Click OK.

11 Delete the text that you just typed, type **S607**, and then press Tab.

S607 meets the data validation rule; the alert box does not appear.

12 Close the table.

AC2000E.1.4

Creating and Modifying a Lookup Field

So far in this lesson, you have learned several ways to make tables more efficient and to simplify data entry. Default values, validation rules, and input masks that direct user input are useful, but Lookup fields are another tool that can help users enter the proper values into a field.

If the values to be entered into a field will come from a well-defined list of values, such as the contents of a field in another table, you can create a Lookup field based on that list. Rather than asking the user to type a value into a field, the Lookup field gives the user a list from which to choose the value. You create a Lookup field with the Lookup Wizard. Using the Wizard, you can pull the values in the Lookup field from an existing table or query, or you can type a new list of values.

You can change the values in an existing Lookup field by adding new values to the field on which the list is based. You can also change the Lookup field by running the Lookup Wizard again and either selecting a new field to provide values or creating your own list. If the Lookup Wizard is still open and you want to modify the values in the list, click the Back button until you reach the dialog box where you type the values in the list or choose the table or query from which to draw the values.

In this exercise, you make the DepartmentID field in tblPurchaseOrder a Lookup field.

1   Open tblPurchaseOrder in Design view.

2   In the Data Type column, click in the DepartmentID row, click the down arrow that appears, and then click Lookup Wizard.

The first Lookup Wizard dialog box appears.

> If you click the I Will Type In The Values That I Want option, the Lookup Wizard allows you to type the values that you want in the Lookup field.

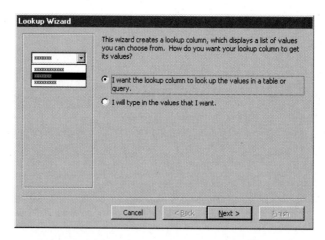

3   Click Next.

The wizard will draw the values for the Lookup field from an existing table or query. The next Lookup Wizard dialog box appears, as shown on the following page.

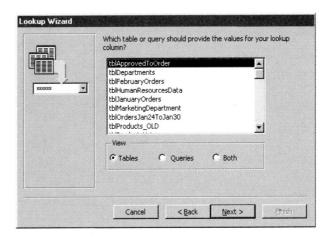

4   Click tblDepartments, and click Next.

The values for the Lookup field will come from tblDepartments. The next Lookup Wizard dialog box appears.

> You can remove a selected field from the Selected Fields list by clicking the < (Remove) button.

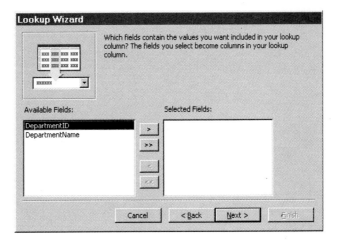

5   In the Available Fields list, click DepartmentName, click the > (Add) button, and then click Next.

Access will use the values in the DepartmentName field for the Lookup field. The next Lookup Wizard dialog box appears.

> The width of the column in this dialog box will be the width of the actual Lookup field.

> The key column is the primary key field from the table that contains the values for the Lookup field. You can add the primary key field to the Lookup field from this dialog box even if you did *not* add it to the Selected Fields list in the previous Lookup Wizard dialog box.

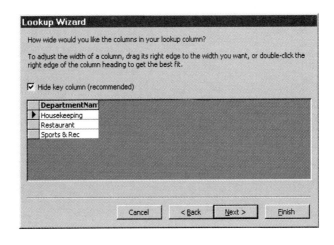

You can also double-click the edge of the column to resize it.

6   Move the mouse pointer over the right edge of the DepartmentName cell until the pointer turns into a resizing double-headed arrow, drag the edge of the column to the right until the entire field name (*DepartmentName*) is visible, and then click Next.

The Lookup field will be wide enough to show all the items in the list. The next Lookup Wizard dialog box appears with DepartmentID already in the What Label Would You Like For Your Lookup Column? box.

7   Click Finish to use the label *DepartmentID* for the Lookup field.

An alert box appears, indicating that you must save changes before the relationships can be created.

8   Click Yes.

9   Display tblPurchaseOrder in Datasheet view.

The 0 appears in the DepartmentID column because that is the default value for the field. Default values are discussed earlier in this lesson.

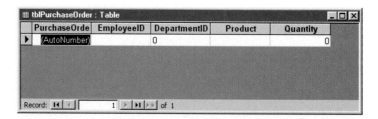

10   Click in the DepartmentID field, and click the down arrow that appears.

A list of possible values for the field appears.

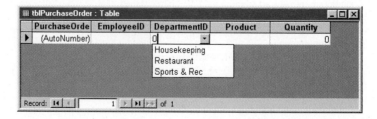

11   Close the table.

AC2000E.5.1
AC2000E.5.3

You can create many-to-many relationships, which are more complicated than either one-to-one or one-to-many relationships. Many-to-many relationships are discussed in Lesson 2, "Creating Custom Queries."

Creating a Relationship

The Lakewood Mountains 01 database includes tblApprovedToOrder, a table that lists the names, titles, and contact information for Lakewood Mountains Resort employees who are approved to place orders. The database also contains a table called tblHumanResourcesData that lists confidential information for each employee, such as date of hire, salary, and hours worked per week. Access provides a way to connect these tables so that an employee listed in one table is also in the other. This connection, or **relationship**, reduces errors in the database by requiring that all employees approved to place orders are actual employees listed in the data for the human resources department.

The simplest type of relationship in a database is a **one-to-one relationship**, which means that each record in one of the tables has only one related record in the other table. In the example above, each employee is listed only once in tblApprovedToOrder and in tblHumanResourcesData. An employee should not be approved to order twice, nor should an employee have more than one salary history in the human resources table. To create a one-to-one relationship, the tables must share a primary key field that contains a unique value for each record in the database. In the example of tblApprovedToOrder and tblHumanResourcesData, both tables have an employee ID field as a primary key field.

Tables can also be in a **one-to-many relationship**, where a record in one table has one or more associated records in another table. For example, in an inventory table, there is only one product code and product description for each inventory item. However, this same product can be ordered many times by a customer (for example, on different dates), so the same product code and description could be listed many times in a table of product orders.

When you have two tables in a relationship, regardless of the type of relationship, you should consider enforcing **referential integrity** between the tables. When you enforce referential integrity, you require that a record in one of the tables have one or more matching records in the other table. For example, there must be an employee ID in tblHumanResourcesData that matches the employee ID entered in tblApprovedToOrder. In practical terms, it means an employee must be hired and entered into the human resources table before he or she can be approved to place orders.

You can refine referential integrity by also setting the **cascade update** or **cascade delete** function. Cascade update changes the contents of the table on the *many* side of the relationship to reflect any changes to values in the primary key field of the table on the *one* side. For example, if an employee in tblHumanResourcesData was given a new employee ID, the record with that employee's ID number in tblApprovedToOrder would be updated with the new number.

Cascade delete, by contrast, removes records from the table on the *many* side of the relationship whenever a related record on the *one* side is deleted. For example, if the employee with employee ID 206 left the company and that record was deleted from tblHumanResourcesData, the record in tblApprovedToOrder associated with employee 206 also would be deleted.

important

You can use cascade update without harming your database, but cascade delete might remove data from your tables. Use it with caution, and only after you've backed up your data!

In this exercise, you create a one-to-one relationship between tblHumanResourcesData and tblApprovedToOrder, enforce referential integrity, and set cascade update between the two tables.

Relationships

1   On the Database toolbar, click the Relationships button.

The Relationships window appears.

2   On the Relationship toolbar, click the Show Table button, add tblHumanResourcesData and tblApprovedToOrder to the Relationships window, and then close the Show Table dialog box.

Field lists for tblHumanResourcesData and tblApprovedToOrder appear in the Relationships window.

The field lists in the Relationships window can be resized so that you can see all the fields in each list. Move the mouse pointer over the edge of the field list until the pointer turns into a horizontal, vertical, or diagonal double-headed arrow, and drag the edge to resize the field list.

3   From the tblHumanResouresData field list, drag the EmployeeID field on top of the EmployeeID field in the tblApprovedToOrder field list.

The Edit Relationships dialog box appears.

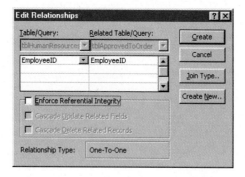

4   Select the Enforce Referential Integrity check box, select the Cascade Update Related Fields check box, and then click Create.

The Edit Relationships dialog box closes, and the Relationships window becomes visible again.

The line between the EmployeeID fields of the two tables and a 1 next to each field list indicate that the two tables are in a one-to-one relationship.

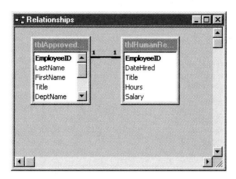

5   Save and close the Relationships window.

Lesson Wrap-Up

This lesson covered how to create an index, normalize a table, define data validation rules, create input masks, set default field values, create Lookup fields, and set cascade options in Access 2000.

If you are continuing to the next lesson:

Close

● Click the Close button in the top-right corner of the Database window.

The Lakewood Mountains 01 database closes.

If you are not continuing to the next lesson:

Close

● To quit Access for now, click the Close button in the top-right corner of the Access window.

Access and the Lakewood Mountains 01 database close.

Lesson Glossary

cascade delete A function that, between tables in a one-to-many relationship, deletes related records in the *many* tables when records are deleted in the *one* table.

cascade update A function that, between tables in a one-to-many relationship, updates related records in the *many* tables when records are changed in the *one* table.

data validation rules Limits or conditions set on the data entered into a field.

default value In a new record, a value that Access automatically enters into a certain field.

index A set of fields for which Access tabulates information and uses the stored information to perform queries or sort the results based on the contents of those fields.

input mask A property that sets the format for storing field data.

Lookup field A field that requires a user to select a value from a pre-defined list. Also refers to a field that the Table Analyzer Wizard inserts in a table when two tables have been split to maintain a connection between the split tables.

normalization A process that Access performs (through the use of the Table Analyzer Wizard) to minimize or eliminate duplicated information in a database.

one-to-many relationship A relationship that exists between two tables when each record in one table has one or more matching records in the other table.

one-to-one relationship A relationship that exists between two tables when each record in one table has one matching record in the other table.

primary key A field that contains a unique value for each record.

referential integrity A system of rules that Access uses to ensure that relationships between records in related tables are valid and that related data is not accidentally deleted or changed.

relationship A connection between two tables related by the data in at least one primary key field.

sort To organize the contents of fields in a specific order, such as alphabetical or numerical.

table The database object that holds all the data in the database and makes it available for viewing or manipulation.

validation text The message that Access displays when the user enters a value that does not meet the data validation rule.

Quick Quiz

1   What is a one-to-one relationship?

2   How do you define a data validation rule for a field?

3   What does the Table Analyzer Wizard do?

4   What is an input mask?

5   What are the advantages of setting a default value for a field?

6   How do you create a Lookup field?

7   How do you index a field?

8   How can you update table data based on changes in related tables?

9   How do you define a default value for a field?

10   What is referential integrity?

Putting It All Together

Exercise 1: Normalize tblOrdersJan24ToJan30 to create two tables. Name the table that contains the order information **tblJan24To30Orders,** and do not give the table a primary key. Name the table that contains the vendor contact information **tblVendorAddresses.** Close the new tblOrders-Jan24ToJan30 query.

Exercise 2: In this exercise, you modify tblFebruaryOrders so that it is easier to use. Add a validation rule to the OrderDate field so that the user must enter a date later than 01/01/00 or else a message that says *The order must have been placed after January 1, 2000* will appear. Create an input mask for the Code field that requires the user to enter two letters before and three letters after a dash. (Hint: Use the symbol *L*.) Set a default value of $19.95 for the Price field. Add a Lookup field to the EmployeeID field that draws its values from the EmployeeID field in tblApprovedToOrder. Save and close tblFebruaryOrders.

Exercise 3: Create a one-to-many relationship between tblApprovedTo-Order and tblJanuaryOrders. (Hint: You create a one-to-many relationship in the same way that you create a one-to-one relationship.) Set cascade update between tblApprovedToOrder and tblJanuaryOrders so that if an employee's ID changes, tblJanuaryOrders will be updated automatically. Save and close the Relationships window.

LESSON 2

Creating Custom Queries

After completing this lesson, you will be able to:

✔ *Specify criteria in multiple fields.*

✔ *Modify query properties.*

✔ *Apply filters to a query.*

✔ *Calculate totals in a query.*

✔ *Specify criteria in a totals query.*

✔ *Create an action query.*

✔ *Create a parameter query.*

✔ *Create a crosstab query.*

✔ *Create a PivotTable.*

✔ *Join tables to create a query.*

✔ *Create a many-to-many relationship.*

Tables store data, but you use a **query** to retrieve that data efficiently. A query is a database object that you use to extract specific records from the database and display the records in various ways. The most basic type of query is a **select query**, which extracts records from one or more tables and displays them in a single datasheet, form, or report.

In this lesson, you learn how to use some of the different queries available in Microsoft Access. If database users need to total or average records found by a query, you can create a **totals query** to do the calculations automatically. You can let users enter their own query criteria with a **parameter query**. You can automate tasks that take a long time to do manually—such as creating tables, updating existing tables, deleting table records, or adding records to tables—by using an **action query**. You can use a **filter** with a query to show only records of interest to you. You will also learn how to use records from two or more tables in a single query.

If your query returns financial data, you can use a **crosstab query** to display the data in a spreadsheet-like format. The **PivotTable**, which presents data in the same way that a crosstab query does, allows you to reorganize data dynamically. You can also use a query to extract multiple related records from tables in a **many-to-many relationship**.

To complete the procedures in this lesson, you will need to use a file named Lakewood Mountains 02 in the Access Expert Practice folder that is located on your hard disk. You will also need to have Microsoft Excel 95 or later installed on your computer.

For additional information about opening the practice file for this lesson, see the "Using the CD-ROM" section at the beginning of this book.

Sample files for the lesson

AC2000E.3.4

Specifying Criteria in Multiple Fields

In Access, you create and modify queries using the Query Design view window. This window displays the field lists of tables that are available to use in the query. The lower half of the Query Design view window, called the Design grid, shows which fields have been used in the query. The Query Design view window also allows you to set individual properties for each field, providing numerous options for customizing queries.

When you create a query, you can set criteria in one or more fields to restrict the records included in the results. The more criteria you set, the more specific the query. For example, if you have a table of all the orders placed by your employees, you could use a query to return records for only those orders placed after February 2, 2000 (by using the Criteria row in the OrderDate field) and by a certain employee (by using the Criteria row in the EmployeeID field).

When you add criteria to more than one query field, Access will find only the records that meet both the first criterion *and* the second criterion. If you want Access to find records that meet the first criterion *or* the second criterion, you type the first criterion in the Criteria row of the first field and the second criterion in the Or row of the second field. For example, if you have a table of all the orders placed by your employees, you could use a query to return records for orders placed after February 2, 2000 (by using the Criteria row in the OrderDate field) *or* orders with numbers higher than 1049 (by using the Or row in the Order# field).

In this exercise, you open the Lakewood Mountains 02 database and run a query with multiple criteria to find every order placed by employee S606 after January 15, 2000. You then add another criterion to further limit the query to orders with numbers below 1040.

Open

1   On the Database toolbar, click the Open button, navigate to the Access Expert Practice folder on your hard disk, and then open the Lakewood Mountains 02 database.

2   On the Objects bar, click Queries, and double-click Create Query In Design View.

The Query Design view window appears with the Show Table dialog box open.

3   In the Show Table dialog box, click tblJanuaryOrders, and click Add.

The tblJanuaryOrders field list appears in the top half of the Query Design view window.

4   Click Close.

The Show Table dialog box closes.

The Design view window for queries (Query Design view window) is different from the Design view window for tables (Table Design view window) used in Lesson 1, "Customizing Tables."

You can also move fields to the Design grid by double-clicking the field name in the field list.

5 Scroll down until the EmploymentID field is visible, and drag the EmployeeID field from the tblJanuaryOrders field list to the first blank Field cell in the Design grid.

6 Repeat step 5 for the Code, Order#, and OrderDate fields (in that order).

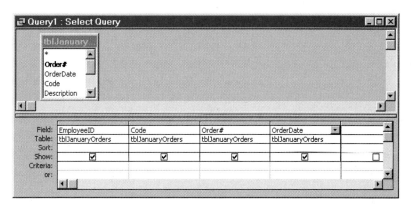

7 In the EmployeeID column, click in the Criteria row, and type **S606**.

The query will find records for employee S606.

You can specify date criteria using any valid date format: *1/15/00; 15-Jan-00; Saturday, January 15, 2000*; and so on.

8 In the OrderDate column, click in the Criteria row, and type **>1/15/00**.

The query will also find records for orders placed after January 15, 2000.

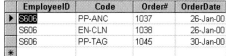

Run

9 On the Query Design toolbar, click the Run button.

The query runs, and all orders placed by employee S606 after January 15, 2000, appear.

	EmployeeID	Code	Order#	OrderDate
▶	S606	PP-ANC	1037	26-Jan-00
	S606	EN-CLN	1038	26-Jan-00
	S606	PP-TAG	1045	30-Jan-00
*				

View

10 On the Query Datasheet toolbar, click the View button.

The query appears in Design view.

11 In the Order# column, click in the Criteria row, and type **<1040**.

Access automatically places quotation marks (" ") around the text and number signs (#) around the date that will be used to restrict data.

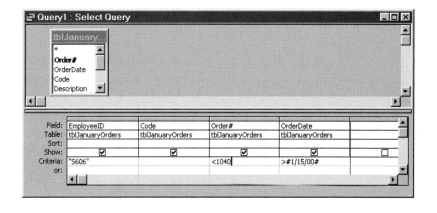

12   On the Query Design toolbar, click the Run button.

All orders by employee S606 with numbers less than order #1040 and placed after January 15, 2000 appear.

EmployeeID	Code	Order#	OrderDate
▶ S606	PP-ANC	1037	26-Jan-00
S606	EN-CLN	1038	26-Jan-00
*			

Save

13   On the Query Datasheet toolbar, click the Save button.

The Save As dialog box appears.

14   In the Query Name box, type **qryMultipleCriteria**, and click OK.

Access saves the query.

Close

15   Click the Close button in the top-right corner of qryMultipleCriteria.

The query closes.

AC2000E.3.5

Modifying Query Properties

When you create a query, Access assigns default properties (such as data type) to some of the fields in the query based on the properties of the table fields referenced by the query. While those properties can't be changed, Access does allow you to set four properties for each field: **description, format, input mask,** and **caption.**

Property	Description
description	A description of the field (up to 255 characters).
format	The data type (such as currency, date/time, number, and so on) used to determine how data in the field will be displayed. This property does not affect how the data is stored.
input mask	A template used to enter search criteria in a parameter query.
caption	The text displayed as the field's column header in the query results. If this property is left blank, Access uses the name of the field as the caption.

> **Input masks are discussed in more detail in Lesson 1, "Customizing Tables."**

The Lakewood Mountains 02 database contains qryJanuaryOrdersByDate, which, when run, gives a list of the items ordered in January, the date of the order, and the order number. After examining the results of qryJanuaryOrdersByDate, you decide that the name of the OrderDate field takes up more space than is necessary. In this exercise, you modify qryJanuaryOrdersByDate by changing the caption from *OrderDate* to *Date.*

1   In the Database window, click qryJanuaryOrdersByDate, and click Design on the Database window toolbar.

The query opens in Design view.

Run

2 On the Query Design toolbar, click the Run button.

The query runs, and the query results appear with *OrderDate* as the caption for the first column.

View

3 On the Query Datasheet toolbar, click the View button.

The query appears in Design view with OrderDate already selected in the Field row of the Design grid.

Properties

4 On the Query Design toolbar, click the Properties button.

The Field Properties dialog box appears.

The Field Properties dialog box can also be displayed by right-clicking any cell in the Field row and clicking Properties on the shortcut menu that appears.

When the Caption box is blank, the field name—in this case, *OrderDate*—will be used as the caption by default.

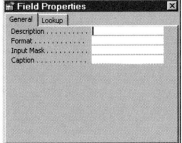

5 Click in the Caption box, and type **Date**.

6 Close the Field Properties dialog box.

Run

7 On the Query Design toolbar, click the Run button.

The query results appear, with *Date* as the caption for the first column.

Setting *Date* as the caption does not change the field name in the Query Design view window.

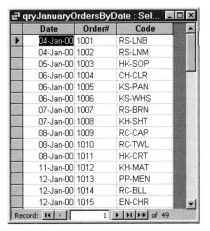

8 Save qryJanuaryOrdersByDate.

AC2000E.3.1

You can add new records to a table of filtered records. The new records will be included in the original table after the filter is removed.

Applying Filters to a Query

A filter is a rule or set of rules that limit which records will be displayed when you run a query. Filtering accomplishes the same task as specifying criteria, but in a more limited way. A filter has two advantages over using criteria to limit query results.

- Applying a filter doesn't require you to modify the query by adding or changing criteria.

- You can turn a filter on and off, while you would need to change query criteria and rerun the query to get the same result.

In Access, you have two different methods for creating a filter. To filter by form, you first choose the field and then the specific value by which you want to filter. Alternatively, to filter by selection, you create a filter using whatever value is currently selected.

Apply Filter

To turn the filter on and off, you use the Apply Filter and Remove Filter buttons. These two buttons are actually the same button; the button picture stays the same but the button name does not. To apply a filter, you click the Apply Filter button. To remove the filter, you click the same button—now called the Remove Filter button—again.

Remove Filter

You can combine a query and a filter to perform quick searches. For example, qryJanuaryOrdersByDate contains the Order#, Code, EmployeeID, and Date fields. Suppose the inventory manager at Lakewood Mountains Resort wants to use this query to display records for particular employees. She can quickly apply a filter that, in effect, says "display the records for employee S606 only." Applying a filter in this manner is faster than adding *EmployeeID = S606* as a criterion to the query.

In this exercise, you use the Filter By Form button to display the order records for employee S606 in qryJanuaryOrdersByDate and the Filter By Selection button to display all orders placed on January 12, 2000.

1   Display qryJanuaryOrdersByDate in Design view.

2   Drag the EmployeeID field from the tblJanuaryOrders field list to the first blank cell in the Field row. You might have to resize the Query Design view window so that the first blank cell is visible.

Run

3   On the Query Design toolbar, click the Run button.

The query runs, and the EmployeeID field appears in the results.

Filter By Form

4   On the Query Datasheet toolbar, click the Filter By Form button.

The Filter By Form window appears.

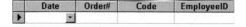

5   Click in the EmployeeID column, click the down arrow that appears, scroll down, and then click S606.

The filter will display records for employee S606.

Apply Filter

6   On the Query Datasheet toolbar, click the Apply Filter button.

Access filters the query, and only the records for employee S606 appear.

Date	Order#	Code	EmployeeID
12-Jan-00	1015	EN-CHR	S606
13-Jan-00	1018	EN-STR	S606
13-Jan-00	1019	EN-BLN	S606
26-Jan-00	1037	PP-ANC	S606
26-Jan-00	1038	EN-CLN	S606
30-Jan-00	1045	PP-TAG	S606

Remove Filter

7   On the Query Datasheet toolbar, click the Remove Filter button.

Access removes the filter, and qryJanuaryOrdersByDate shows all the records again.

8   In the Date field, click in any record for an order placed on January 12, 2000.

Filter By Selection

9   On the Query Datasheet toolbar, click the Filter By Selection button.

All the orders placed on January 12, 2000, appear.

OrderDate	Order#	Code	EmployeeID
12-Jan-00	1013	PP-MEN	R221
12-Jan-00	1014	RC-BLL	S505
12-Jan-00	1015	EN-CHR	S606
12-Jan-00	1016	CH-RPP	S607

Remove Filter

10   On the Query Datasheet toolbar, click the Remove Filter button.

Access removes the filter, and qryJanuaryOrdersByDate shows all the records again.

11   Save and close qryJanuaryOrdersByDate.

AC2000E.3.2

Calculating Totals in a Query

Queries display information based on the criteria that you set. A totals query not only displays the data, but it also performs calculations on the data. Although the name *totals query* suggests that this kind of query always displays a sum, a totals query can use one of several Access calculation functions, or aggregate functions, in the query criteria. An **aggregate function** reflects a property of your data as a whole, such as an average or sum, rather than individual values. Access includes several aggregate functions, the most common of which are described in the following table.

This Function	Will
Sum	Total all values in a field.
Avg	Average all values in a field.
Min	Display the lowest value in a field.
Max	Display the highest value in a field .
Count	Total the number of values in a field.
Group By	Organize query results.

Group By is the default aggregate function.

Access interprets all records that do not contain a value as *Null*, or blank, not as a zero. This interpretation can cause problems because many aggregate functions will not include records with a Null value. For example, the Count function will count only records that do not contain Null. In addition, mathematical expressions using a Null record will have a Null result.

In general, aggregate functions apply to all the records in a table. However, you can also apply aggregate functions to individual groups of records. To group records by different categories within a field, you use the Group By aggregate function in the Total row. For example, if the head of the marketing department at Lakewood Mountains Resort needed to know the total amount spent on salaries for all the marketing reps, the Group By, Count, and Sum aggregate functions could be used to group all the employees by title, count the employees in each group, and sum their salaries.

In this exercise, you use aggregate functions to perform calculations in a query created from tblMarketingDepartment.

1   Double-click Create Query In Design View.

The Query Design view window appears with the Show Table dialog box open.

2   Add tblMarketingDepartment to the Query Design view window, and close the Show Table dialog box.

3   Drag the EmployeeID and Salary fields from the field list to the first two Field cells in the Design grid.

Totals

4   On the Query Design toolbar, click the Totals button.

The Total row appears in the Design grid with Group By set as the default function.

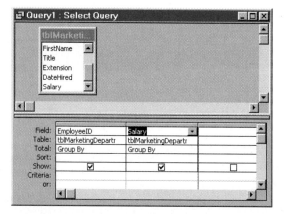

5   In the EmployeeID column, click in the Total row, click the down arrow that appears, and then click Count.

The query will count the number of employee ID numbers.

6   In the Salary column, click in the Total row, click the down arrow that appears, and then click Sum.

The query will add the values in the Salary field. The Query Design view window should look similar to the illustration on the following page.

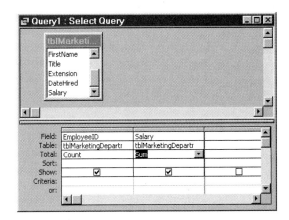

7 On the Query Design toolbar, click the Run button.

The query runs, and a count of the employee ID numbers and the total amount of all salaries appear.

Run

The field name changes to a combination of the aggregate function and the original field name.

CountOfEmplo	SumOfSalary
14	$454,680.00

8 Display the query in Design view.

9 Drag the Title field from the field list to the first blank cell in the Field row.

10 On the Query Design toolbar, click the Run button.

The query runs, and the salary totals appear sorted by title.

Run

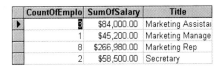

CountOfEmplo	SumOfSalary	Title
3	$84,000.00	Marketing Assistai
1	$45,200.00	Marketing Manage
8	$266,980.00	Marketing Rep
2	$58,500.00	Secretary

11 Save the query as **qrySalaryByTitle**.

Specifying Criteria in a Totals Query

To further customize a totals query, you can include a **criteria expression** to limit or specify the kind of information that the query returns. If you want to limit the records that are counted in a totals query, you add a criteria expression to the Criteria row for a field with Group By set as the aggregate function. For example, if you wanted to count the number of housekeeping employees at Lakewood Mountains Resort with employee numbers above H103, you would type >*H103* in the Criteria cell of the EmployeeID column.

In this exercise, you add a criteria expression to qrySalaryByTitle so that the query results will show the sum of the salaries for just marketing reps.

1 Display qrySalaryByTitle in Design view.

2 In the Title column, click in the Criteria row, and type **=Marketing Rep**.

Run

3 On the Query Design toolbar, click the Run button.

The query runs, and the number of marketing reps and the sum of all their salaries appear.

CountOfEmplo	SumOfSalary	Title
3	$266,980.00	Marketing Rep

4 Close qrySalaryByTitle without saving changes.

tip

If you have trouble getting the query results that you want when you use multiple criteria, try setting one criterion and running the query. After you verify that the criterion works correctly, add another criterion and run the query again. You can continue this process for each criterion that you add. For example, you could first run a query to find all the employees in the housekeeping department. If that query worked, you could add another criterion to find housekeeping employees who were hired after a particular date.

AC2000E.3.6

Creating an Action Query

An action query modifies or creates a table. You create an action query when you want to change a large amount of data in an existing table. You can leave the changed data in the existing table or you can create a new table in which to store the changed records. Four types of action queries are available in Access: **make-table query, update query, append query,** and **delete query.**

Action Query Type	Description
Make-table query	Creates a new table containing the selected records.
Update query	Updates the selected records in one or more tables.
Append query	Adds the selected records to the end of one or more tables.
Delete query	Deletes the selected records from one or more tables.

The table that you create using a make-table query will not inherit the properties or primary key setting from the existing table.

A make-table query works by selecting records and creating a new table containing those records. As a result, make-table queries are useful for quickly making a backup copy of an existing table. You can also use a make-table query to create a table that contains old records or records from a specific period.

You do not create a new table until you click the Run button.

important

Like all action queries, a make-table query will change your database permanently, so Access lets you view the result of the query before running it. This intermediate step allows you to check the contents of the new table. To see the results of your make-table query without creating a new table, display the query in Datasheet view.

Append queries are queries that take records from an existing table or query and add those records to the end of an existing table. For example, if a Lakewood Mountains Resort employee were traveling and gathered contact information for three new suppliers, the employee could store the contact information in a new table and, after returning to the resort, use an append query to add the records in the traveling table to the end of the main suppliers table.

For an update query to work, the tables must be in a one-to-many relationship. In the example here, tblVendors is on the *one* side, and tblJanuaryOrders, tblFebruaryOrders, and tblMarchOrders are on the *many* side.

Update queries are queries that change existing values in one or more tables. For example, a vendor might change its company name. Rather than go through every record in the order-tracking tables in the database, you could change the company name in tblVendors and then create an update query to automatically change the vendor's name in tblJanuaryOrders, tblFebruaryOrders, and tblMarchOrders.

Delete queries can only be used to delete specific records, not the fields within the records.

As the name suggests, a delete query permanently removes records from a table. You create the query exactly as you would create a standard select query, but instead of displaying the records found by the query, Access deletes the selected records from the table affected by the query.

In this exercise, you create a backup copy of tblJanuaryOrders by using a make-table query, and then you use a delete query to remove all records of orders placed before January 7.

1   Double-click Create Query In Design View.

The Query Design view window appears with the Show Table dialog box open.

2   Add tblJanuaryOrders to the Query Design view window, and close the Show Table dialog box.

3   Double-click the title bar of the tblJanuaryOrders field list.

Access selects all the items in the tblJanuaryOrders field list.

4   Drag the selected field list to the first cell in the Field row.

All the fields from tblJanuaryOrders appear in the Design grid with each field in a separate column.

5   On the Query menu, click Make-Table Query.

The Make Table dialog box appears.

The Make Table dialog box also allows you to add a new table to another database by clicking the Another Database option and typing the name of the other database in the File Name box.

6   In the Table Name box, type **tblBackupJanuaryOrders**, and click OK.

The new table will be named tblBackupJanuaryOrders. The Query Design view window displays *Make Table Query* on the title bar.

You can also copy a table by clicking the table in the Database window, clicking the Copy button, clicking the Paste button, and then typing a new table name in the Paste Table As dialog box.

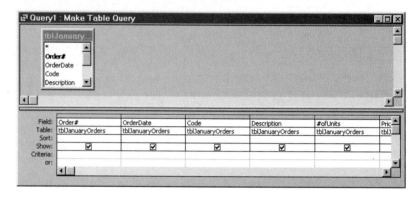

7   On the Query Design toolbar, click the View button.

View

The query runs, and the results appear without creating a new table.

This is what the new table will look like, but it is not the new table. You do not create the new table until you click the Run button in step 9.

8   Display the query in Design view.

9   On the Query Design toolbar, click the Run button.

Run

An alert box appears, indicating that 49 rows will be pasted into the new table.

10 Click Yes.

11 Close the query without saving changes.

12 Display the list of tables in the Database window, and double-click tblBackupJanuaryOrders, the duplicate of tblJanuaryOrders that you just created.

13 Close the table.

14 Display the list of queries in the database window, and double-click Create Query In Design View.

15 Add tblBackupJanuaryOrders to the Query Design view window, and close the Show Table dialog box.

16 Drag the OrderDate field to the first Field cell in the Design grid.

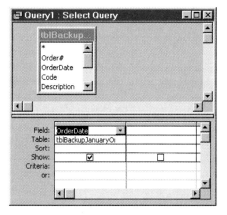

The criterion you type in the Criteria cell tells Access what records to delete—in this case, all orders placed before January 7, 2000.

17 Click in the Criteria cell of the OrderDate column, and type **<#01/07/00#**.

The query will delete orders placed before January 7, 2000.

18   On the Query menu, click Delete Query.

The Query Design view window displays *Delete Query* on the title bar.

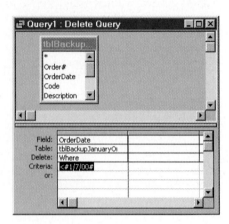

Run

19   On the Query Design toolbar, click the Run button.

An alert box appears, telling you that six records will be permanently deleted if you proceed.

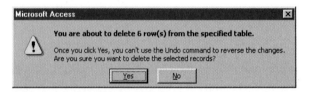

20   Click Yes.

Access deletes the records.

21   Close the query without saving changes.

AC2000E.3.3

Creating a Parameter Query

You might find that you use certain queries repeatedly, changing only the criteria to display different results. For example, you might want to create a query that will find orders made to particular companies, but not always the same company. Creating a separate query for each company would require a lot of work and crowd the Database window unnecessarily. To make it easier to run such a query, you can add a message that prompts the user for the criteria to use in the query. This prompt will appear when the query runs and can tell users what type of value that they need to enter. For this example, the message would prompt the user for the name of the company. This type of query is called a parameter query.

> If the list of potential values is small, the list can be included in the message itself.

You can run a parameter query either from the Database window or from the Query Design view window. Each time the query runs, the Enter Parameter Value dialog box appears. You enter the desired criterion in the box and click OK to display the appropriate query results.

You can also set a parameter prompt for crosstab queries, which you learn about in the next section of this lesson.

Parentheses (()) and curly brackets ({}) function differently from square brackets ([]) and cannot be used to define a parameter in a Criteria cell.

A parameter query is a type of select query, meaning that it finds records from one or more tables and is set up in the same way as any other select query. To add criteria prompts to the query, you specify a prompt in the Criteria row of the desired fields. The prompt text (the message that the user will see) must be enclosed in square brackets and must be different from the field name; however, the text can contain the field name.

Typically, parameter queries are used to limit the query to a single record, but you can also use a **wildcard** in query criteria so that several matching records might result. A wildcard is a single character, usually specified by an asterisk (*), that represents one or more other characters. For example, you can use a wildcard to design a query to display the names of all employees whose last names begin with a certain letter. To prompt the user to enter the first letter of the names that they want to see, you would type the following expression in the Criteria cell of the Last Name column:

```
Like [First letter of last name:] & "*"
```

The text *First letter of last name:* will appear in the prompt, and the ampersand (&) indicates that Access will link the letter that the user types with an asterisk (the wildcard). If the user wants to search for employees with last names that start with the letter A and types an *A* into the dialog box, for example, the criterion that the query would use would be

```
Like "A*"
```

Using A* as the criterion, the query would return any record containing a last name beginning with the letter A.

You can also design a query that searches for a particular letter *anywhere* in a field. For example, if you wanted to find all employees with a certain letter in their last name, you could type a query like this:

```
Like "*" & [Letter in last name:] & "*"
```

The text *Letter in last name:* will appear in the prompt, and the ampersand (&) indicates that an asterisk (the wildcard) will be placed before and after the letter when the query is run.

In this exercise, you create a parameter query based on tblFebruaryOrders that prompts for the employee ID number so that a user can find all the orders placed by a specific employee just by typing the employee's ID number in the dialog box.

1   Double-click Create Query In Design View.

The Query Design view window appears with the Show Table dialog box open.

2   Add tblFebruaryOrders to the Query Design view window, and close the Show Table dialog box.

3 Drag the EmployeeID, Order#, #ofUnits, and Price fields (in that order) from the field list to the first four cells of the Field row.

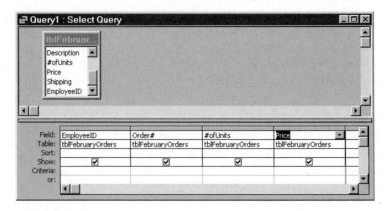

4 In the EmployeeID column, click in the Criteria row, and type **[Enter Employee ID]**.

Run

5 On the Query Design toolbar, click the Run button.

The Enter Parameter Value dialog box appears, containing the message that you typed in step 4.

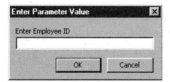

6 In the Enter Employee ID box, type **S606**, and click OK.

The query runs, and the orders placed by employee S606 in February appear.

EmployeeID	Order#	#ofUnits	Price
S606	1059	1	$199.99
S606	1071	4	$15.95
S606	1072	2	$49.95
S606	1073	5	$49.95
S606	1082	1	$2,000.00
0			

7 Save the query as **qryFebruaryOrdersParameterQuery**, and close it.

Creating a Crosstab Query

A crosstab query displays summarized values (sums, counts, and averages) from one field in a table and groups them by one set of facts listed down the left side of the datasheet and another set of facts listed across the top of the datasheet. In a crosstab query, data items are combined, displayed in a spreadsheet-like format, and used to analyze trends and make comparisons.

Crosstab queries display data, but you cannot use them to change that data.

Access uses data from three fields to create a crosstab query: one field to provide the values for the row headings, one field to provide values for the column headings, and one field to provide the values for the body of the query. In the illustration below, the row headings are the vendor IDs, the column headings are the employee IDs, and the body of the crosstab query shows how much each employee spent with each vendor.

Crosstab queries are great for financial data, but you can also use them to present attendance data (name, date, and presence/absence), event times (runner, date, and time), and many other data combinations.

You can create a crosstab query by using a wizard, or you can design one yourself. The Crosstab Query Wizard takes you step by step through the process of creating a crosstab query. Crosstab queries are unique in Access because they are actually easier to design manually than with the wizard.

To use the Crosstab Query Wizard, display the list of queries in the Database window, and click the New button on the Database window toolbar. In the New Query dialog box, click Crosstab Query Wizard.

Designing a crosstab query manually means that you must define each component of the query. You begin the query by adding tables to the Query Design view window and dragging the desired field names to the Field row in the Design grid. You then determine which fields to use for the row headings, the column headings, and the body of the crosstab for the query.

In this exercise, you create a crosstab query using tblOrdersJan24ToJan30.

1 Double-click Create Query In Design View.

 The Query Design view window appears with the Show Table dialog box open.

2 Add tblOrdersJan24ToJan30 to the Query Design view window, and close the Show Table dialog box.

3 Drag the EmployeeID and VendorID fields from the field list to the first two cells in the Field row.

Query Type

You can also click Crosstab Query
on the Query menu to designate
the query as a crosstab query.

4   On the Query Design toolbar, click the Query Type down arrow, and
click Crosstab Query.

The Total and Crosstab rows appear in the Design grid. The Query
Design view window displays *Crosstab Query* on the title bar.

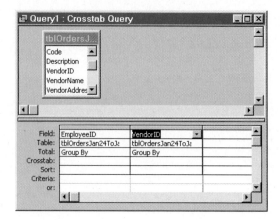

The Total row and the aggregate
functions that you can use in the row
are discussed earlier in this lesson.

In the fields designated as the
row headings and column headings,
you must leave Group By in the
Total row.

5   In the EmployeeID column, click in the Crosstab row, click the down
arrow that appears, and then click Column Heading.

The query will use employee ID numbers as column headings.

6   In the VendorID column, click in the Crosstab cell, click the down
arrow that appears, and then click Row Heading.

The query will use the vendor ID numbers as row headings.

7   Click in the first blank cell in the Field row, and type
Total: [#ofUnits]*[UnitCost].

The value in this field will be the result of multiplying the value in the
#ofUnits field by the value in the UnitCost field.

8   In the same column that you used in step 7, click in the Total row, click
the down arrow that appears, and then click Sum.

9   In the same column that you used in step 8, click the Crosstab row,
click the down arrow that appears, and then click Value.

Access will compute the total cost of each order and use the results to
calculate the contents of the crosstab query body.

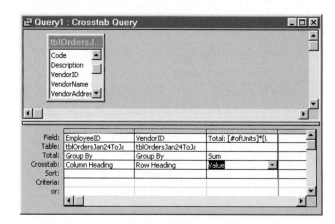

Run

10   On the Query Design toolbar, click the Run button.

The query runs, and the results show how much each employee spent with each vendor between January 24 and January 30.

VendorID	H102	H103	R221	R234
CH	$13.90		$5.00	$29.90
EN				
HK				
KC				
KS				
PP			•	
RC	$129.90		$39.95	
RS		$100.00		

> **If you want to stop a long query after you begin to run it, press Ctrl+Break.**

11   Save the query as **qryTotalByVendorCrosstab**, and close it.

Creating a PivotTable

A PivotTable is a special form that allows you to analyze data with Microsoft Excel. Using a PivotTable, you can change the way columns and rows are organized and then perform calculations on the corresponding columns or rows. In one sense, a PivotTable is a more advanced crosstab query. But instead of creating several crosstab queries to emphasize different aspects of your data, you can recognize a single PivotTable quickly and without prior preparation to illustrate your points. Reorganizing data allows you to emphasize different aspects of the data on the fly. For example, you might organize order data to emphasize orders by employee, then by month, and then by vendor.

> **important**
>
> You must have Excel 2000 installed on your computer to use PivotTables.

For example, consider tblOrdersJan24ToJan30, which includes a VendorID field, an EmployeeID field, and a Total field. You can create a PivotTable that will show the EmployeeID numbers in the left column and the VendorID values in the top row. In the center, the table can show the total purchases for each employee from each company. Such an analysis could show that an employee has gotten into the habit of ordering from a particular company and is not shopping around for the best price on some items. This PivotTable would look similar to the following illustration.

Worksheet in PivotTable Form

	A	B	C	D	E	F	G	H
1								
2								
3	Sum of Total	VendorID						
4	EmployeeID	CH	EN	HK	KC	KS	PP	RC
5	H102	16.85						179.8
6	H103							
7	R221	7.95						89.
8	R234	32.85						
9	R455							27.8
10	S504				209.5	100.95		
11	S505				26.9			
12	S606		115.9	47.85			34.95	
13	S607					11.85	114.7	
14	Grand Total	57.65	115.9	284.25	100.95	11.85	149.65	297.

Sheet1

You could reorganize the contents of the PivotTable by dragging the VendorID field below the EmployeeID field to show the total amount of goods that each employee ordered from each vendor.

When you reorganize a PivotTable, Access automatically recalculates the values in the body of the PivotTable.

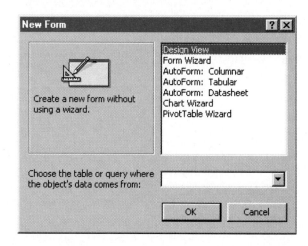

You create a PivotTable to present data that would fit into a crosstab query, with the added benefit of having more than one field providing column and row heading values. The PivotTable will organize the data based on the contents of the first field providing values for the column headings, then the second, and so forth. If the column headings were Month and Vendor, for example, the PivotTable would list all the Vendors that were ordered from in the first month, then all the vendors that were ordered from in the second month, and so on.

Unlike most wizards in Access, there is no manual counterpart to the PivotTable Wizard; the only way to create a PivotTable is by using the Wizard. In this exercise, you create a PivotTable based on tblOrdersJan24ToJan30.

1   Display the list of forms in the Database window, and click New on the Database Window toolbar.

The New Form dialog box appears.

You can also open th New Form dialog box by clicking Form on the Insert menu.

New Form

Create a new form without using a wizard.

Design View
Form Wizard
AutoForm: Columnar
AutoForm: Tabular
AutoForm: Datasheet
Chart Wizard
PivotTable Wizard

Choose the table or query where the object's data comes from:

OK   Cancel

2 Click PivotTable Wizard, and click OK.

The first PivotTable Wizard dialog box appears.

3 In the PivotTable Wizard dialog box, read the introductory text, and click Next.

The next PivotTable Wizard dialog box appears.

4 Click the Tables/Queries down arrow, and click Table: tblOrdersJan24ToJan30.

The fields in tblOrdersJan24ToJan30 appear in the Available Fields list with EmployeeID already selected.

If you select a table or query in the New Form dialog box, that table or query will appear in the Tables/ Queries box in this PivotTable Wizard dialog box.

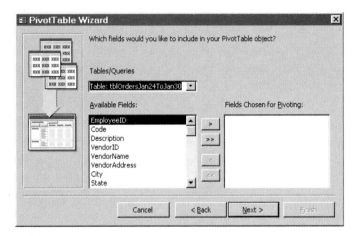

5 Click the > (Add) button.

You can also double-click a field in the Available Fields list to add it to the Fields Chosen For Pivoting list.

The EmployeeID field moves to the Fields Chosen For Pivoting list.

6 Add the VendorID and Total fields to the Fields Chosen For Pivoting list, and click Next.

Microsoft Excel starts, and the next PivotTable Wizard dialog box appears.

If the Office Assistant appears, right-click the Assistant, and click Hide on the shortcut menu that appears.

If you click Finish at this point, a blank PivotTable will appear. No data will appear until you tell Access how to arrange the data by clicking the Layout button.

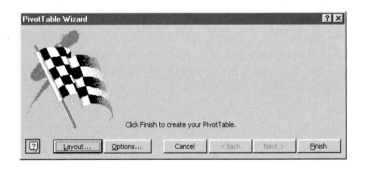

7   Click Layout.

The next PivotTable Wizard dialog box appears with the three fields that you selected listed on the right side of the dialog box.

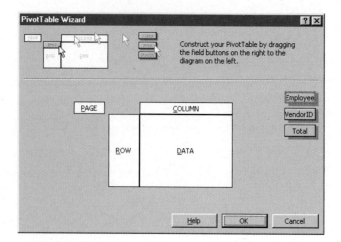

8   Drag the EmployeeID field to the Row area. (You will see only the word *Employee*.)

9   Drag the VendorID field to the Column area.

10   Drag the Total field to the Data area.

The name of the Total field changes to *Sum of Total*, and the layout of the PivotTable is complete.

The Page area, which is not used in this exercise, can by used as a filter for the PivotTable as a whole. For example, you could use the Department field in the Page area to have the PivotTable show records for only one department at a time.

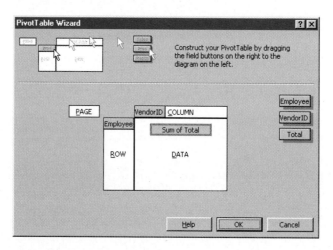

11   Click OK.

The same PivotTable Wizard dialog box that you saw in step 6 appears.

12 Click Finish.

The PivotTable appears in Access in a PivotTable Form window. The PivotTable shows how much each employee spent with each vendor.

The employees are listed by employee ID, and the vendors are listed by vendor ID.

If you display the form in Design view, the PivotTable will appear as one control that you can move around the form just like any other form control.

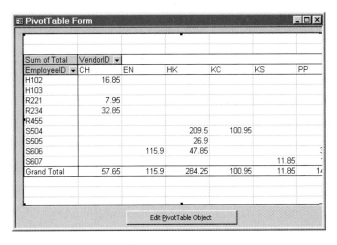

If you try to use the Office Assistant or Help menu at this point, you start Excel Help instead of Access Help.

13 Click Edit PivotTable Object.

The PivotTable appears as an Excel worksheet, and the PivotTable toolbar appears.

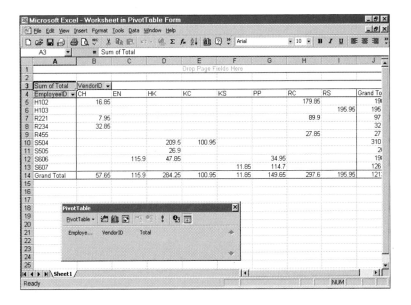

Docking the PivotTable toolbar is not an essential step in editing a PivotTable; it simply moves the PivotTable toolbar out of the way.

14   Drag the PivotTable toolbar up until the toolbar is docked at the top of the Excel window.

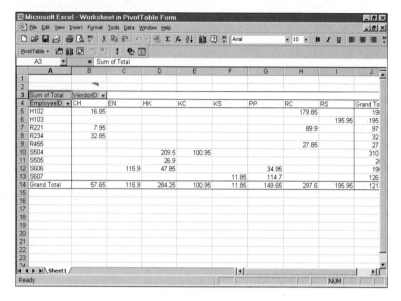

15   Click the Select All button (the blank gray box to the left of the column A header and above the number row headers).

Select All

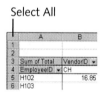

Access selects all the rows and columns in the PivotTable worksheet.

16   Right-click anywhere on the Excel worksheet, and click Format Cells on the shortcut menu that appears.

The Format Cells dialog box appears, with the Number tab already selected.

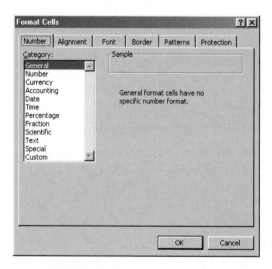

An example of the format that you
select will appear in the Sample box
to the right of the Category list.

17   In the Category list, click Currency, verify that the Currency format uses a dollar sign and two decimal places, and then click OK.

The Format Cells dialog box closes. The PivotTable now displays all values in Currency format with a dollar sign and two decimal places.

18   Close the Excel window.

19   Save the form as **frmPurchasePivot**, and close it.

AC2000E.3.8

Joining Tables to Create a Query

An easy way to select records that have matching data in two or more tables is to **join** the tables. When you join tables that are already in a one-to-many relationship, the primary key field—which appears in both tables and contains a unique value for each record—of the table on the one side is used to display matching records from the table on the many side. This approach is much easier than specifying query criteria.

For example, the inventory manager at Lakewood Mountains Resort wants to create a query that will display all orders for a given month along with the name and address of the vendor for each order. This approach is possible if both the orders table for that month and the vendors table contain the VendorID field, which can be used as the primary key. Access creates a one-to-many relationship between the tables using the VendorID field.

You can join tables in three ways:

The default is to include rows only
when the joined field matches in
both tables.

- You can specify to include rows in the query only when the joined field produces matches in both tables.
- You can specify to include all rows from the first table and only those records from the second table that match the join field in the first table.
- You can specify to include all rows from the second table and only those records from the first table that match the join field in the second table.

To specify these and other join properties, you use the Join Properties dialog box, which you open by clicking Join Properties on the View menu while in the Query Design view window.

Show Tables

tip

If you want to use a field other than the primary key as the join field, click the Show Tables button on the Relationship toolbar, and drag the field name in the first table's field list on top of the desired field in the second table's field list. You can also use the Join Properties dialog box to specify different fields for the left and right columns.

In this exercise, you create a query that joins the VendorID field in tblMarchOrders with the VendorID field in tblVendors. The resulting query will display the vendor name and address fields from tblVendors for only those records that have a matching VendorID in tblMarchOrders. As a result, the vendor's name and address will appear for any orders placed in March. You also change the join properties and sort the records according to their VendorID.

> In the Show Table dialog box, you can quickly add two or more tables to the query by clicking the name of the first table, holding down the Ctrl key, and clicking the name of the second table. Then click the Add button.

1   Create a new query in Design view, add tblMarchOrders and tblVendors to the Query Design view window, and then close the Show Table dialog box.

   The relationship between tblMarchOrders and tblVendors is shown by a line.

2   Drag all the fields *except* the VendorID field from the tblMarch-Orders field list to the Field row.

tip

To select all but one or two fields from a field list, you can double-click the title bar in the table list to select all fields, hold down the Ctrl key, and then click the field or fields that you do not want to include.

3   Drag all the fields *except* the VendorID and Phone fields from the tblVendors field list to the Field row.

4   Run the query.

   Access compares the VendorID fields in the two tables. Every record in tblMarchOrders and tblVendors that contains a matching VendorID field appears in the query results.

> Notice that the VendorID field itself doesn't appear in the results of the query.

Order#	OrderDate	Code	Description	#ofUnits	Price
1050	3/28/00	HK-BLB	Light Bulbs (50)	1	$15.95
1091	3/22/00	HK-BRR	Mini Refrigerator	6	$75.00
1065	3/12/00	KH-BED	Trundle Bed	5	$89.95
1051	3/4/00	PP-TME	Timesheets (100)	1	$9.95
1056	3/29/00	PP-STY	Hotel Stationary (500)	1	$15.95
1081	3/19/00	PP-MNU	Room Service Menu (500)	1	$49.95

5   Display the query in Design view.

6 On the View menu, click Join Properties.

The Join Properties dialog box appears.

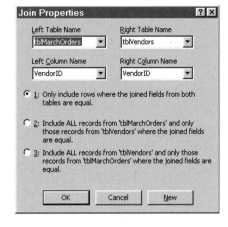

7 Click option 3, and click OK.

The query results will include all records from tblVendors and only matching records from tblMarchOrders.

8 Run the query.

All the records in tblVendors (even those without matching records in tblMarchOrders) and all the matching records in tblMarchOrders appear. The illustration below has been modified to display the join.

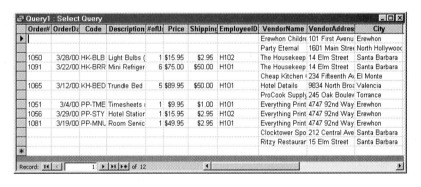

9 Display the query in Design view.

10 On the View menu, click Join Properties.

The Join Properties dialog box appears.

11 Click option 1, and click OK.

12 Run the query.

Only the records that match in both tblVendors and tblMarchOrders appear.

13 Click any field in the OrderDate column.

Sort Ascending

You can also sort by pointing to Sort on the Records menu and clicking Sort Ascending or Sort Descending.

14   On the Query Dataseet toolbar, click the Sort Ascending button.

The records are sorted in ascending order by Order Date.

Order#	OrderDate	Code	Description	#ofUnits	Price	Shipping
1051	3/4/00	PP-TME	Timesheets (100)	1	$9.95	$1.00
1065	3/12/00	KH-BED	Trundle Bed	5	$89.95	$50.00
1081	3/19/00	PP-MNU	Room Service Menu (500)	1	$49.95	$2.95
1091	3/22/00	HK-BRR	Mini Refrigerator	6	$75.00	$50.00
1050	3/28/00	HK-BLB	Light Bulbs (50)	1	$15.95	$2.95
1056	3/29/00	PP-STY	Hotel Stationary (500)	1	$15.95	$2.95

15   Save the query as **qryMarchOrdersWithVendorInfo**, and close it.

AC2000E.3.7

The process for creating indexes is discussed further in Lesson 1, "Customizing Tables."

tip

When you index a field, you create an ordered list of every value in that field. Access can then use the index to work more efficiently. Rather than check each record in a table to find the value called for by the query, Access can search the index and find the value in much less time. Indexing fields when you set query criteria is very effective, as is indexing fields on either side of a join.

AC2000E.1.5

Byte, integer, and long integer do not allow for decimal values.

Using Other Data Formats

The Field Size property limits the amount of disk space reserved for any field with a Number data type. As shown in the following table, number fields can be set in several ways.

Setting	Range	Storage
Byte	0 to 255 (no decimal places).	1 byte
Integer	−32,768 to 32,767 (no decimal places).	2 bytes
Long Integer	−2,147,483,648 to 2,147,483,647 (no decimal places).	4 bytes
Single	-3.4×10^{38} to 3.4×10^{38} (7 decimal places).	4 bytes
Double	-1.797×10308 to 1.797×10308 (15 decimal places).	8 bytes
Replication ID	N/A.	16 bytes
Decimal	$-10 \wedge 28-1$ to $10 \wedge 28-1$ (28 decimal places).	12 bytes

Replication ID numbers can be used in database replication, which is discussed in Lesson 7, "Using Database Tools."

(continued)

continued

Unless you want to restrict the amount of numerical data that can be entered, you should select either Long Integer or Double because both of these settings allow very long numbers. It is important to be careful when changing field size because values larger than the field size will be replaced with a **Null** value. Null is the value given to records that do not contain any data, instead of a zero. Records with a Null value are not included in calculations.

To change the Field Size property for a field with a Number data type:

1   Display the table in Design view.

2   Click in the row for the field that you want to change.

3   In the Field Properties section, click in the Field Size box, click the down arrow that appears, and then select the data type that you want.

AC2000E.5.2

Creating a Many-to-Many Relationship

Normally when you create a relationship, it is a one-to-one relationship, where one record in a table has one matching record in another table, or a one-to-many relationship, where one record in a table has many matching records in another table. To join tables, which was discussed in the previous section, you use a one-to-many relationship.

You can also create **many-to-many relationships**, which are more complex than either one-to-one relationships or one-to-many relationships. The best way to explain a many-to-many relationship is with an example. The inventory manager at Lakewood Mountains Resort occasionally purchases products at a discount from a variety of distributors instead of directly from the manufacturer. So, she creates a products table that uses one product Code to display multiple products listed in tblProductList, a one-to-many relationship. Then she creates a query that displays every distributor listed in tblDistributors from which she can purchase a product. This approach is a many-to-many relationship because it creates multiple (many) records for each record in the products table, which allows for multiple (many) distributor records for a single product.

> One-to-one and one-to-many relationships are discussed in Lesson 1, "Customizing Tables."

The trick to creating a many-to-many relationship between two tables is to create a third table, called a **junction table**, which allows multiple records to be displayed for each record in a pair of existing tables. The illustration on the next page shows a sample junction table in Design view.

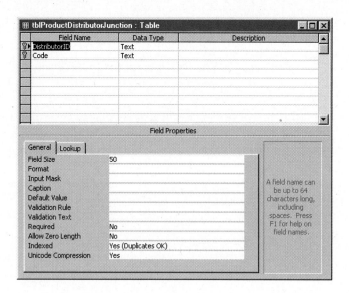

You can add other fields to the junction table without affecting the many-to-many relationship.

Note that the Junction table contains two fields: the Code field, which is the primary key from tblProductList, and the DistributorID field, which is the primary key from tblDistributors. Also note that both fields in the junction table are still primary key fields.

In this exercise, you define two one-to-many relationships: one between tblProductsList and tblProductsDistributorJunction (the junction table), and the second between tblDistributors and tblProductsDistributor-Junction. You use those relationships and the records in the junction table to create a query that displays which products are available from which distributors and to describe the products.

Relationships

1   On the Database toolbar, click the Relationships button.

     The Relationships window appears.

2   On the Relationship toolbar, click the Clear Layout button.

![Clear Layout icon]

Clear Layout

     An alert box appears, asking if you want to clear the Relationships window.

3   Click Yes

     The Relationships window clears.

Clearing the Relationships window does not mean that you have deleted all the relationships in the database, just that you can't see them. This step is not necessary; it just makes it easier to see the new relationships.

4   Click the Show Table button.

     The Show Table dialog box appears.

Show Table

You can select more than one table in the Show Table dialog box by holding down the Ctrl key and clicking the tables that you want to add.

The primary key field for each table appears in bold.

5 Add tblDistributors, tblProductDistributorJunction, and tblProductsList to the Relationships window, and close the Show Tables dialog box.

The field lists for the three selected tables appear in the Relationships window.

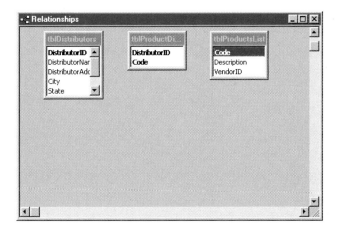

6 Drag the DistributorID field from the tblDistributors field list on top of the DistributorID field in the tblProductDistributorJunction field list.

The Edit Relationships dialog box appears.

Note that the relationship type in the Edit Relationships dialog box is one-to-many.

7 Select the Enforce Referential Integrity check box, and click Create.

Access creates a one-to-many relationship, with tblDistributors on the one side and tblProductDistributorJunction on the many side.

8 Drag the Code field from the tblProductsList field list to the Code field in the tblProductDistributorJunction field list.

The Edit Relationships dialog box appears.

9 Select the Enforce Referential Integrity check box, and click Create.

Access creates a one-to-many relationship, with tblProductsList on the one side and tblProductDistributorJunction on the many side.

10 Save and close the Relationships window.

11 Create a query in Design view that includes the Code and Description fields from tblProductsList and the DistributorID field from blDistributors.

12 In the Code column, click in the Sort row, click the down arrow that appears, and then click Ascending.

The query results will be sorted in ascending order based on the contents of the Code column.

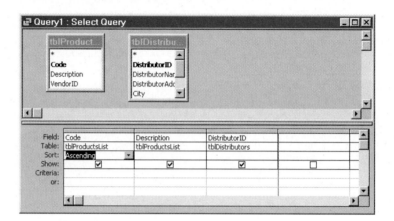

13 Run the query.

The query results appear.

Notice that the same product descriptions appear multiple times with different distributor names, and the same distributor names appear multiple times with different product descriptions.

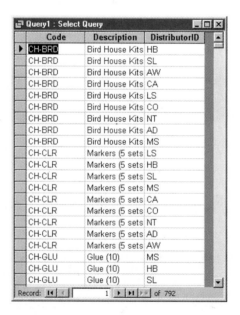

14 Save the query as **qryDistributorProducts**, and close it.

Lesson Wrap-Up

This lesson covered how to specify query crieria; modify query properties; filter query results; use calculations in a query; create an action query, parameter query, or crosstab query; use a PivotTable to analyze data; join tables to create a query; and use a many-to-many relationship with a query.

If you are continuing to the next lesson:

Close

● Click the Close button in the top-right corner of the Database window.

The Lakewood Mountains 02 database closes.

If you are not continuing to the next lesson:

Close

● To quit Access for now, click the Close button in the top-right corner of the Access window.

Access and the Lakewood Mountains 02 database close.

Lesson Glossary

action query A query that automates database actions that might take a long time to do manually.

aggregate function A function—such as Add or Average—that can be used in a totals query to perform calculations on data.

append query A type of action query that adds selected records to the end of a table.

caption The text displayed in query results as the field's column heading.

criteria expression A rule that Access uses to pick records to appear in a query or filtered table.

crosstab query A query that displays summarized values (sums, counts, and averages) from one field in a table and groups them by one set of facts listed down the left side of the datasheet and another set of facts listed across the top of the datasheet.

delete query A type of action query that deletes records from an existing table.

description A query field property that gives a user space to enter a summary of a field's contents (optional).

filter A rule or set of rules that limit which records will be displayed when you run a query.

format The data type (such as currency, date/time, or number) used to determine how data in a field will be displayed. This property does not affect how the data is stored.

input mask A template used to enter search criteria in a parameter query.

join To combine fields and records from two tables in a single query.

junction table A table that makes many-to-many relationships possible by containing both of the primary key fields for the two tables in the relationship.

make-table query A type of action query that creates a new table with selected records.

many-to-many relationship A relationship between two tables where multiple records in the first table are related to multiple records in the second table.

Null A value given to records that do not contain any data, instead of a zero. Records with a Null value are not included in calculations.

parameter query A select query that requires the user to enter the criterion that is used to find records in the tables.

PivotTable A type of form that you can use to dynamically view and reorganize table data on a Microsoft Excel worksheet.

query A type of database object that can be used to locate specific records and present the results in various ways.

select query The most basic type of query, which finds records from one or more tables and displays them in a single datasheet, form, or report.

totals query A query that performs calculations on the data returned by a query.

update query A type of action query that updates values in a table based on changed information in a related table.

wildcard A single character, usually specified by an asterisk (*), that represents one or more other characters, and can be used to find more than one result in a query.

Quick Quiz

1   How do you find the average value of data in a field?
2   What does a make-table query do?
3   What is a parameter query?
4   How do you filter query results using the Filter By Form button?
5   How do you change the join properties of a query?
6   What happens when you add criteria to two query fields?
7   What is a crosstab query?
8   How do you specify criteria in a totals query?
9   What is a many-to-many relationship?

Putting It All Together

Exercise 1: Modify qryJanuaryOrdersByDate so that the captions for the Order# and EmployeeID fields include spaces and the format of the Date field is Short Date. Run the query, and use filter by selection to find all orders placed by employee R234. Remove the filter, and filter the query by form to find all orders for the item with the code *PP-CRD*. Add a parameter to the query that says *Day in January* to prompt users to enter the date for which they want to see orders. Run the query to find orders placed on January 8. Save and close the query.

Exercise 2: Using tblJanuaryOrders, create a query that shows the total amount (including shipping) spent by each employee (listed by employee ID) during the month of January. Sort the query results in ascending order by the amount in the Total field. Run the query. Restrict the query results to just restaurant employees. (Hint: All restaurant employees have an employee ID number that begins with the letter *R*.) Run the query again. Save the query as **qryJanEmployeeTotals**, and close it.

Exercise 3: Using tblFebruaryOrders, create a query that shows the total cost of orders (including shipping) placed by housekeeping employees to The Housekeeper Helper. (Hint: All housekeeping employees have employee ID numbers that start with *H*, and all Housekeeper Helper products have a code that starts with *HK*.) Run the query. Use a make-table query to save the query results as **tblFebruaryTotals**. Change the query into a crosstab query that uses the employee ID numbers as row headings, the codes as column headings and the Total field as the value. Run the query, save it as **qryFebruaryTotalsCrosstab**, and close it.

Exercise 4: Create a PivotTable using tblFebruaryTotals that you created in Exercise 3. Use the employee IDs as the row headings, the codes as the column headings, and the Total field as the data in the PivotTable. Save the PivotTable as **frmFebPivot**, and close it.

Exercise 5: Create a query that joins the EmployeeID field in tblApprovedToOrder to the EmployeeID field in tblFebruaryTotals. Run the query. Change the join properties to display all records in tblApprovedToOrder and only matching records in tblFebruaryOrders, and run the query again. Close the query without saving changes.

LESSON 3

Customizing Forms

After completing this lesson, you will be able to:

✔ *Create a form in Design view.*

✔ *Add a list to a form.*

✔ *Customize form sections.*

✔ *Insert a graphic in a form.*

✔ *Modify control properties.*

✔ *Create a subform.*

✔ *Create a switchboard.*

In Microsoft Access, you can use a **form** to simplify working with data. Forms are specialized database objects that you use to view, add, and edit data in a format that is more attractive and user-friendly than a table. If people who are not familiar with Access use your database, forms are a good way to make it easy for them to understand and work with the data in the database.

You create a form using the data in a table or query. Forms have a unique relationship with their underlying table or query; when you enter data into a form, the data is also added to the table or query that the form is based on, and vice versa. By customizing the forms in a database, you can simplify the entry of data into the database and improve the accuracy of the new data.

In this lesson, you'll learn how to modify forms and simplify data entry. If you add lists to forms, users can click the information that they want to add, instead of typing it. You can also divide the form into sections so that certain information—such as copyright warnings, titles, or instructions—is repeated at different intervals throughout the form. If users need information from two or more related forms, you can add a **subform** to a form to display the related information. You can also enhance the forms in your database by adding graphics, such as logos or diagrams. To further simplify navigation in Access, you'll also learn how to create a customized form called a **switchboard** that has buttons users can click to open database objects or perform actions, such as closing the database.

To complete the procedures in this lesson, you will need to use files named Lakewood Mountains 03 and LMRsmall in the Access Expert Practice folder that is located on your hard disk.

For additional information about opening the practice file for this lesson, see the "Using the CD-ROM" section at the beginning of this book.

Sample files for the lesson

AC2000E.2.1

Creating a Form in Design View

In Access, you can create a form in three different ways: using AutoForm, the Form Wizard, or Design view. Of these three, AutoForm is the easiest way to create a form, although this technique only allows you to select the layout of the form and the table or query on which the form is based. To use AutoForm, display the list of forms in the Database window, click New on the Database window toolbar, and select the AutoForm layout that you want for your form.

The Form Wizard gives you more choices than AutoForm. When you use the Form Wizard, you can select the tables and queries that provide the contents of the form, which fields will appear in the form, and the style and layout of the form.

> Forms can be opened in two views. Form view displays the actual data in the form, and Design view allows you to modify the design of the form.

Of the three ways to create a form, using Design view gives you the most options. You start by identifying the table or query on which the form will be based. Then Access displays a field list for the table or query that you selected and a blank form containing only a **Detail section**, which is the section of the form where records appear. You customize the form by adding **controls**, which display data, perform actions, and enhance the appearance and functionality of the form.

> You can select consecutive field names in the field list by clicking the first field name, holding down the Shift key, and then clicking the last field name. To select nonconsecutive field names, hold down the Ctrl key, and click the fields that you want to use.

There are three different types of controls that you can use on forms: bound, unbound, and calculated. A **bound control** contains information from a field in the table or query from which the form gets its data. To add bound controls to a form, you display the field list—a box containing the field names from the underlying table or query—and drag the desired field names to the form. When you add a field to a form, Access adds two bound controls: a **text box** and a **label**. The text box contains the data from the field in the table or query, and the label provides a description of the data, usually the name of the field.

Unlike a bound control, an **unbound control** is not related to the underlying table or query. Unbound controls can include lines, rectangles, buttons, labels, and more. Although bound controls are made up of labels and text boxes, you can also add labels and text boxes to a form as unbound controls. When you add a text box to a form, it always appears with a label. However, you can add a label to a form without also adding a text box. To create unbound controls, you use the tools in the **toolbox**, a floating toolbar that can be opened and closed by clicking the Toolbox button on the Form Design toolbar.

Toolbox

> Remember, field names are always surrounded by brackets ([ ]) in an expression.

A **calculated control** uses an expression to calculate its value based on the data in one or more of the fields on the form. For example, if you wanted to calculate 5 percent sales tax for an order, you might create an expression like =[OrderTotal]*.05. Expressions always start with an equal sign and use the same operators that you use in most basic math problems. The table on the next page lists the operators and field naming conventions for expressions in calculated controls.

Symbol	Use
+	Addition
-	Subtraction
*	Multiplication
/	Division
\	Integer division (the remainder is discarded)
mod	Modulo division (the remainder is the result)
[*fieldname*]	Name of the field

Control names can be up to 64 characters long.

When you create a control, Access assigns that control a name. On a form with a lot of controls, control names make it easier for you to find the control that you want. The default name that Access assigns a control reflects the type of control and the field (if any) to which the control is bound. For example, a command button might be named *Command15*, an unbound text box might be named *Text17*, and a text box bound to the EmployeeID field would be named *EmployeeID*. If you know the name of the control that you want, you can select it by clicking the Object down arrow on the Formatting toolbar and clicking the control name.

Object
down arrow

Names
of the
controls on
the form

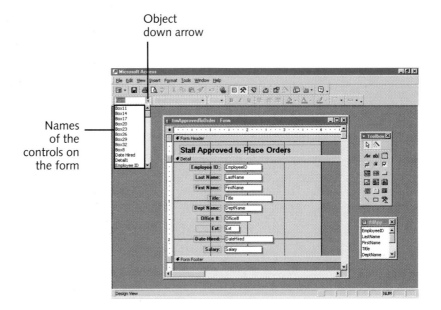

In this exercise, you open the Lakewood Mountains 03 database and use Design view to create a form based on tblFebruaryOrders.

Open

1 On the Database toolbar, click the Open button, navigate to the Access Expert Practice folder on your hard disk, and then open the Lakewood Mountains 03 database.

2 Display the list of forms in the Database window, and click New on the Database window toolbar.

The New Form dialog box appears with Design View already selected.

You can also open a blank form by double-clicking Create Form By Using Design View in the Database window. However, this technique does not give you a chance to select the table or query to use as the basis for the form. As a result, you have to use the property sheet for the form to open a field list for the underlying table or query.

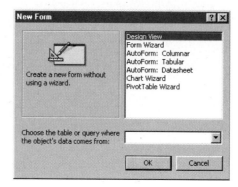

3 Click the Choose The Table Or Query Where This Object's Data Comes From down arrow, scroll down, click tblFebruaryOrders, and then click OK.

The form opens with the field list for tblFebruaryOrders and the toolbox already open.

The grid and dotted background appear by default when the form is in Design view. If you want to remove them, click Grid on the View menu.

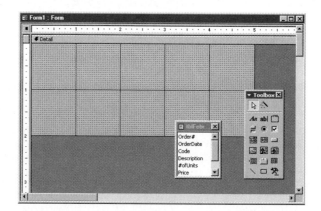

You can drag the toolbox and the field list to any location in the Access window. To make the toolbox into a toolbar, drag it on top of the other toolbars.

4 In the toolbox, verify that the Control Wizard tool is deselected.

Control Wizard

5   In the field list, click Order#, and drag it until the left edge of the mouse pointer is halfway between the 1- and 1.5-inch marks on the horizontal ruler.

When you add a field to a form, the left edge of the box mouse pointer shows where the left edge of the text box will be, with the label to the left.

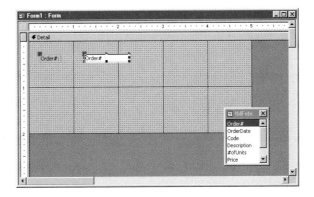

In these illustrations, the toolbox has been moved out of the way to make room for the controls.

6   In the field list, click OrderDate, and drag it until the left edge of the mouse pointer is aligned with the 3.5-inch mark on the horizontal ruler.

Notice that dragging a field to the form does not remove it from the field list. You can add the same field to a form more than once.

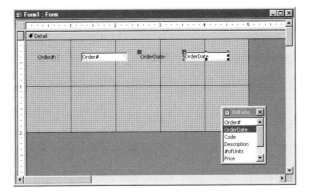

7   In the field list, scroll down, click EmployeeID, and drag it below the Order# text box until the left edge of the mouse pointer is aligned with the left edge of the Order# text box.

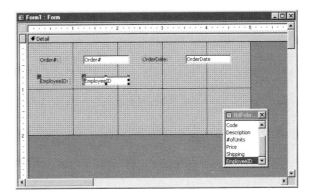

8 In the field list, click #ofUnits, and drag it below the OrderDate text box until the left edge of the mouse pointer is aligned with the left edge of the OrderDate text box.

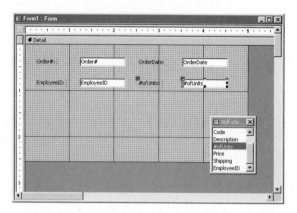

9 In the field list, click Price, and drag it below the #ofUnits text box until the left edge of the mouse pointer is aligned with the left edge of the #ofUnits text box.

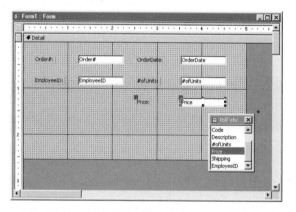

ab|

Text Box

10 In the toolbox, click the Text Box tool, and click below the Price text box, aligning the plus sign (+) on the mouse pointer with the left edge of the Price text box.

An unbound control appears.

In this example, the new control is named Text7 and contains the word *Unbound* in the text box to show that it is an unbound control. The name of your control might not match the name of the control in the illustration.

In these illustrations, the field list for tblFebruaryOrders has been moved out of the way to make room for the controls.

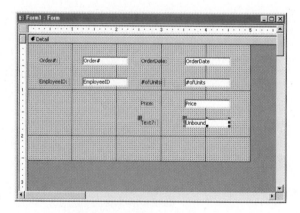

11   Click the new label, move the mouse pointer over the center of the label until the pointer turns into an insertion point, and then click the mouse.

An insertion point appears in the label text.

When you click any blank area in the form, you deselect all the controls in the form.

12   Delete the existing text, type **Subtotal:**, and then click any blank area in the form.

13   Click the new text box, move the mouse pointer over the center of the text box until the pointer turns into an insertion point, and then click the mouse.

The text in the control disappears.

This expression multiplies the value in the Price field by the value in the #ofUnits field.

14   Type **=[Price]*[#ofUnits]**.

15   Move the mouse pointer over the bottom edge of the Detail section until the pointer turns into a resizing double-headed arrow, and drag the edge of the section down about one inch.

The Detail section increases in size.

16   In the field list, click Shipping, and drag it below the Subtotal text box until the left edge of the mouse pointer is aligned with the left edge of the Subtotal text box.

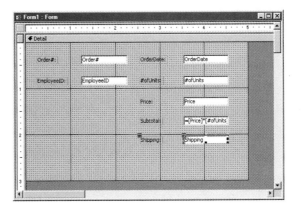

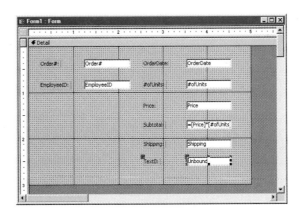

abl

Text Box

17   In the toolbox, click the Text Box tool, and click just below the Shipping text box, aligning the plus sign (+) on the mouse pointer with the left edge of the Shipping text box.

An unbound control appears.

Your form does not need to exactly match the illustration shown here.

18   Click the new label, move the mouse pointer over the center of the label until the pointer turns into an insertion point, and then click the mouse.

An insertion point appears in the label text.

19   Delete the existing text, type **TOTAL**, and then click any blank area in the form.

20   Click the new text box, move the mouse pointer over the center of the text box until the pointer turns into an insertion point, and then click the mouse.

The text in the control disappears.

This expression multiplies the value in the Price field by the value in the #ofUnits field and adds the value in the Shipping field.

21   Type **=[Price]*[#ofUnits]+[Shipping]**.

22   Display the form in Form view.

The order cost appears in the Subtotal text box, and the order cost plus shipping appears in the TOTAL text box.

The numbers in the Subtotal and TOTAL text boxes are not formatted as currency with a dollar sign and two decimal points. You will change the format of the text in these controls later in the lesson.

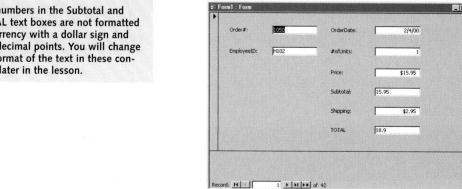

23   Save the form as **frmFebruaryOrders**.

Adding a List to a Form

You can improve the effectiveness of a form by adding controls that display a list of choices so that users can click the information that they want instead of having to type it. Using a list helps speed up data entry and can prevent the errors that lead to incorrect results in sorts, filters, and queries. Access has two types of controls that can display a list of options in a form: list boxes and combo boxes.

A **list box** displays a list of options. The list is always open, and the value that you select is limited to the choices in the list. You can scroll through the list by using the arrow buttons next to the list.

A **combo box** is a text box with a list box attached that lets the user either type a value or select one in the list. The list is visible only when the user clicks the down-arrow, as shown below. Unlike the list in a list box, the list in a combo box is not open all the time. As a result, combo boxes take up less space than list boxes.

Combo boxes in forms are similar to Lookup fields in tables. Creating Lookup fields is discussed in Lesson 1, "Customizing Tables."

Priority:	
	Regular
	2-3 Days
	Overnight

When you create a list box or combo box, you can type the items in the list or pull them from an existing table or query. If you want to display a limited number of items in the list and the items will not change, you can define a **value list**, which is a list that you create for the list box or combo box. If you pull the values from an existing table or query, the list box or combo box becomes a bound control. If you use a value list, the list box or combo box is an unbound control.

You cannot pull data from an existing table or query *and* set a value list for the same list box or combo box.

In this exercise, you add a list box and a combo box to frmFebruaryOrders. The list box will draw its values from a table, while the combo box will draw its values from a list that you create.

A list box can be changed to a combo box or text box, and a combo box can be changed to a list box or a text box. To change a box type, click Change To on the Format menu and click the type of object that you want the box to become.

1   Display frmFebruaryOrders in Design view.

2   In the toolbox, click the List Box tool, and click below the EmployeeID text box, aligning the plus sign (+) on the mouse pointer with the left edge of the EmployeeID text box.

List Box

A list box appears in the form.

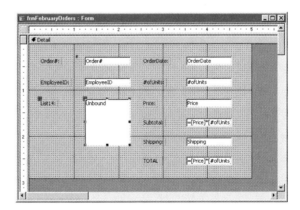

3   Resize the new list box to about half its original height.

4   Click the new label, move the mouse pointer over the center of the label until the pointer turns into an insertion point, and then click the mouse.

An insertion point appears in the label text.

5   Delete the existing text, and type **Code:**.

6   Double-click the edge of the list box.

The List Box property sheet appears.

7   Click the Data tab, if necessary.

The title bar of the property sheet includes *List14,* which is the name that Access gave the list box. Don't worry if your list box does not have the same number as the one in the illustration.

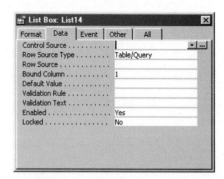

8   Click in the Control Source box, click the down arrow that appears, and then click Code.

The data in the list box will be related to the Code field in tblFebruaryOrders (so that the list will select the correct code for the current order).

9   In the Row Source Type box, verify that Table/Query is selected.

The data in the list box will come from a table or query.

10   Click in the Row Source box, click the down arrow that appears, scroll down, and then click tblProductsList.

The data in the list box will come from tblProductsList.

The list box becomes a bound control after you select a table to provide data to the list.

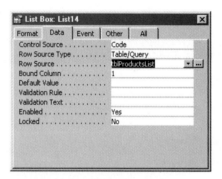

11   Close the List Box property sheet.

Combo Box

12 In the toolbox, click the Combo Box tool, and click below the Code list box, aligning the plus sign (+) on the mouse pointer with the left edge of the Code list box.

A combo box appears in the form.

Note that the combo box already contains a down arrow even though no value list has been defined for the control. Until you create a value list, a blank list will appear when you click the down arrow in Form view.

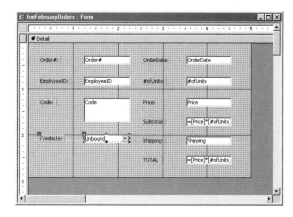

13 Click the new label, move the mouse pointer over the center of the label until the pointer turns into an insertion point, and then click the mouse.

An insertion point appears in the label text.

14 Delete the existing text, and type **Priority:**.

You can also change the label text in the Caption box on the Format tab in the property sheet for the label.

15 Double-click the edge of the combo box.

The Combo Box property sheet appears, with the Data tab selected.

16 Click in the Row Source Type box, click the down arrow that appears, and then click Value List.

17 Click in the Row Source box, and type **Regular;2-3 Days;Overnight**.

These are the values that will appear when you click the down arrow in the combo box.

The semicolons (;) in the value list tell Access that each item is a separate entry in the combo list.

The combo box is not a bound control; the data in the list comes from the value list that you enter in step 17.

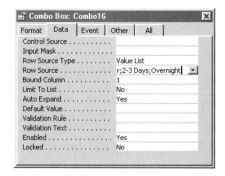

18 Close the Combo Box property sheet.

19 Display the form in Form view.

The Code list box displays all the codes from tblProductsList, and the Priority combo box allows you to enter your own value or click the down arrow to select one of the three default values.

> If you type a new value in the Priority text box, the value will not be added to the value list.

20   Click the Priority down arrow.

A list containing the values that you typed in step 17 appears.

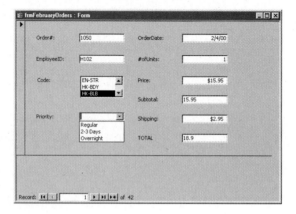

21   Save the form.

AC2000E.2.4

Customizing Form Sections

One way to customize a form is to divide it into sections. You can divide forms into five sections—**Form Header, Page Header,** Detail, **Page Footer,** and **Form Footer**—each of which display information in a different place in the form.

> The Page Header and Page Footer sections are not visible when the form is in Form view; they appear only when the form is printed.

Section	Use
Form Header	Displays information at the top of the first page of the form.
Page Header	Displays information at the top of every printed page.
Detail	Displays records in the body of the form.
Page Footer	Displays information at the bottom of every printed page.
Form Footer	Displays information at the bottom of the last page of the form.

When you create a form in Design view, the Detail section appears by default. Every form must have a Detail section to display data from the form's underlying table or query. You can add the other form sections by using the Page Header/Footer or Form Header/Footer commands on the View menu. Form headers and footers and page headers and footers must be added and removed from the form in pairs. For example, you cannot add a page header without also adding a page footer. You can, of course, have all five sections in the same form.

Access treats each section as a distinct object within the database, with its own properties. When the section is selected, the bar above the section, which contains the name of the section, changes to white text on a black background. When you select a section, you can modify the properties for the section, such as background color and size, by clicking the buttons on the Formatting toolbar. To see all the available section properties, you can open a property sheet for the section by double-clicking the section bar, double-clicking any blank area in the form section, or double-clicking the section selector, the gray box to the left of the section bar on the vertical ruler.

Section
selector

In this exercise, you use a form header to add a title to frmFebruaryOrders.

1   Display frmFebruaryOrders in Design view.

2   On the View menu, click Form Header/Footer.

A form header and form footer appear in the form.

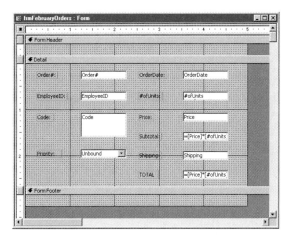

3   Move the mouse pointer over the bottom edge of the Form Header section until it turns into a resizing double-headed arrow, and drag the edge down a half-inch.

The Form Header section increases in size by a half-inch.

Label

4   In the toolbox, click the Label tool, and click in the center of the Form Header section at the one-inch mark on the horizontal ruler.

A label, indicated by a blinking insertion point, appears in the Form Header section.

5   Type **February Orders**, and click any blank area in the form.

6   Click the February Orders label, change the font size to 14 points, and then make the font bold.

When you remove page headers and footers or form headers and footers, Access deletes all the information in the section.

You might need to resize the form window to see both the form header and the form footer.

Modifying the font will work if the label is selected, but not if the text in the label is selected.

7 Resize the February Orders label so that all the label text is visible.

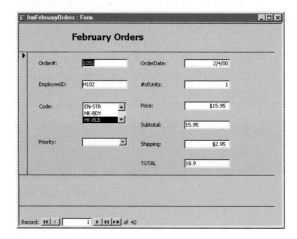

8 Display the form in Form view.

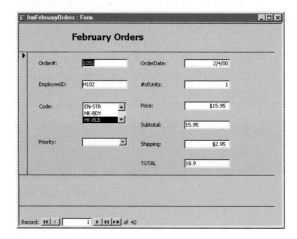

The blank area at the bottom of the form is the Form Footer section.

9 Save the form.

AC2000E.2.2

Inserting a Graphic in a Form

You can enhance the appearance of your forms by using graphics. For example, you could add your company logo to a form so that whenever you or another user prints a record, your company logo is also printed. You can also use graphics to call attention to areas of the form or provide information about sections of the form.

The standard installation of Microsoft Office 2000 includes the Microsoft Clip Gallery, from which you can select from thousands of images in a variety of categories, such as business, communications, science, and technology. You can also insert graphics created in other programs.

To open the Microsoft Clip Gallery, click Object on the Insert menu, click Microsoft Clip Gallery, and then click OK.

Images can be stored in a number of different formats depending on how the image was created and how it will be used. Access supports all of the popular image formats, such as GIF (Graphics Interchange Format), TIFF (Tagged Image File Format), JPEG (Joint Photographic Experts Group), and BMP (bit map). The LMRsmall graphic that you use in this exercise is in the TIFF format.

In this exercise, you add a small version of the Lakewood Mountains Resort logo to the Form Header section of frmFebruaryOrders so that the logo will appear on any printed records.

1 Display frmFebruaryOrders in Design view.

2 In the Form Header section, click any blank area.

3 On the Insert menu, click Picture.

The Insert Picture dialog box appears.

> You can also double-click the graphic to insert it into the form.

4 In the Insert Picture dialog box, navigate to the Access Expert Practice folder on your hard disk, verify that LMRsmall is selected, and then click OK.

Access inserts the graphic into the top-left corner of the Form Header section.

> If you don't like the placement of the graphic, you can move it just as you would any other control on a form.

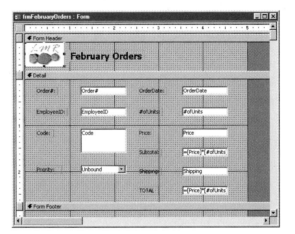

5 Display the form in Form view.

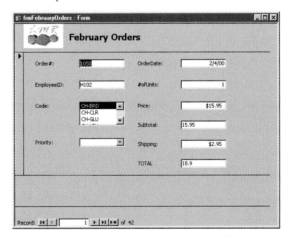

6 Save the form.

AC2000E.2.3

Modifying Control Properties

Every control in a form has its own set of properties, which set how the control appears, the data it contains, and how it responds when clicked, right-clicked, or double-clicked. You can modify some properties for a control—mostly those for the appearance of the control—by clicking the control and using the buttons on the Formatting toolbar. To see all the available properties for a control, you can open the property sheet for the control by double-clicking the edge of the control.

If you select more than one control at once, you can change the properties for all the controls at the same time by using the Formatting toolbar or the Multiple Selection property sheet. To open a property sheet when more than one control is selected, right-click one of the selected controls, and click Properties on the shortcut menu that appears. You cannot open a Multiple Selection property sheet by double-clicking the edge of one of the selected controls.

In this exercise, you modify the properties of the Subtotal and Total controls on frmFebruaryOrders so that the values in the controls appear in currency format, with a dollar sign and two decimal places.

> You can select more than one control by holding down the Shift key and clicking the controls that you want to select.

1   Display frmFebruaryOrders in Design view.

2   In the Detail section, click the Subtotal text box, hold down the Shift key, and click the TOTAL text box.

3   Right-click the TOTAL text box, and click Properties on the shortcut menu that appears.

     The Multiple Selection property sheet appears.

4   Click the Format tab, if necessary.

5   In the Format text box, click the down arrow, scroll down, and then click Currency.

> The Multiple Selection property sheet shows only those properties that all the selected controls have in common.

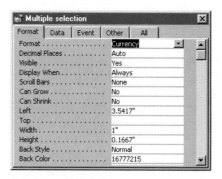

6   Close the Multiple Selection property sheet.

7 Display the form in Form view.

The values in the Subtotal and TOTAL text boxes are now displayed in currency format, with a dollar sign and two decimal places.

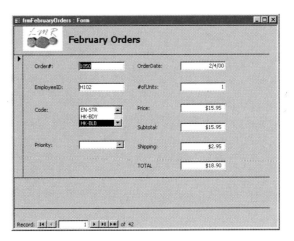

8 Save and close the form.

AC2000E.2.5

Modifying Form Properties

As with controls and form sections, the form as a whole also has its own set of properties that you can adjust using the property sheet for the form. Forms have numerous properties that you can set and modify. For example, you can set the reaction of the form when the user right-clicks it, the color of the form, the source for the form, and whether users can add or edit data in the form.

You can open the property sheet for the form by double-clicking the form selector, which is the gray box at the intersection of the horizontal and vertical rulers.

The black box in the form selector indicates that the form is selected.

Form selector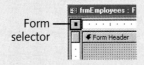

(continued)

continued

In the property sheet for the form, there are five tabs, each listing different categories of properties for the form.

Category	Use
Format	Defines how the form appears.
Data	Defines properties such as the source of the values on the form, whether the form allows filters, and so on.
Event	Defines how the form will respond when acted upon by the user.
Other	Defines miscellaneous properties like the form's name.
All	Displays all the properties for the form in the same list.

To find out more about a particular property, click in the box for the property and press F1.

To modify form properties

1   Display the form in Design view.

2   Double-click the form selector.

3   In the property sheet, click the desired tab.

4   Click in the box for the property that you want to change.

5   Type the new value for the property.

    Or

    Click the down arrow that appears, and click the new value for the property.

6   Close the property sheet.

AC2000E.2.6

Creating a Subform

In the simplest sense, a subform is a form within a form. Subforms are an easy way to see data from two different forms without having to switch back and forth between the forms. For example, a form that contains a list of the employees who are approved to place orders might contain a subform that shows the orders placed by each employee. So, when the record in the **main form**—the form that contains the subform—is for employee S606, the subform would show only the orders placed by employee S606, as shown on the following page.

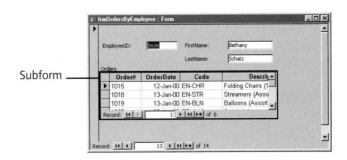

Subform

When a subform shows only the correct records for the record in the main form, it means that the subform and main form are synchronized. For synchronization to happen, the tables or queries underlying the form and the subform must be in a one-to-many relationship. The table underlying the main form must be on the *one* side of the one-to-many relationship, and the table underlying the subform must be on the *many* side of the one-to-many relationship. You should create this one-to-many relationship before you add a subform to the main form. To create the relationship, you drag the primary key field for the table underlying the main form to the field containing the same information in the table underlying the subform.

If you find that the main form data and the subform data are not synchronized—meaning that there is data in the subform that is not related to the record in the main form—you can fix the problem yourself by checking the relationships between the two tables underlying the form and subform. An unrelated subform will show every record from the underlying table, instead of just those records related to the record in the main form. If you or someone else deletes this relationship, the form and subform data will no longer by synchronized. You can synchronize the form and subform again by creating the one-to-many relationship again.

You can create a subform by using the Subform Wizard, dragging the form that you want to use as the subform onto the main form, or using the Subform/Subreport tool, as you do in the following exercise.

The two related fields that contain the same data do not have to have the same name. For example, one field could be called *Employee#* while the other could be called *Employee Identification Code.*

You start the Subform Wizard by selecting the Control Wizards button, clicking the Subform/Subreport tool, and clicking in the form where you want the Subform to go.

In this exercise, you create a relationship between tblApprovedToOrder and tblJanuaryOrders and add a subform to frmOrdersByEmployee (which is based on tblApprovedToOrder), showing related records from tblJanuary-Orders. As a result for each employee listed in tblApprovedToOrder, there will be a subform showing all the orders in tblJanuaryOrders made by that employee.

Relationships

1   On the Database toolbar, click the Relationships button.

The Relationships window appears.

All the relationships in the database are hidden. To show the relation-ships, click the Show All Relationships button on the Relationship toolbar. To clear the Relationships window again, click the Clear Layout button on the Relationship toolbar.

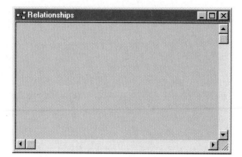

Show Table

2   On the Relationship toolbar, click the Show Table button.

The Show Table dialog box appears.

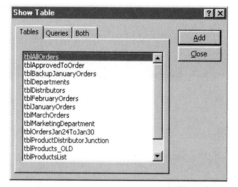

3   Add tblApprovedToOrder and tblJanuaryOrders to the Relationships window, and close the Show Table dialog box.

Field lists for tblApprovedtoOrder and tblJanuaryOrders appear in the Relationships window.

The line between the two EmployeeID fields indicates that the two fields contain the same data. You might have to scroll down in the tblJanuary-Orders field list to see the EmployeeID field.

The field lists in the Relationships window can be moved around the window by clicking the title bar. You can also resize the boxes so that all the fields in each list are visible.

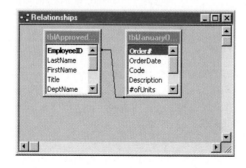

4   Double-click the line between the two field lists.

The Edit Relationships dialog box appears.

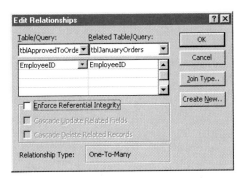

Referential integrity is discussed in Lesson 1, "Customizing Tables."

5   Select the Enforce Referential Integrity check box, and click OK.

The Edit Relationships dialog box closes.

6   In the tblJanuaryOrders field list, scroll down until the EmployeeID field is visible.

The 1 next to the EmployeeID field in the tblApprovedToOrder field list and the infinity sign (∞) next to the EmployeeID field in the tblJanuary-Orders field list indicate that the two tables are now in a one-to-many relationship.

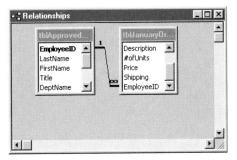

7   Save and close the Relationships window.

8   Open frmOrdersByEmployee in Design view.

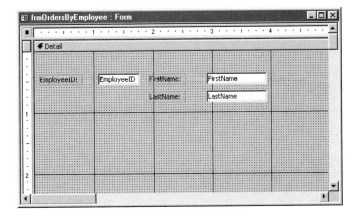

Subform/Subreport

9   In the toolbox, click the Subform/Subreport tool, and click at the left edge of the form at the 1-inch mark on the vertical ruler.

A subform appears in the form.

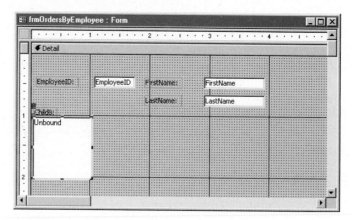

10 Resize the subform so that its right edge is at the 4-inch mark on the horizontal ruler.

Access will not automatically resize the subform to show all the fields in the related form. For example, tblJanuaryOrders has eight fields but only four of them will be visible in the 4-inch-wide subform that you create in step 10. You should always resize subforms to the desired width.

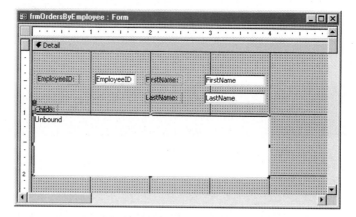

11 Click any blank area in the form.

12 Double-click the edge of the subform.

The Subform/Subreport property sheet appears.

13 Click the Data tab, if necessary.

14 In the Source Object box, click the down arrow, scroll down, and then click Table.tblJanuaryOrders.

The subform will get its data from tblJanuaryOrders.

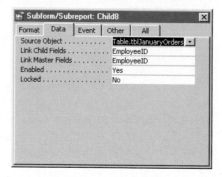

15 Close the Subform/Subreport property sheet.

16 Click the new label, move the mouse pointer over the center of the label until the pointer turns into an insertion point, and then click the mouse.

17 Delete the existing text, and type **Orders**.

18 Display the form in Form view.

The orders placed by employee H101 appear in the subform.

You can navigate through the records in the subform by using the scroll bar on the right edge of the subform or the navigation buttons in the bottom-left corner of the subform.

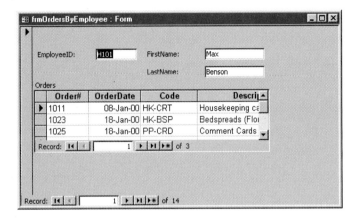

19 Save and close the form.

AC2000E.2.7

Creating a Switchboard

If you create a database using the database wizards included with Access, Access creates a switchboard for the database. A switchboard is a special type of form with buttons that users can click to view, edit, or add data to the database's forms, reports, queries, and other objects.

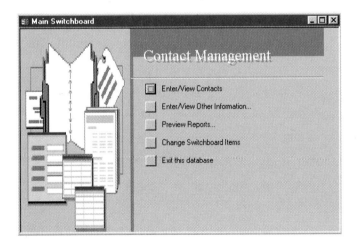

Each item in the first page of the switchboard links to other pages on the switchboard or to an action such as closing the current database without quitting Access. For example, clicking the Enter/View Contacts button in the switchboard shown above opens a form that allows you to enter new records and view existing records in a table of contact information.

You can set your database so that the switchboard—instead of the Database window—appears when you start Access. You'll learn how to set this startup option in Lesson 7, "Using Database Tools."

2000 New!

You can create a switchboard for databases that were not created using a database wizard.

Some database users find using a switchboard to navigate in the database easier than using the Database window. In this sense, a switchboard is a friendly interface for users—typically, the people who will be entering data into forms or printing reports. Creating a switchboard for users can also keep them out of the database window—especially Design view for forms and reports—and prevent them from accidentally making design changes. Users can always close the switchboard and use the Database window to navigate through the database, but switchboards are a friendlier interface.

In earlier versions of Access, you had to create a database with a wizard to use the **Switchboard Manager,** a tool that allows you to add, modify, and delete switchboard controls. In Access 2000, you can run the Switchboard Manager in any database—even those that were not created using a database wizard. The Switchboard Manager is a multilayered tool that you use to create all the parts of the switchboard. When you start the Switchboard Manager, the first dialog box that appears is the Switchboard Manager dialog box.

In the Switchboard Manager, the terms *switchboard* and *switchboard page* are often used interchangeably.

You can click the Make Default button to change the page that first appears when you open the switchboard.

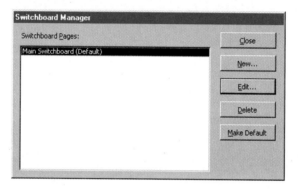

You use the Switchboard Manager dialog box to create the pages in the switchboard, not the items on the pages. You click New to add a new page to the list of pages, Edit to modify an existing one, and Delete to remove a page from the switchboard. If you click Edit, the Edit Switchboard Page dialog box appears.

The Switchboard Name box tells you which page of the switchboard you are editing.

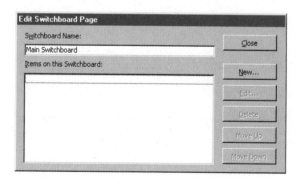

You use the Edit Switchboard Page dialog box to specify which items (buttons) will appear on the page. If you click New or Edit in the Edit Switchboard Page dialog box, the Edit Switchboard Item dialog box appears.

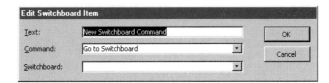

You use the Edit Switchboard Item dialog box to set the function and location of each item in the switchboard.

important

When you create a switchboard, Access adds a form named *Switchboard* to the list of forms in the Database window. You can have only one Switchboard form per database, although that one switchboard can have many pages and layers. In addition to the *Switchboard* form, Access creates a table named *Switchboard Items*. Don't rename either of these objects or else the switchboard will become unusable.

In this exercise, your goal is to make it easier to use the Lakewood Mountains 03 database. Many of the people who use the database use it only to enter data into the forms in the database. You decide to create a switchboard named *Enter/View Form Data* with links to frmFebruaryOrders and frmVendors.

1   On the Tools menu, point to Database Utilities, and click Switchboard Manager.

A dialog box appears, indicating that Access couldn't find a valid switchboard and asking if you would like to create one.

2   Click Yes.

The Switchboard Manager appears with Main Switchboard (Default) already selected.

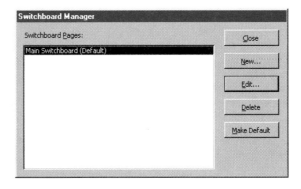

The only page in the switchboard is the Main Switchboard (Default) page.

3   Click Edit.

The Edit Switchboard Page dialog box appears.

The Main Switchboard page does not currently contain any items.

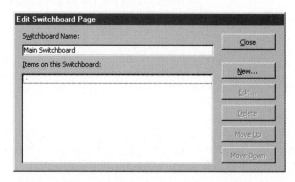

4   Click in the Switchboard Name box, delete the existing text, and type **Enter/View Form Data**.

The name of your main switchboard page will be *Enter/View Form Data*.

5   Click New.

The Edit Switchboard Item dialog box appears.

6   In the Text box, type **Enter/View February Orders**.

The first button on the Enter/View Form Data switchboard page will be called Enter/View February Orders.

7   Click the Command down arrow, and click Open Form In Add Mode.

The form will open in Add mode, meaning that you can enter data. The Switchboard box changes to a Form box.

8   Click the Form down arrow, and click frmFebruaryOrders.

The button will open formFebruaryOrders in Add mode.

9   Click OK.

The Edit Switchboard Item dialog box closes, and Enter/View February Orders is added to the Items On This Switchboard list.

10   Click New.

The Edit Switchboard Item dialog box appears.

11   In the Text box, type **Enter/View Vendors**.

The second button on the Enter/View Form Data switchboard page is called *Enter/View Vendors*.

12   Click the Command down arrow, and click Open Form In Edit Mode.

The form will open in Edit mode, meaning that you can view existing records and enter data. The Switchboard box changes to a Form box.

13   Click the Form down arrow, and click frmVendors.

The button will open frmVendors in Add mode.

14 Click OK.

The Edit Switchboard Item dialog box closes, and Enter/View Vendors is added to the Items On This Switchboard list.

You can reorganize the order of the items on the switchboard by clicking the Move Up and Move Down buttons.

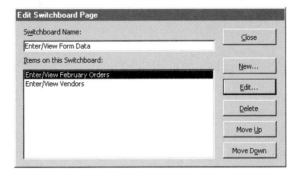

15 Close the Edit Switchboard Page dialog box and the Switchboard Manager dialog box.

16 Display the list of forms in the Database window, if necessary, and double-click Switchboard.

The Edit/View Form Data switchboard appears with the two buttons that you just created.

The title bar for the window contains the name of the switchboard, in this case, Enter/View Form Data.

The name of the database for which the switchboard was created appears above the buttons in the switchboard by default.

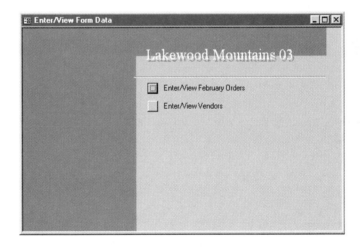

You do not have to double-click the buttons in a switchboard.

This form is in Add mode, meaning you can only add new data, not view existing data.

17 Click Enter/View February Orders.

A blank form for frmFebruaryOrders appears.

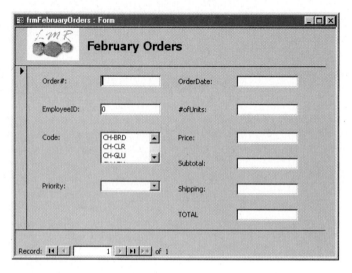

18 Close frmFebruaryOrders.

19 Click Enter/View Vendors.

frmVendors appears with the first record visible.

This form is in Edit mode, meaning that you can view the existing data *and* add new data. To display a blank record, click the New Record button.

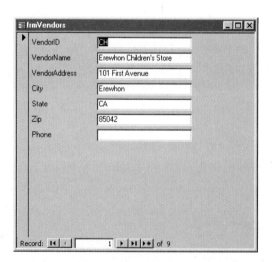

20 Close frmVendors, and close the switchboard.

Lesson Wrap-Up

This lesson covered how to customize forms, form sections, and form controls; add list boxes, combo boxes, and graphics to forms; and create subforms and switchboards in Access 2000.

If you are continuing to the next lesson:

Close

●   Click the Close button in the top-right corner of the Database window.

The Access Core 03 database closes.

If you are not continuing to the next lesson:

Close

●   To quit Access for now, click the Close button in the top-right corner of the Access window.

Access and the Access Core 03 database close.

Lesson Glossary

bound control A control based on the values from a field in a table or query.

calculated control A control that calculates its value using an expression based on the contents of other fields in the form.

combo box A control that allows users to either pick values from an existing list or enter a value not on the list.

controls Objects in a form that display data, perform actions, or enhance the design of the form.

Detail The section of a form that contains the records from the underlying table or query.

form A database object created from the data in an underlying table or query that simplifies viewing, adding, and editing the data in the database.

form footer The section of a form that appears at the bottom of the last page of the form.

form header The section of a form that appears at the top of the first page of the form.

label A type of control that contains text. Labels are often paired with text boxes.

list box A control that allows users to select a value for a field from a list, but prevents the user from entering a value not on the list.

main form A form that displays the records on the *one* side of a one-to-*many* relationship and has a subform that displays the records on the many side of a one-to-many relationship.

page footer The section of a form that appears at the bottom of every printed page of the form.

page header The section of a form that appears at the top of every printed page of the form.

subform A form within a main form that displays the records on the *many* side of a one-to-many relationship.

switchboard A special type of form that allows users to find and perform common database functions through a simple interface.

Switchboard Manager A tool that allows you to add, modify, and delete switchboard controls.

text box A type of control that contains data. Text boxes are often paired with labels.

toolbox A floating toolbar that contains a collection of tools that can be used to modify and create controls.

unbound control A freestanding control that is not connected to data in an underlying table or query.

value list A list used as the source for a list box or combo box.

Quick Quiz

1   How do you insert a graphic in a form?

2   What is a list box?

3   What happens when you add a page header and page footer to a form?

4   Why would you use a combo box instead of a list box?

5   How do you display the property sheet for a control?

6   How do you start the Switchboard Manager?

7   What is a subform?

8   What is a switchboard?

9   Why would you use Design view to create a form, instead of AutoForm or the Form Wizard?

Putting It All Together

Exercise 1: Create a new form in Design view from tblPurchaseOrder. Include the PurchaseOrderID, Product, and Quantity fields. Add a list box named Employee ID that displays the EmployeeID field from tblApprovedToOrder. Add a page header and page footer, add a label that reads *Purchase Order* to the Page Header section, and then insert the LMRsmall logo to the left of the label. Save the form as **frmNewPurchaseOrder**, and close it.

Exercise 2: Open frmVendors, and add the data from tblMarchOrders as a subform with a label reading *Orders*. (Hint: Set up the one-to-many relationship between tblVendors and tblMarchOrders first.) Display frmVendors in Form view, and scroll through the vendor records to see which vendors have already received orders. Save and close the form.

Exercise 3: Extend the capabilities of the switchboard that you created in this lesson. Open the Switchboard Manager and edit the Enter/View February Orders item so that it opens frmFebruaryOrders in Edit mode instead of Add mode. Add a new item to the switchboard named *Close Database* that uses the command Exit Application. Close the Switchboard Manager.

LESSON 4

Customizing Reports

After completing this lesson, you will be able to:

✔ *Create and modify a report in Design view.*

✔ *Add sections to a report.*

✔ *Sort and group report data.*

✔ *Modify report properties.*

✔ *Add and modify report controls.*

✔ *Create a subreport.*

✔ *Synchronize report data.*

A **report** is a type of object that you can use to organize and view the data in a database. Reports are like forms in that reports display table and query data. Unlike forms, however, you cannot add or edit data using a report—only view or print data. Reports make it possible for users to view data, without allowing them to change the data and possibly create errors in the database.

Microsoft Access includes many options for customizing reports to suit your needs and making the data easy for users to understand. With Access, you can:

■ Divide the report into sections, which allows you to specify information to appear at the top and bottom of each report page and at the beginning and end of the report as a whole.

■ Sort and group report data, which changes how data is organized in the report.

■ Add controls to perform calculations or to show data from a table or query.

■ Modify report and control properties, which changes the report's appearance and behavior.

■ Add subreports to show records from a related table or query.

For additional information about opening the practice file for this lesson, see the "Using the CD-ROM" section at the beginning of this book.

Sample files for the lesson

To complete the procedures in this lesson, you will need to use a file named Lakewood Mountains 04 in the Access Expert Practice folder that is located on your hard disk.

AC2000E.4.3

Creating and Modifying Reports in Design View

The quickest and easiest way to design a basic report is by using Auto-Report, which allows you to choose only the general layout of the report and the table or query that the report is based on. Another way to create a report is by using the Report Wizard, which allows you more flexibility than AutoReport. With the Report Wizard, you can choose the table or query that you want to base the report on, the fields from the table or query that you want to include, different techniques of grouping and sorting the data in the report, the layout and style of the report, and the name of the report. Once you have created a report using either of those techniques, you can customize the report in Design view.

However, you can also use Design view to create reports by displaying a blank report and adding report elements manually. Although using AutoReport or the Report Wizard is easier, creating a report in Design view offers you more flexibility and design options.

When you create a report in Design view, you add controls to the report to enhance the appearance of the report. A control is an object on a report that displays data, such as command buttons, list boxes, labels, and combo boxes. You can add bound, unbound, and calculated controls to a report by dragging the desired control from the toolbox—a special toolbar that contains tools used to modify and create controls—to the blank report.

To use AutoReport, click New on the Database window toolbar, and click either AutoReport: Columnar or AutoReport: Tabular in the New Report dialog box.

To use the Report Wizard, double-click Create Report Using Report Wizard, and follow the instructions in the wizard.

Reports can be displayed in two views besides Design view: Print Preview and Layout view. Print Preview shows how the entire report and its data will appear when printed, and Layout view shows just the layout for the first page of the report. You can switch between these views by using the View button on the toolbar.

Controls are also discussed in Lesson 3, "Customizing Forms."

Control	Use
Bound	Retrieves and displays information from an underlying table or query.
Unbound	Displays information such as instructions, labels, and images and is not related to an underlying table or query.
Calculated	Displays information calculated from an expression based on data in the other controls or the underlying table or query.

In this exercise, you open the Lakewood Mountains 04 database and use Design view to create a report based on tblJanuaryOrders.

Open

1   On the Database toolbar, click the Open button, navigate to the Access Expert Practice folder on your hard disk, and then open the Lakewood Mountains 04 database.

2 On the Objects bar, click Reports, and click New on the Database window toolbar.

The New Report dialog box appears with Design View already selected.

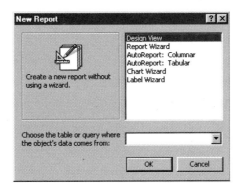

3 Click the Choose The Table Or Query Where The Object's Data Comes From down arrow, scroll down, click tblJanuaryOrders, and then click OK.

A new report appears in Design view with the toolbox and the field list for tblJanuaryOrders already open.

In this exercise, all the controls that you add to the report are bound controls based on tblJanuaryOrders. You add unbound controls to the report later in this lesson.

The field list and toolbox can be moved by clicking the title bar and dragging.

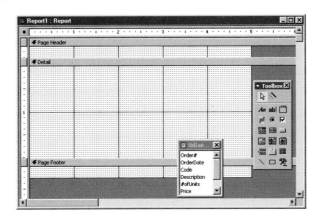

4 In the field list, click EmployeeID, and drag it until the left edge of the mouse pointer is about a quarter inch from the top edge of the Detail section and aligned with the 1-inch mark on the horizontal ruler.

When moving a control from the field list to the report, the mouse pointer turns into a box. When you click, the left edge of the box is where the left edge of the text box will be, with the label to its left.

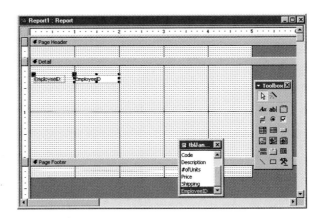

5   In the field list, scroll up, click Order#, and then drag the field until the left edge of the mouse pointer is aligned with the left edge of the EmployeeID text box.

6   In the field list, click OrderDate, and then drag the field until the left edge of the mouse pointer is aligned with the left edge of the Order# text box.

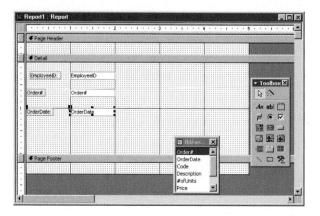

7   In the field list, click Code, and drag the field until the left edge of the mouse pointer is between the 3- and 3.5-inch marks on the horizontal ruler.

8   In the field list, click Description, and drag the field until the left edge of the mouse pointer is aligned with the left edge of the Code text box.

Your report will not exactly match the illustration shown here.

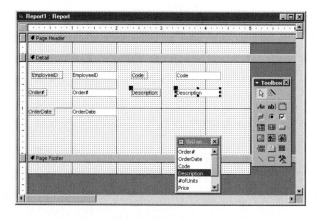

9   Save the report as **rptJanuaryOrders**.

Adding Sections to a Report

AC2000E.4.5

To make a report easier to understand, you can divide it into sections, which display information at different intervals in the report. All blank reports in Access include three sections: a page header, a page footer, and a Detail section. The Detail section contains the main body of the report, and the Page Header and Page Footer sections appear at the top and bottom of every printed page, respectively. Users often add column headings and labels to these sections. For example, if you created a report that shows Lakewood Mountains Resort's February reservations, you might put the resort's logo in the page header and *February 2000* in the page footer so that they would appear on every printed page of the report.

Report headers and footers and page headers and footers must be added or removed from a report as a pair.

Report sections can have the same raised and sunken effects as individual cells in a table.

Report Header and **Report Footer** sections work differently than the Page Header and Page Footer sections. Instead of appearing on every page of the report, the report header appears only once at the beginning of the report and the report footer appears only once at the end of the report. The report header is a good place to add a title to your report, while the report footer is a good place to add information such as who created the report.

Report sections have fewer properties than individual controls or the report as a whole. The color of the section can be set using the Fill/Back Color button on the Formatting toolbar, but all other properties—such as the name of the section, whether data in a group can be split between pages, if the selection will have a special effect, if a macro will run when the report is printed, whether the section will adjust automatically to show all the data in the section, and more—must be set using the property sheet for the section. To open the property sheet for section, you double-click any blank area in the section, the section bar, or the section selector, which is the gray box to the left of the section bar on the vertical ruler.

Section — selector

Access creates relatively small header and footer sections, but you can change the height of the section to accommodate the controls that you add to it. To increase or decrease the height of a section, move the mouse pointer over the bottom edge of the section until the pointer turns into a resizing double-headed arrow, and drag down to increase the section height or drag up to decrease the section height. To adjust the width of the report, move the mouse pointer over the right edge of the report until the pointer turns into a resizing double-headed arrow, and drag the edge of the section to the left or right.

Resizing Double-Headed Arrow

You can change the width of an entire report, but you cannot change the width of just one section.

In this exercise, you add a report header and footer to rptJanuaryOrders, adjust the height of the report header, and then add a label.

1 On the View menu, click Report Header/Footer.

A report header and report footer appear in the report.

To see the report footer, you might need to move the mouse pointer over the bottom edge of the report window until a vertical double-headed arrow appears and drag the bottom edge down. You can also click the Maximize button to enlarge the size of the report window.

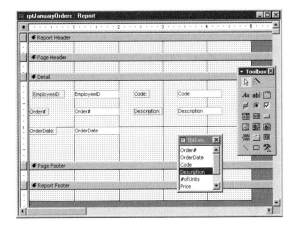

2   Move the mouse pointer over the bottom edge of the Report Header section until the pointer turns into a resizing double-headed arrow, and drag the edge down about a quarter inch.

Aa

Label

3   In the toolbox, click the Label tool, click in the center of the Report Header section about one inch from the left edge, and then type **Lakewood Mountains**.

4   Click any blank area in the report.

> You can change the font size and style by using the buttons on the Formatting toolbar.

5   Click the label, change the font size to 14 points, change the font to bold, and then resize the label so that all the text is visible.

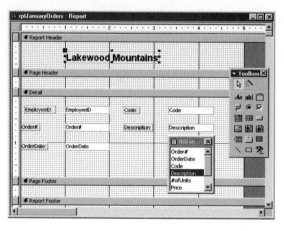

6   Save the report.

Sorting and Grouping Report Data

To better organize the information in your report, you can **group** the data into categories. Grouping data allows you to arrange records based on one or more common fields so that they are easier to read. For example, if you created a report to show orders placed at Lakewood Mountains Resort in January 2000, you could group the data by EmployeeID, which would organize all of the orders placed by the first employee together, and then the second, and so forth. All orders placed by a single employee would appear grouped together.

> Unlike page and report headers and footers, group headers and footers can be added to a report individually instead of as a pair.

When you group data in your report, you can give the group a **group header** or **group footer**. The group header displays information at the beginning of each group of data, and a group footer displays information at the end of the group. A group header usually contains the field by which report data is grouped, called the **grouping field**, and a group footer can be used to calculate totals or other summaries for each group. Using the example in the last paragraph, you could use the group footer to display a count of all orders placed by each employee and the total cost of those orders.

Group headers and footers take the name of the field by which they are grouped. In the following illustration, the group header and footer are called EmployeeID Header and EmployeeID Footer because EmployeeID is the grouping field. In this example, the employee's ID number appears bold in the group header, the orders made by the employee appear in the Detail section, and the group footer (if it contained any information) appears last. Although it is currently blank, the group footer could be used to total the number of orders made by each employee.

Unlike page headers and footers and report headers and footers, you can add a group header without also adding a group footer and vice versa.

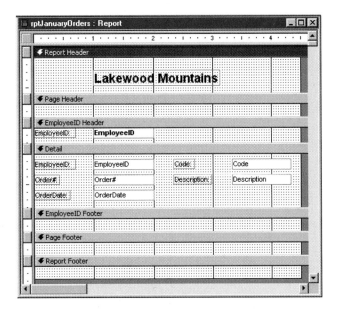

Sorting And Grouping

You set grouping fields in the Sorting And Grouping dialog box, which can be opened by clicking the Sorting And Grouping button on the Report Design toolbar.

You can group using the contents of up to 10 fields or expressions in the report.

tip

If you set more than one grouping field, Access assigns top priority to the field at the top of the list, and then to the field in the next line, and so forth.

To remove a sorting or grouping level, click the row selector for the sorting or grouping level, and press Delete. If you delete a group, you also delete all the headers and footers associated with the group.

After you have set a field as a grouping field, the properties for the group appear in the bottom half of the Sorting And Grouping dialog box. The group properties indicate whether a group header and group footer have been created and how the group will be sorted. Sorting changes the order in which a field's contents are organized. By default, Access organizes data in ascending order—from the lowest value to the highest value. You can change the sort to descending—from the highest to the lowest value—in the Sort Order column of the Sorting And Grouping dialog box.

In this exercise, you set a grouping order for rptJanuaryOrders, add a group header and a group footer to the report, change the color of the group header, and then display the report contents in Print Preview.

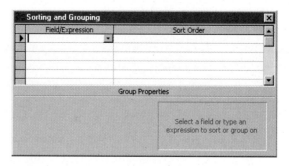

Sorting And Grouping

1   On the Report Design toolbar, click the Sorting And Grouping button.

The Sorting And Grouping dialog box appears with the insertion point already in the first cell in the Field/Expression column.

To remove a group, click the Sorting And Grouping button on the toolbar. In the Sorting And Grouping dialog box, click the row selector of the field to be removed, and press Delete.

2   In the first cell in the Field/Expression column, click the down arrow, and click EmployeeID.

EmployeeID becomes a grouping field, and the properties for the group appear in the bottom section of the Sorting And Grouping dialog box.

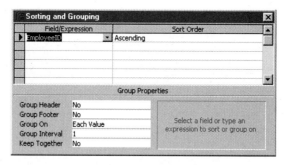

3   In the Group Properties section, click in the Group Header box, click the down arrow that appears, and then click Yes.

An EmployeeID Header section appears in rptJanuaryOrders.

4   In the Group Properties section, click in the Group Footer box, click the down arrow that appears, and then click Yes.

An EmployeeID Footer section appears in rptJanuaryOrders.

5 Close the Sorting And Grouping dialog box.

The report now has an EmployeeID header and an EmployeeID footer.

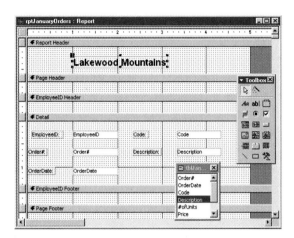

View

6 On the Report Design toolbar, click the View button.

The report appears in Print Preview.

Notice that the View button and the Print Preview button are identical. You can press either to see the report in Print Preview.

The records in the report are organized by employee ID.

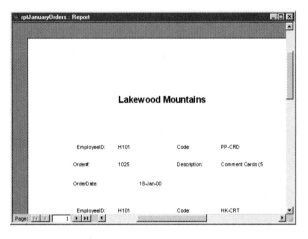

View

Copy

Paste

7 On the Print Preview toolbar, click the View button.

The report appears in Design view.

8 Click the EmployeeID text box (not the EmployeeID label), and click the Copy button on the Report Design toolbar.

9 Click in the EmployeeID Header section, and click the Paste button on the Report Design toolbar.

The EmployeeID label and text box appear in the EmployeeID Header section.

10 Click any blank area in the EmployeeID Header section.

The EmployeeID bar turns dark, indicating that the section is selected.

Fill/Back Color

11 On the Formatting toolbar, click the Fill/Back Color down arrow, and click a yellow square.

The background of the EmployeeID Header section turns yellow.

View

12   On the Report Design toolbar, click the View button.

The report appears in Print Preview.

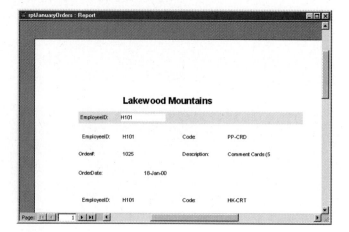

View

13   On the Print Preview toolbar, click the View button.

The report appears in Design view.

14   Save the report.

AC2000E.4.2

Modifying Report Properties

As with other database objects, reports have properties that you can adjust using the property sheet for the report. You can set report properties to change the report's appearance, specify how the report acts when a user clicks, double-clicks, or right-clicks the report, or define the table (or other source) from which the report gets its data. For example, you could allow users to right-click the body of a report to display the report in Print Preview. You could also create different versions of a report, with different information highlighted according to users' needs.

You can display the property sheet for a report by double-clicking the report selector, which is the gray box at the intersection of the horizontal and vertical rulers. The property sheet lists all the available properties for a report and allows you to change them. To find out more about a particular property, click in the box for the property, and press F1.

Report
selector

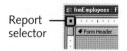

> The caption is not printed when you print the report.

In a report, the caption property sets the **caption** that appears on the report window title bar when the report is in Print Preview. In this exercise, you add a caption to rptJanuaryOrders.

1   Double-click the report selector.

A black square appears in the report selector, indicating that the report is selected. The Report property sheet appears.

2   In the Report property sheet, click the Format tab, if necessary.

3   Click the Caption box, if necessary, and type **January Orders**.

4   Close the Report property sheet.

5   On the Report Design toolbar, click the View button.

View

The report appears in Print Preview, with the caption appearing in the title bar for the report window.

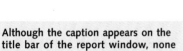

Although the caption appears on the title bar of the report window, none of the text in the report changes.

Caption

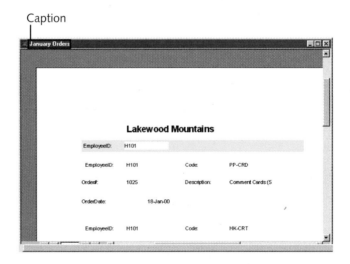

6   On the Report Design toolbar, click the View button.

View

The report appears in Design view.

7   Save the report.

AC2000E.4.4

Adding and Modifying Report Controls

The end goal of a report is to present the data in the database in an attractive and easy-to-use format. You can use controls to enhance and customize the appearance of your reports. Earlier in this lesson you created a report by using bound controls, which contain the data in the report. You can use unbound controls, such as lines, rectangles, and page breaks, to set off the data in your report. For example, page breaks, which force Access to print the next records on a new page, can be placed in a group footer to cause each group of records to be printed on a separate page.

AC2000E.4.1

Another way to customize a report is to add a graphic, which is also a type of unbound control. To insert a picture while the report is in Design view, click Picture on the Insert menu, navigate to the location of the picture you want to add, and then click OK.

Inserting a picture into a report is discussed in the "Inserting a Graphic in a Form" section in Lesson 3, "Customizing Forms."

After you've added controls to your report, you can modify the controls in two ways:

■   Select the control and use the buttons on the Formatting toolbar to adjust properties, such as the color and font of the control.

■   Double-click the edge of the control to open the property sheet for the control. The property sheet contains all the available properties for the control, such as the appearance of the control, the response of the control to certain actions like printing or clicking, and the contents of the control.

In this exercise, you add a page break control to the EmployeeID Footer section of rptJanuaryOrders—which will cause each group of records to be printed on a separate page—and change the font of the EmployeeID control to extra bold.

1   Scroll down so that the EmployeeID footer is visible, if necessary.

Page Break

2   In the toolbox, click the Page Break tool, and click just above the Page Footer bar.

A page break, which looks like a dotted line, appears in the EmployeeID Footer section.

You only need to position a page break vertically; Access places the page break against the left margin by default.

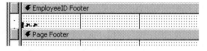

3   In the EmployeeID Header section, double-click the edge of the EmployeeID text box (not the EmployeeID label).

The Text Box property sheet appears.

4   Click the Format tab, if necessary.

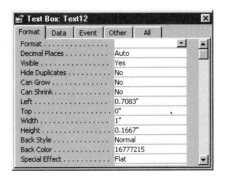

5   Scroll down, click in the Font Weight box, click the down arrow that appears, and then click Extra Bold.

6   Close the Text Box property sheet.

View

7   On the Report Design toolbar, click the View button.

The report appears in Print Preview with the employee ID in the EmployeeID Header section in extra bold font.

View

8   On the Print Preview toolbar, click the View button.

The report appears in Design view.

9   Save and close rptJanuaryOrders.

AC2000E.4.6

Creating a Subreport

A **subreport** is a report that appears inside another report, called the **main report**. The main report contains records on the *one* side of a one-to-many relationship, and the subreport displays related records from the table on the *many* side. This makes it easy to view data from different tables without switching back and forth between the tables. For example, in a report that lists employees in a department, a subreport could show the orders made by each employee. In the report below, the subreport rptAllOrders displays the orders made by employee H101, whose name and employee ID appear in the main report, rptOrdersByEmployee.

> You can add as many subreports as you want to the main report.

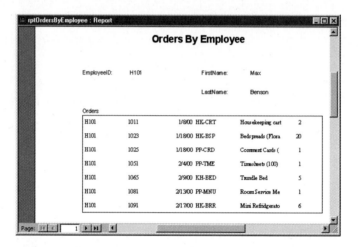

> To create a subreport, you can also open the main report in Design view and drag the report you want to use as the subreport from the Database window to the desired location in the main report.

Before you create a subreport, you should create the reports that you want to use as the subreport and the main report. Then you can use the Subform/Subreport tool in the toolbox to create a Subform/Subreport control in the report at the location where you want the subreport. You can then display the Subform/Subreport property sheet to specify the database object that you want to use as the source object for the subreport.

In this exercise, you add rptAllOrders to rptOrdersByEmployee as a subreport.

1 Open rptOrdersByEmployee in Design view.

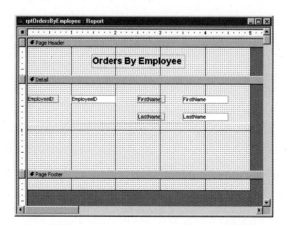

Subform/Subreport

2   In the toolbox, click the Subform/Subreport tool, and click near the left edge of the report at the 1-inch mark on the vertical ruler.

A subreport control appears in the report.

When you add a subreport control to a report, Access gives the control the name *Child* and a number. Don't worry if your subreport does not have the same number as the one in the illustration.

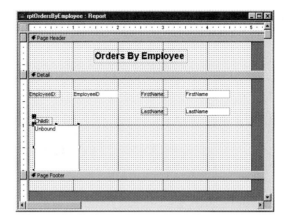

3   Drag the right edge of the subreport to the right until the subreport is the same width as the report.

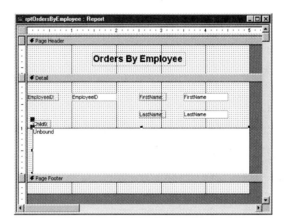

4   Double-click the edge of the subreport box (not the subreport label).

The Subform/Subreport property sheet appears.

5   Click the Data tab, if necessary.

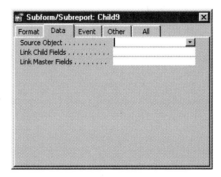

6   In the Source Object box, click the down arrow, and click Report: rptAllOrders.

7 Close the Subform/Subreport property sheet.

rptAllOrders appears in the subreport.

Although the column headings in the Page Header section of the subreport are visible in Design view, the sections do not appear when the subreport is in Print Preview. Access does not print the page header and footer of a subreport.

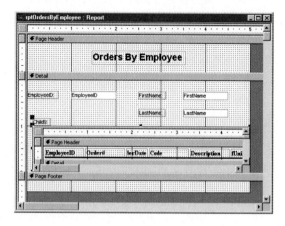

8 Click the subreport label, move the mouse pointer over the center of the label until the pointer turns into an insertion point, and then click the mouse.

An insertion point appears in the label text.

9 Delete the existing text, and type **Orders**.

10 On the Report Design toolbar, click the View button.

The report appears in Print Preview.

View

You do not have to resize the subreport in Design view to have all the orders visible in the subreport in Print Preview.

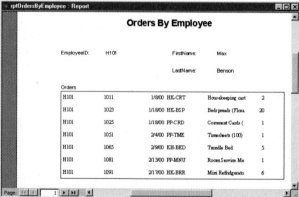
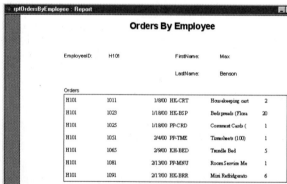

11 On the Report Design toolbar, click the View button.

The report appears in Design view.

View

12 Save and close rptOrdersByEmployee.

AC2000E.4.6

Synchronizing Report Data

When you add a subreport to a report, Access will automatically **synchronize** the data in the subreport with the data in the report, meaning that the records in the subreport correspond to the information in the report. For example, in the previous exercise, in the section of the report for employee H101, the subreport displayed only records from employee H101 instead of all the records in the subreport.

Sometimes the data in the report and subreport fall out of sync—meaning that there is data in the subreport that is not related to the record in the main report. An unrelated subreport will show every record from the underlying table. To fix the synchronization, you check the relationship between the tables that the report and subreport are based on. If the tables underlying the report and subreport are not in a one-to-many relationship, the data in the report and subreport will not match.

You can check the relationship between the underlying tables by clicking the Relationships button on the Database toolbar. In the Relationships window, the two underlying tables should have a line between them— from the primary key field in the table on the *one* side of the relationship to the field containing the same data in the table on the *many* side. The two related fields that contain the same data do not have to have the same name. For example, one field could be called *Employee#* while the other could be called *Employee Identification Code*.

In this exercise, you create a relationship between tblApprovedToOrder and tblAllOrders to ensure the tables underlying rptAllOrders and rptOrdersByEmployee are related properly.

> By default, Access synchronizes data between tables and the queries that are based on those tables whenever a query is run.

Relationships

1 On the Database toolbar, click the Relationships button.

The Relationships window appears.

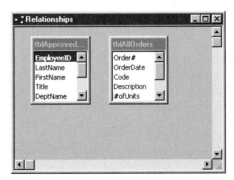

> A relationship is shown by a line connecting the two field lists.

2 Scroll down in the tblAllOrders field list until EmployeeID is visible.

3 Drag the EmployeeID field name from tblApprovedToOrder on top of the EmployeeID field name in tblAllOrders.

The Edit Relationships dialog box appears.

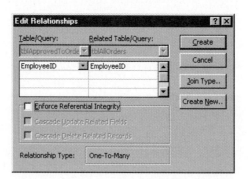

4 Select the Enforce Referential Integrity check box, and click Create.

A line representing the relationship between the tables appears in the Relationships window.

The 1 next to the field list for tblApprovedToOrder indicates that the table is on the *one* side of the one-to-many relationship. The infinity sign (∞) next to the tblAllOrders field list indicates that it is on the *many* side.

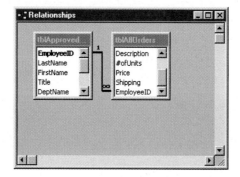

5 Save and close the Relationships window.

Lesson Wrap-Up

This lesson covered how to customize reports, add sections to a report, sort and group report data, modify report properties, add and modify report controls, create subreports, and synchronize subreport data in Access 2000.

If you are continuing to the next lesson:

Close

● Click the Close button in the top-right corner of the Database window.

The Lakewood Mountains 04 database closes.

If you are not continuing to the next lesson:

Close

● To quit Access for now, click the Close button in the top-right corner of the Access window.

Access and the Lakewood Mountains 04 database close.

Lesson Glossary

caption The text that appears on a report window title bar when the report appears in Print Preview. The caption is not printed when you print the report itself.

group To organize report contents based on the values in one or more fields.

group footer The section of a report that appears at the bottom of grouped data and is commonly used to calculate totals or other summaries for each group.

group header The section of a report that appears at the top of grouped data and commonly contains the field by which the data are grouped.

grouping field A field by which Access organizes report data.

main report A report with a subreport that displays the records on the *one* side of a one-to-many relationship.

report A database object used to print data in an attractive and easy-to-read format.

report footer A section of a report that appears at the bottom of the last printed page of the report.

report header A section of a report that appears at the top of the first printed page of the report.

subreport A report within a report that displays the records on the *many* side of a one-to-many relationship.

synchronize To ensure that the tables, which provide data to a report and its associated subreport, are related by the correct field.

Quick Quiz

1   How do you synchronize subreport data?

2   How do you create a report in Design view?

3   What is the difference between a report and a form?

4   Why would you divide a report into sections?

5   How do you add a page break to a report?

6   How do you modify the properties for an entire report?

7   What is a subreport?

8   What three sections do all reports include by default?

9   How do you modify the properties of a report control?

10   How can you tell if a report and subreport are not synchronized?

Putting It All Together

Exercise 1: Create a report in Design view based on tblApprovedToOrder that shows the employee ID, first name, and last name for each employee approved to place orders. Add a subreport to the report that displays each employee's orders from rptAllOrders. Display the report in Print Preview. Save the report as rptApprovedOrders, and close it. Verify that tblApproved-ToOrder and tblAllOrders are in a one-to-many relationship, with tblApprovedToOrder on the *one* side of the relationship.

Exercise 2: Open rptEmployeeOrders and group the data by EmployeeID and by OrderDate. Sort the OrderDate field in descending order. Add a report header and report footer to the report. Add a page break to the report footer. Add a label to the report header that reads *Employee Orders*, change the font to 20 points, and resize the label so that all the text is visible. Display the report in Print Preview before closing it.

LESSON 5

Using Databases on the Internet

After completing this lesson, you will be able to:

✔ *Create a hyperlink.*

✔ *Export a form to HTML.*

✔ *Create a data access page using AutoPage.*

✔ *Create a data access page using the Page Wizard.*

✔ *Group and sort data on a data access page.*

You can use the World Wide Web (the "Web") to enhance and display the information in a Microsoft Access database. You can place connections to the Web inside your database. Using Access, you can add a **hyperlink** to your database to display an object, another file, a Web page, or an e-mail composition window. Hyperlinks are especially useful for database users who reference Web pages, such as online catalogs, while using the database.

To make the data in a database available for viewing on the Web, you can export data to an HTML file. HTML is an acronym for Hypertext Markup Language, which is a language used for defining the formatting and special handling of text, images, and objects on a Web page. As an HTML file, the data in your database can be viewed by many users without also allowing them to modify the database itself. If you do want users to modify the database using the Web, you can create a **data access page**, a type of database object new in Access 2000. With a data access page, users can view, edit, manipulate, and add data to the database using a **Web browser**, a program that makes it possible to view files on the Web.

To complete the procedures in this lesson, you will need to use a file named Lakewood Mountains 05 in the Access Expert Practice folder that is located on your hard disk. You will also need to have Microsoft Internet Explorer 4 or later installed, although Internet Explorer 5.0 is preferable.

2000 New!

Data access pages (sometimes referred to simply as pages) are new in Access 2000.

Sample files for the lesson

For additional information about opening the practice file for this lesson, see the "Using the CD-ROM" section at the beginning of this book.

AC2000E.6.1

Switchboards are discussed in Lesson 3, "Customizing Forms."

Creating a Hyperlink

With one click of the mouse, hyperlinks allow users to connect to Web sites, other objects in an Access database, or other non-Access files, such as Microsoft Word documents or Microsoft Excel worksheets. Hyperlinks are the fastest way to open database objects or non-Access files. They are preferable to switchboards if database performance is more important than the switchboard interface. You can also create an **e-mail hyperlink**, which, when clicked, will start the user's e-mail program and display a message composition window with a specific e-mail address already entered. The user can then write and send the e-mail message normally.

To add hyperlinks to your database, you must first set the Hyperlink data type for the field where you want the hyperlink. Then, in Datasheet view or Form view, you specify the Web addresses, files, or database objects that the user can view by clicking the hyperlink.

To understand how you can use hyperlinks to enhance a database, consider the employees at Lakewood Mountains Resort who are responsible for ordering supplies for the resort. Some of the companies that supply the resort have put their catalogs on Web sites, complete with secured pages that buyers can use to place orders. If you add hyperlinks for each company's Web site to the database, employees can easily order supplies by simply clicking a hyperlink.

Links are created by using the Insert Hyperlink dialog box, which makes it possible for you to link to many different items.

- The Existing File Or Web page icon lets you select a Web page or a non-Access file for the hyperlink.
- The Object In This Database icon lets you connect to an object in the current database.
- The Create New Page icon lets you create a new Web page to use for the hyperlink.
- The E-mail Address icon helps you create an e-mail hyperlink, which creates a new message to an address that you choose.

In the illustration on the next page, the option to link to an existing file or Web page is selected.

You can use the ScreenTip button to add text that will appear when the user's mouse pointer hovers over the hyperlink.

The Text To Display box contains the name of the hyperlink.

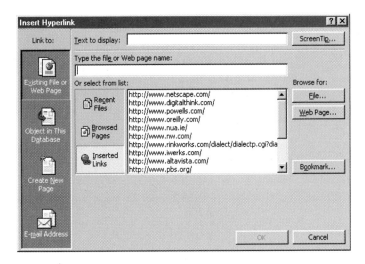

In this exercise, you open the Lakewood Mountains 05 database and create a hyperlink to open a query that displays every order placed with a particular vendor.

Open

1   On the Database toolbar, click the Open button, navigate to the Access Expert Practice folder on your hard disk, and then open the Lakewood Mountains 05 database.

2   Open tblVendors in Datasheet view.

3   In the record for Party Eternal, scroll to the right, and click in the Orders field.

4   On the Insert menu, click Hyperlink.

The Insert Hyperlink dialog box appears.

You can also press Ctrl+K to open the Insert Hyperlink dialog box.

5   In the Link To box, click the Object In This Database icon.

The available object types in the current database appear.

The icons for Reports, Pages, Macros, and Modules are faded because there are no objects of these types in the Lakewood Mountains 05 database.

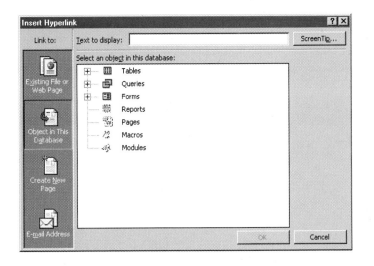

6 Click the plus sign (+) next to Queries.

A list of the queries in the database appears.

To hide the list of queries, click the minus sign (-) next to Queries.

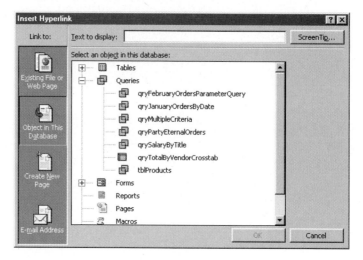

7 Click qryPartyEternalOrders, and click OK.

A hyperlink for qryPartyEternalOrders appears in tblVendors.

If you do not want the hyperlink text to be *qryPartyEternal*, you can type the desired text in the Text To Display box in the Insert Hyperlink dialog box.

8 Click the hyperlink.

The results of qryPartyEternalOrders appear, showing all orders made to Party Eternal.

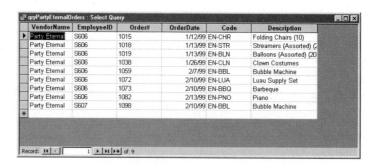

9 Close qryPartyEternalOrders.

10 Close tblVendors.

Exporting a Form to HTML

To make database objects available to users who don't have Access or who aren't used to working with databases, you can save tables, forms, and reports as HTML documents. Users can view HTML documents on the Web or on an **intranet**—a network within an organization used to share company information and resources among employees—by using a Web browser such as Internet Explorer. The standard Access or Microsoft Office 2000 installation includes the Internet Explorer 5.0 Web browser.

Saving a database object in another file format (like HTML) is called **exporting.** When you export a table, form, or report to HTML, users can view but not change the data. As a result, you should try to export forms instead of tables because forms are formatted more attractively in HTML than tables. If you export a report to HTML, Access creates a separate HTML document for each printed page of the report.

> HTML files created from database objects aren't stored in the database. They are saved as separate files in a location of your choice.

In this exercise, you export a form to an HTML document named Vendor_List_Form and open that document using Internet Explorer.

1   Display the list of forms in the Database window, and click frmVendors.

2   On the File menu, click Export.

The Export Form To dialog box appears.

> The Export Form To dialog box shows the contents of the My Documents folder by default. Your My Documents folder might have different contents than the one shown here.

3   Navigate to the Access Expert Practice folder on your hard disk.

4   Click in the File Name box, delete the existing text, and then type **Vendor_List_Form**.

The HTML document will be named Vendor_List_Form.

> When you export a database object to HTML, it isn't necessary to use the Leszynski naming conventions. However, you shouldn't include spaces in the name of an HTML file; most Web browsers cannot read file names that contain spaces.

5   Click the Save As Type down arrow, click HTML Documents (*.html;*.htm), and then click Save.

The HTML Output Options dialog box appears.

> The HTML Output Options dialog box allows you to select a template that controls the appearance of the HTML page. If you want to use a template, click the Browse button and (in the standard Access installation) navigate to C:\Program Files\Microsoft Office\Templates\ 1033\Webs\. This path was created with the assumption that your hard disk is drive C.

The Internet Explorer button might be part of the Quick Launch bar on the Windows taskbar. If so, you can start Internet Explorer by clicking this button.

You can also open the Open dialog box by pressing Ctrl+O.

6   Click OK.

7   On the Windows taskbar, click Start, point to Programs, and then click Internet Explorer.

Internet Explorer starts.

8   On the File menu, click Open.

The Open dialog box appears.

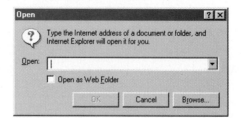

9   Click Browse.

The Microsoft Internet Explorer dialog box appears.

10   Navigate to the Access Expert Practice folder on your hard disk, click Vendor_List_Form, and then click Open.

The Open dialog box appears.

11   Click OK.

The form appears as an HTML document.

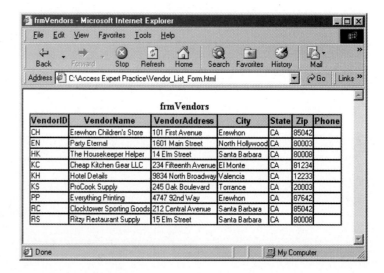

12   Quit Internet Explorer.

AC2000E.6.3

Creating a Data Access Page Using AutoPage

When you export a database object to a Web page, users can view the object using a Web browser, but they cannot make any changes to the data. To make it possible for users to edit the data on a Web page, you can create a special type of Web page called a data access page (page). New in Access 2000, data access pages allow users to view, update, append, and delete data in the database on the Web or on an intranet.

important

To use data access pages properly, you need to have Internet Explorer 5.0 or later installed on your computer. Internet Explorer 5.0 comes with the standard Office 2000 installation, but if it isn't installed on your computer, you can download it from *www.microsoft.com* or ask your system administrator for help. You can use Internet Explorer 4 or later to view data access pages, but most of the editing capabilities for data access pages won't be available.

To make a database available for editing on the Web or an intranet, you must first publish the database and the data access pages to a Web or intranet server and set up user passwords and permissions. This procedure involves some Web server administration procedures that are beyond the scope of this course. However, the general procedures for creating data access pages are the same whether you post pages on the Web or save them on your local computer.

You can display data access pages in either Page view or Design view. In Page view, you can modify the data in the data access page.

tip

If you've already created data access pages and saved them to your local hard disk, you can open the pages in FrontPage 2000 and then use the Publish Web command on the File menu to publish the page on a Web server. Additional resources for using FrontPage to publish a page to a Web or intranet server include *Microsoft FrontPage 2000 Step by Step* and the *Microsoft FrontPage 2000 Step by Step Courseware Expert Skills Student Guide*, both published by Microsoft Press.

You can create data access pages by using AutoPage, by using a wizard, or from scratch in Design view. AutoPage is the fastest way of creating a data access page, although it does not give you much control over the contents or appearance of the page. If you use AutoPage to create a data access page, you only select the table or query from which the page will pull data. Data access pages created with AutoPage use a columnar layout, which has two columns, with labels on the left and the record data in text boxes on the right.

In this exercise, you use AutoPage to create a data access page based on tblMarketingDepartment.

1   Display the list of pages in the Database window.

2   On the Database window toolbar, click New.

The New Data Access Page dialog box appears.

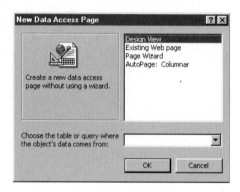

3   Click AutoPage: Columnar.

4   Click the Choose the Table Or Query Where The Object's Data Comes From down arrow, scroll down, and then click tblMarketingDepartment.

5   Click OK.

The data access page appears in Page view.

This data access page is formatted using the Straight Edge theme, which is the default format. To change the format, display the page in Design view, click Theme on the Format menu, click the theme that you want to use, and then click Yes.

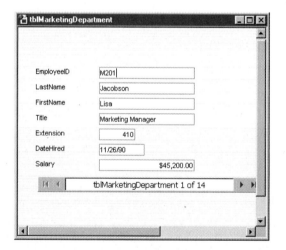

Access saves the page in the current folder and places a shortcut to the page in the list of pages in the Database window. Rest the mouse pointer on the shortcut to display the path to the folder where the page is saved.

6   Save the page as **MarketingDepartment**, and close it.

AC2000E.6.3

Creating a Data Access Page Using the Page Wizard

You can use the Page Wizard to create a more advanced data access page than you can with AutoPage. The Page Wizard steps you through the process of creating the data access page, beginning with choosing the tables and queries that will provide data for the data access page. The Page Wizard also prompts you to group and sort the contents of the data access page.

Grouping and sorting the contents of data access pages is very much like grouping and sorting report data. The field that you choose as the **grouping level** determines how the data appears on the page based on the content of one or more fields. For example, in a data access page that lists orders and the employees who placed them, you could group the orders by employee so that orders placed by the same employee would be grouped together. You could then sort the groups so that records for a specific field would be in alphabetical or numerical order. Assuming that the employees were sorted in ascending order by employee ID number, the group for the person with the lowest employee number would be first and the group for the person with the highest employee number would be last.

> **You can filter records in a data access page in the same way that you filter other database objects.**

important

Adding grouping levels to a data access page makes the page read-only.

After you add grouping levels to a data access page, the page is divided into several sections. Each section has its own **navigation bar**, a toolbar with controls that allow you to move from record to record, or to particular records on the page. For example, on a data access page of orders grouped by employee ID, there would be a navigation bar to move from a group for one employee ID to a group for another. Within each employee ID group, you use a different navigation bar to move from order to order.

In this exercise, you use the Page Wizard to create a data access page based on tblAllOrders.

1   Double-click Create Data Access Page By Using Wizard.

The Page Wizard appears.

> **The query or table that appears in the Tables/Queries box when you open the Page Wizard might be different than the one in the illustration.**

2   Click the Tables/Queries down arrow, scroll up, and then click Table: tblAllOrders.

The fields in tblAllOrders appear in the Available Fields list.

3   Click the >> (Select All) button, and click Next.

All the fields in tblAllOrders move from the Available Fields list to the Selected Fields list. The next Page Wizard dialog box appears.

To add a grouping level, click the field that you want to use as the grouping level, and click the > (Add) button. You can add more than one grouping level to a data access page.

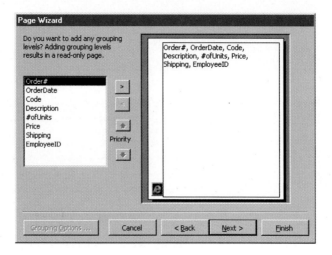

4   Click Next to accept no grouping.

The next Page Wizard dialog box appears.

You can change the sort order from ascending to descending by clicking the Sort button to the right of the box where you specify the field that you want to sort.

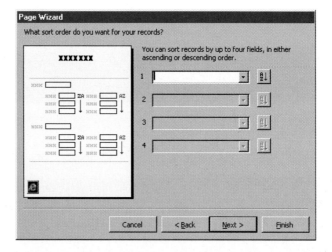

5   Click the down arrow in the first box, click Order#, and then click Next.

Access will sort records in the data access page in ascending order by the values in the Order# field. The next Page Wizard dialog box appears with tblAllOrders already entered in the What Title Do You Want For Your Page? box, as shown on the next page.

If you select the Do You Want To Apply A Theme To Your Page? check box, the Theme dialog box will appear after you click Finish so that you can choose a theme (format) for your page.

Although you can use spaces in the name of your data access page, you shouldn't. Many Web browsers don't accept spaces in a URL, so if the page name is part of the URL, the page won't be accessible from the Web.

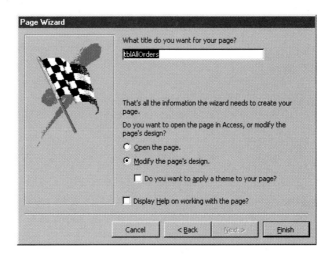

6   In the What Title Do You Want For Your Page? box, type **All_Orders**, click the Open The Page option, and then click Finish.

The data access page appears in Page view with the first record, for order number 1001, displayed.

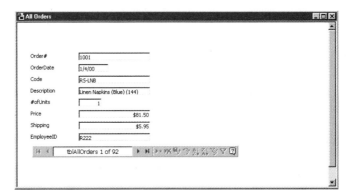

Next Page

7   On the navigation bar, click the Next Page button.

The second record, for order number 1002, appears.

8   Save the data access page as **All_Orders**.

You create data access pages using design tools similar to those for forms and reports.

Creating a Data Access Page in Design View

As with forms and reports, you can also create a data access page in Design view. Many of the tools that you use to create data access pages in Design view are similar to those you use to create forms and reports. Creating a data access page using Design view is a long process, and you might want to use either AutoPage or the Page Wizard to create the data access page and then use Design view to customize the page.

(continued)

continued

You can use Access Help to find
more information about creating a
data access page in Design view.

To create a data access page in Design view

1   Display the list of pages in the Database window.

2   Double-click Create Data Access Page In Design View.

3   On the Page Design toolbar, click the Field List button to display the tables and queries in the database, select the table or query from which you want to add fields to the data access page, and then drag the fields to the page.

And/Or

On the Page Design toolbar, click the Toolbox button, and use the tools in the toolbox to add unbound controls to the data access page.

Field List

Toolbox

AC2000E.6.2

Grouping and Sorting Data on a Data Access Page

In the previous section, you learned how to group and sort the contents of a data access page by creating the page using the Page Wizard. If you create a data access page from scratch, or if you want to change the way a wizard-created data access page organizes its contents, you can group and sort the page contents in Design view.

Demote

Promote

When a data access page is open in Design view, you can remove a grouping level by clicking the control text box and clicking the Demote button on the Page Design toolbar. To add a grouping level, click the text box for the field that you want to add as a grouping level, and click the Promote button on the Page Design toolbar.

You can change the way Access sorts the contents of any section in the data access page by using the Default Sort box in the group properties section of the Sorting And Grouping dialog box. For each field that you want to sort, you type the name of the field, a space, and then *ASC* or *DESC*, depending on whether you want to sort the field in ascending or descending order. For example, to sort the EmployeeID field in ascending order, you would type *EmployeeID ASC*. You do not have to surround the field name with brackets ([]). If you want to sort using more than one field, separate the entries with a comma.

You can clear a sort order section by
deleting the Default Sort property of
that section.

You can open the Sorting And
Grouping dialog box by clicking the
Sorting And Grouping button on the
Design toolbar.

In this exercise, you change the grouping levels and sort orders assigned to the All_Orders data access page to see which employees have made orders from which vendors.

1   Display the All_Orders data access page in Design view, as shown on the following page. You might have to scroll up to see the *Click Here And Type Title Text* text.

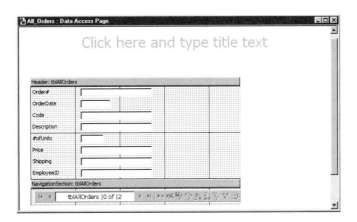

2   Close any toolbars, including the toolbox, that appear.

3   Click the *Click Here And Type Title Text* text.

     Access deletes the text, and a blinking insertion point appears.

4   Type **All Orders**.

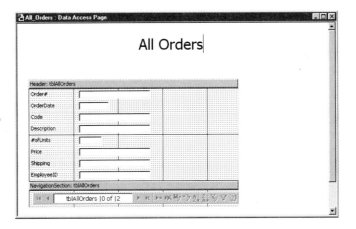

Promote

Make sure to click the OrderDate text box, not the label. If you click the OrderDate label, the Promote button will not be available.

The separate section indicates that Access will group the contents of the data access page by the values in the OrderDate field.

5   Click the OrderDate text box, and click the Promote button on the Page Design toolbar.

     OrderDate moves out of the Header: tblAllOrders section into its own section—named Header: tblAllOrders-OrderDate—above the Header.

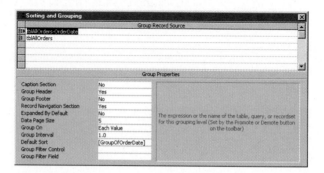

Sorting And Grouping

6   On the Page Design toolbar, click the Sorting And Grouping button.

The Sorting And Grouping dialog box appears.

7   Click in the tblAllOrders row.

The group properties for the tblAllOrders section appear in the Group Properties section.

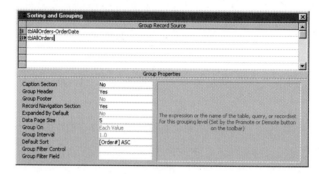

8   In the Group Properties section, click in the Default Sort box, delete the existing text, and then type **EmployeeID ASC**.

Access will sort the records in ascending order based on the contents of the EmployeeID field.

9   Close the Sorting And Grouping dialog box.

View

10   On the Page Design toolbar, click the View button.

The data access page appears in Page view grouped by the OrderDate field.

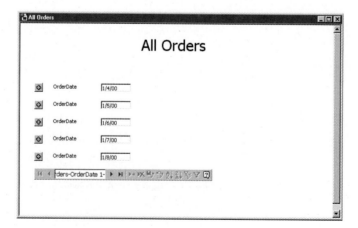

Next Record

Expand

11 On the navigation bar, click the Next Record button.

The records for the next five order dates appear.

12 Click the Expand control next to the 1/12/00 order date.

The orders placed on 1/12/00 appear, sorted by EmployeeID.

On grouped data access pages, you can view specific data by expanding and collapsing group headers.

You can sort records in a group while the page is in Page view by clicking the Sort Ascending or Sort Descending button on the Page View toolbar. You will lose the sort order when you close the page.

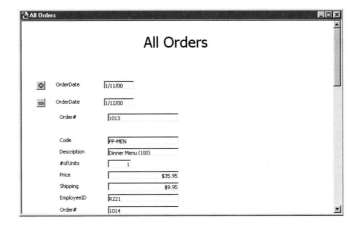

13 Save and close the data access page.

Lesson Wrap-Up

This lesson covered how to create hyperlinks to connect other database objects or to a Web page, export database objects to HTML, create and modify data access pages, and group and sort the contents of a data access page.

If you are continuing to the next lesson:

Close

● Click the Close button in the top-right corner of the Database window.

The Lakewood Mountains 05 database closes.

If you are not continuing to the next lesson:

Close

● To quit Access for now, click the Close button in the top-right corner of the Access window.

Access and the Lakewood Mountains 05 database close.

Lesson Glossary

data access page (page) A database object that allows users to view, edit, and add table and query data to a database over an intranet or the Web.

e-mail hyperlink A hyperlink that opens an e-mail composition window that has a specific e-mail address already entered.

exporting Saving database objects in a different file format, such as HTML.

grouping level A field used to organize the records in the Detail section of a data access page.

HTML   An acronym for Hypertext Markup Language, which is a language used to define the formatting and special handling of text, images, and objects on a Web page.

hyperlink   An HTML instruction in a database object that displays a specific file, database object, or Web page when clicked.

intranet   A network within an organization used to share company information and resources among employees.

navigation bar   A set of controls on a data access page that allows the user to move from record to record in the Detail section or from value to value in a grouped section.

Web browser   A program that allows you to view files via the World Wide Web.

Quick Quiz

1   What does a hyperlink do?

2   Why would you group the contents of a data access page?

3   How do you change the sort order of records in a section of a data access page?

4   What is a data access page?

5   How do you create a data access page using AutoPage?

6   What is an e-mail hyperlink?

7   How do you display the Insert Hyperlink dialog box?

8   How do you export a form to HTML?

9   What happens when you export a database object to HTML?

Putting It All Together

Exercise 1: Using the Page Wizard, create a data access page based on tblJanuaryOrders. Set EmployeeID as the grouping criterion, sort the page contents in ascending order by the Order# field, and then name the page January_Orders. Open the page in Design view, and change the grouping level from EmployeeID to OrderDate. Save the data access page as **January_Orders**, and close it.

Exercise 2: Export frmApprovedToOrder to an HTML document named **Employees**, and open it using Internet Explorer. After viewing Employees, close Internet Explorer.

Exercise 3: Using AutoPage, create a new data access page from tblPurchaseOrder. Save the page in the Access Expert Practice folder as **Purchase_Order**, and close it. Add a new field to tblProductsList called PlaceOrders. In the first record in the PlaceOrders field, add a link that will open the Purchase_Order data access page. Close tblProductsList.

LESSON 6

Automating Tasks

After completing this lesson, you will be able to:

✔ *Create an AutoKeys macro.*

✔ *Use controls to run a macro.*

✔ *Assign a macro to an event.*

✔ *Assign a macro to a condition.*

✔ *Test and debug a macro.*

A **macro** is a powerful tool that can be used to automate many activities within Microsoft Access. When you create a macro, you define a series of tasks for Access to perform whenever the user triggers the macro. For example, the steps in your macro can maximize or minimize a window, display a message box, open a database object, save the current object, or export an Access table to another database. With some macros, you can specify an event or condition that will trigger the macro, such as clicking the mouse or opening an object.

If you or your users repeat the same series of actions frequently, you can create a macro to perform the actions for you. For example, suppose that you need to print copies of the table containing all the orders placed at Lakewood Mountains Resort each month. You could create a macro to print the orders, which saves time and allows others to print the same records without requiring them to open the table themselves.

There are several types of macros. The difference between the types lies in how the user triggers the macro. If you create an **AutoKeys macro**, users run the macro by pressing a key sequence like Ctrl+2. If you create an **event macro**, Access starts a macro when a user performs a specific action, such as double-clicking a control or right-clicking the Detail section of a form. A **conditional macro** runs when certain criteria, set by the creator of the macro, are met.

To complete the procedures in this lesson, you will need to use a file named Lakewood Mountains 06 in the Access Expert Practice folder that is located on your hard disk.

For additional information about opening the practice file for this lesson, see the "Using the CD-Rom" section at the beginning of this book.

Sample files for the lesson

AC2000E.7.7

Creating an AutoKeys Macro

AutoKeys macros are triggered by pressing a key or sequence of keys (such as F5 or Ctrl+B) assigned to that macro. The sequence of keystrokes that you set for an AutoKeys macro becomes the macro name. For example, a macro named F5 runs when you press F5.

When you name an AutoKeys macro, you use the carat (^) to represent the Ctrl key. For example, a macro named ^b is executed by holding down the Ctrl key and pressing the b key simultaneously. The following table lists the types of key combinations that you can use to run an AutoKeys macro.

Syntax	Description	Example
^*number*	Ctrl + any number	^2
F*	Any function key	F5
^F*	Ctrl + any function key	^F5
+F*	Shift + any function key	+F5

When you create an AutoKeys macro, you need to define what **action** the macro will perform, such as opening an object, maximizing a window, or displaying a message. You also need to provide the information, called **arguments**, that the macro needs to run, such as the name of the database object to be opened, the window to be maximized, or the message to be displayed in a dialog box.

> You do not need to include comments for the macro to work.

You create an AutoKeys macro in the **Macro window**—also called the **Macro Builder**. The default macro window contains two columns in the top half—one where you set the macro actions and the other for comments about each action. You can add other columns to the top of the window, depending on the type of macro that you are creating. The bottom half of the Macro window is the Action Arguments section, where you enter the arguments for the macro action. The arguments that appear in this section depend on the action that you choose.

> There are no arguments in the Action Arguments section of this Macro window because no action has been defined yet.

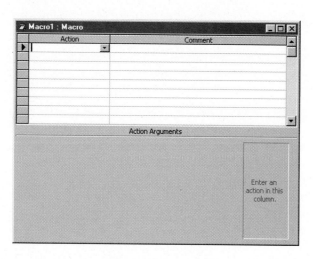

Note that the default Macro window does not include a place to define which key sequence will trigger an AutoKeys macro. To add a Macro Name column to the Macro window, you click the Macro Names button on the Macro Design toolbar. The Macro Name column allows you to specify the key sequence for AutoKeys macros and enter more than one macro into a single macro file. Each row in the Macro window defines one macro.

Macro Names

If you assign an AutoKeys macro to a key sequence that Access already uses to perform a certain task (for example, Access uses ^c as the key sequence for the Copy command), the macro that you create will replace the Access key sequence.

The AutoKeys macro group shown in the illustration includes three macros, ^b, ^c, and ^d.

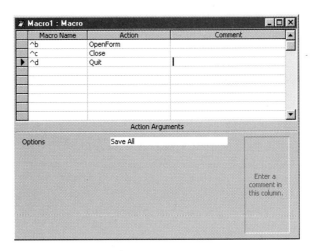

The macro window above is an example of a **macro group**, which is a file that contains more than one macro. For example, all AutoKeys macros are stored in one group, named AutoKeys. If you don't save the AutoKeys group with the name AutoKeys, Access will not recognize the macros as AutoKeys macros, and pressing the assigned key combinations will have no effect.

In this exercise, you open the Lakewood Mountains 06 database and create a series of AutoKeys macros that will open, maximize, minimize, and close frmFebruaryOrders.

Open

Even though a macro group contains more than one macro, a macro group is often simply referred to as a macro.

1   On the Database toolbar, click the Open button, navigate to the Access Expert Practice folder on your hard disk, and then open the Lakewood Mountains 06 database.

2   Display the list of macros in the Database window, and click New on the Database window toolbar.

The Macro window appears.

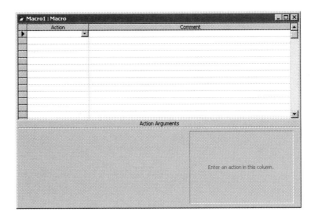

Macro Names

3   On the Macro Design toolbar, click the Macro Names button.

The Macro Name column appears in the Macro window.

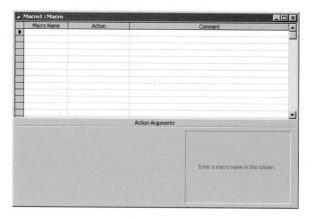

4   In the first cell in the Macro Name column, type **^1**, and press Tab.

The insertion point moves to the first cell in the Action column, and a down arrow appears.

The OpenForm action opens the form that you specify in the Action Arguments section.

5   Click the down arrow, scroll down, and then click OpenForm.

The arguments for the OpenForm action appear in the Action Arguments section.

For more information on any of the actions in the Action Arguments section, click in the box for the action, and press F1.

6   In the Action Arguments section, click in the Form Name box, click the down arrow that appears, and then click frmFebruaryOrders.

The ^1 macro will open frmFebruaryOrders.

7   Click in the second cell in the Macro Name column, type **^2**, and then press Tab.

The insertion point moves to the second cell in the Action column, and a down arrow appears.

8   Click the down arrow, scroll down, and then click Maximize.

The ^2 macro will maximize the open window.

9   Click in the third cell in the Macro Name column, type **^3**, and then press Tab.

The insertion point moves to the third cell in the Action column, and a down arrow appears.

10   Click the down arrow, scroll down, and then click Minimize.

The ^3 macro will minimize the open window.

11   Click in the fourth cell in the Macro Name column, type **^4**, and then press Tab.

The insertion point moves to the fourth cell in the Action column, and a down arrow appears.

12   Click the down arrow, and click Close.

The arguments for the Close action appear in the Action Arguments section.

> The Close action closes the object that you specify in the Object Type and Object Name boxes in the Action Arguments section.

13   In the Action Arguments section, click in the Object Type box, click the down arrow that appears, and then click Form.

14   Click in the Object Name box, click the down arrow that appears, and then click frmFebruaryOrders.

The ^4 macro will close frmFebruaryOrders.

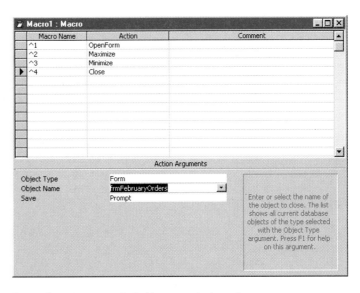

> You do not use the Leszynski naming convention when naming macros.

15   Save the macro as **AutoKeys**, and close it.

The AutoKeys macros will work as soon as you save the macro group.

16   Press Ctrl+1.

frmFebruaryOrders opens.

17   Press Ctrl+2.

Access maximizes frmFebruaryOrders.

18   Press Ctrl+3.

Access minimizes frmFebruaryOrders.

19   Press Ctrl+4.

frmFebruaryOrders closes.

AC2000E.7.6

Using Controls to Run a Macro

You can link a macro to a command button, which you click to run the macro. For example, you might create a command button to run a macro that displays information about an open form or prints the form. You can use the Command Button Wizard to help you create command buttons. When you use a command button to run a macro, you should give the macro and the command button meaningful names so that it is easy for users to find and run the macro.

Command button controls are discussed in Lesson 3, "Customizing Forms."

> ## tip
>
> It might be tempting to write a macro that runs a query displaying orders associated with a specific vendor or employee, but it's actually easier to create a subform that shows the same information. Subforms are discussed in Lesson 3, "Customizing Forms."

In this exercise, you create a command button that runs a macro to print the current record when the button is clicked.

1   Open frmVendors in Design view.

2   On the Form Design toolbar, click the Toolbox button, if necessary.

The toolbox appears.

Toolbox

3   In the toolbox, click the Control Wizards tool.

Control Wizards

4   In the toolbox, click the Command Button tool, and click in the form below the Phone text box.

A command button appears on the form, and the first Command Button Wizard dialog box appears.

Command

If you press Cancel while in the Command Button Wizard, Access creates a button labeled Command without attaching a macro to it. You can delete the command button by clicking the button and pressing Delete.

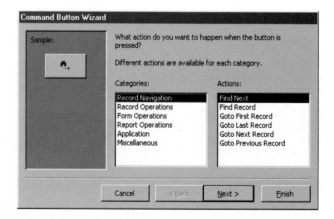

4   In the Categories list, click Miscellaneous.

The Actions list displays the actions that are available in the Miscellaneous category.

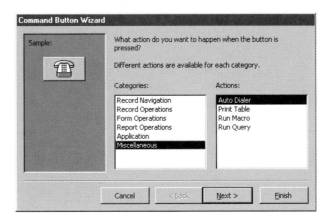

6   In the Actions list, click Run Macro, and click Next.

The command button will run a macro. The next Command Button Wizard dialog box appears, displaying a list of the macros in the database.

Note that each macro in the Auto-Keys group is listed as a separate macro.

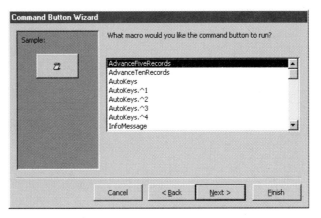

7   Scroll down, click PrintCurrentRecord, and then click Next.

The command button will run the macro named PrintCurrentRecord. The next Command Button Wizard dialog box appears.

The Sample box in the Command Button Wizard shows an example of what the command button would look like with the current settings.

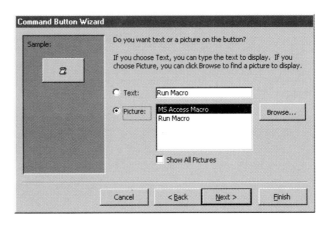

8   Click the Text option, delete the existing text in the box next to the option, type **Print Record**, and then click Next.

The text on the command button will say *Print Record*. The next Command Button Wizard dialog box appears.

When you create a command button, Access names the button using the word *Command* and a number. You can choose a new name for the button in this Command Button Wizard dialog box.

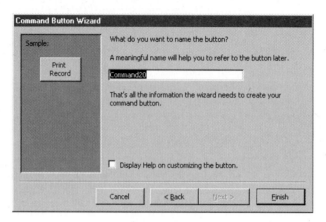

9   Type **PrintRecord**, and click Finish.

PrintRecord is the name of the command button. The Print Record command button appears on frmVendors.

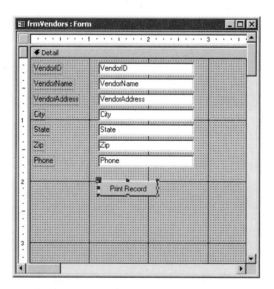

View

10   Display the form in Form view.

11   Click the Print Record command button.

Access prints the record displayed in frmVendors.

12   Save and close frmVendors.

Assigning a Macro to an Event

An **event** is an action performed within a database, such as clicking the mouse button, opening a form, or printing a report. You can create macros that run whenever a certain event occurs. For example, when working with forms, you might repeatedly locate a record in a form, print the record, and then advance to the next record. You could create a macro to automate these steps.

You use the property sheet for the form to choose the event that will trigger the macro. In the example above, you might run the macro whenever the user double-clicks the Detail section of the form.

Access recognizes a large number of events, but the available events vary, depending on the type of object that the event will affect. The following table describes a few of the common events to which macros can be assigned.

Event	Description
OnOpen	Performs an action when an object is opened but before the first record is displayed.
OnCurrent	Performs an action when an object's current record is selected.
OnClose	Performs an action when an object is closed and removed from the screen.
OnClick	Performs an action when a user clicks a specific object.
OnDblClick	Performs an action when a user double-clicks an object.
OnActivate	Performs an action when an object is activated.
OnDeactivate	Performs an action when an object is no longer activated.
BeforeUpdate	Performs an action before a record is updated with changed data.
AfterUpdate	Performs an action after a record is updated with changed data.

In this exercise, you attach two pre-existing macros—InfoMessage and AdvanceTenRecords—to frmAllOrders. You add a message to the InfoMessage macro, which runs when frmAllOrders is opened and causes a message box to appear. The second macro causes frmAllOrders to advance by 10 records when the body of the form is clicked.

1 Open the InfoMessage macro in Design view.

2 In the Action Arguments section, click in the Message box, and type **This form lists all orders for Jan-Dec 2000.**

3 Save and close the macro.

4 Open frmAllOrders in Design view, and double-click the form selector. The Form property sheet appears.

5 Click the Event tab.

This message will appear when the InfoMessage macro runs.

Remember, the form selector is the gray box containing a black square to the left of the horizontal ruler.

6   Click in the On Open box, click the down arrow that appears, scroll down, and then click InfoMessage.

The message that you typed in step 2 will appear when the form is opened.

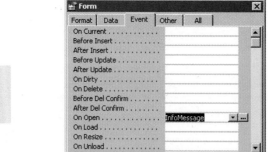

The On Open property will run the InfoMessage macro when you open the form but before the fist record appears.

7   Close the Form property sheet.

8   Double-click the Detail bar.

The Section: Detail property sheet appears.

9   Click the Event tab, if necessary.

10   Click in the On Click box, click the down arrow that appears, and then click AdvanceTenRecords.

The AdvanceTenRecords macro will run when you click any blank area of the Detail section.

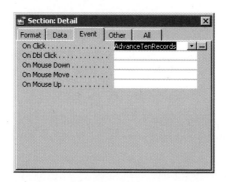

The On Click property will run the AdvanceTenRecords macro when you click in the Detail section.

11   Close the Section: Detail property sheet.

12   Save and close frmAllOrders.

13   In the Database window, double-click frmAllOrders.

The InfoMessage macro runs, displaying the message that you typed in step 2.

14   Click OK.

frmAllOrders appears in Form view, with the first record displayed.

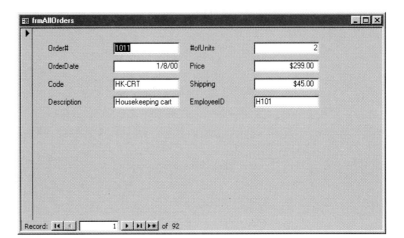

Remember, you can tell which record is displayed by looking at the number in the Record Number box in the bottom-left corner of the form window.

The only section in frmAllOrders is the Detail section, so if you click any blank area in the form, you click the Detail section.

15   Click any blank area in the form.

frmAllOrders advances 10 records to the eleventh record.

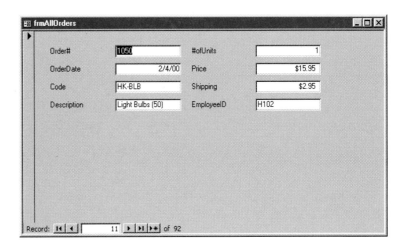

16   Close frmAllOrders.

Assigning a Macro to a Condition

So far, you have created macros that run whenever a key combination is pressed or a specific event occurs, without having the macro examine the contents of records to see if a particular condition exists. Running macros without checking the underlying data can lead to unnecessary macro actions or errors, such as having a blank EmployeeID field in a record. For example, assume Lakewood Mountains Resort requires its employees to get the general manager's approval for any order over $500. Using the techniques learned earlier in this lesson, you could create a macro that displays a reminder to get approval for orders over $500 every time an employee places an order, regardless of the size of the order. If you create a conditional macro, however, you could have the reminder appear only if the order total is more than $500.

Conditions

The conditions that you set for conditional macros use the same character set and syntax as validation rules, which are discussed in Lesson 1, "Customizing Tables."

Conditional macros run only when specific circumstances occur. For example, if an employee enters an order but forgets to enter the Employee ID, a conditional macro could remind the employee to enter the missing information.

To create a conditional macro, you add a Condition column to the Macro window by clicking the Conditions button on the Macro Design toolbar and typing rules for the macros that you want to make conditional.

If the condition that you set is true, the macro will run. For example, if a Lakewood Mountains Resort employee places an order of more than $500, you can use a conditional macro to display a message box reminding the employee to be sure the general manager has approved the order. If the condition is false—that is, if the order is less than $500—the macro will not display the message box.

In this exercise, you create a conditional macro to display a message box with a reminder to get manager approval whenever anyone places an order totaling more than $500.

1   Display the list of macros in the Database window, and click New on the Database window toolbar.

The Macro window appears.

Conditions

2   On the Macro Design toolbar, click the Conditions button.

The Condition column appears in the Macro window.

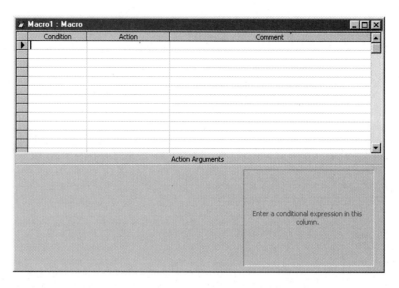

This expression multiplies the number of items ordered by the price of each item and checks to see if the result is more than $500.

3   In the first cell in the Condition column, type **[Quantity]*[Price]>500**, and press Tab.

The condition requires that the order total be greater than $500. The insertion point moves to the first cell in the Action column.

4   Click the down arrow, scroll down, and then click MsgBox.

The macro will display a message box when the total of the current order is greater than $500. The arguments for the MsgBox action appear in the Action Arguments section.

5   In the Action Arguments section, click in the Message box, and type
The general manager must approve this order.

This message will appear when the order total is greater than $500.

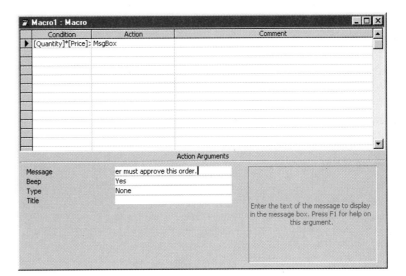

The message can contain up to 255 characters.

Note that a macro name cannot contain spaces.

6   Save the macro as **MoreThan500**, and close it.

7   Open frmPurchaseOrder in Design view.

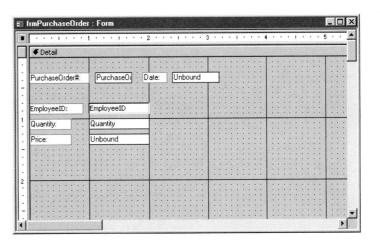

8   Double-click the edge of the Price text box (not the Price label).

The Text Box: Price property sheet appears.

9   Click the Event tab, if necessary.

10   Click in the On Exit box, click the down arrow that appears, and then click MoreThan500.

Access will run the MoreThan500 macro whenever the insertion point moves out of the Price text box.

> If you click the Build button next to the On Exit box, you can use the Macro Builder to create a new macro.

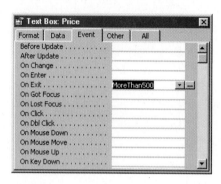

11   Close the Text Box: Price property sheet.

12   Save frmPurchaseOrder.

View

13   Display frmPurchaseOrder in Form view.

The PurchaseOrder# text box is already selected.

14   Press Tab to accept the AutoNumber value for the PurchaseOrder# text box.

The insertion point moves to the Date text box.

15   Type today's date, and press Tab.

The insertion point moves to the EmployeeID text box.

16   Type **R221**, and press Tab.

The insertion point moves to the Quantity text box.

17   Type **6**, and press Tab.

The insertion point moves to the Price text box.

> You should also test the macro to see if it runs when the order total is below $500. Change the number in the Quantity text box to 5, so the order total is not greater than $500. The macro shouldn't run.

18   Type **100**, and press Tab.

The MoreThan500 macro runs, displaying the reminder that the order must be approved by the general manager.

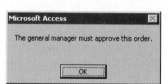

19   Click OK.

The second record in frmPurchaseOrder appears.

20   Close frmPurchaseOrder.

Testing and Debugging a Macro

Creating a macro is like writing a simple computer program. Few computer programs work correctly when they are first written, so you should test your own. The simplest way to test a macro is to run it and observe the results. Depending on the type of macro that you are testing, you can run the macro by pressing the key combination that triggers the macro, clicking the control with the macro attached, or entering a value in the field that causes the conditional macro to run. You can run any type of macro by displaying the list of macros in the Database window, opening the macro that you want to run in Design view, and then clicking the Run button on the Macro Design toolbar.

Run

In the previous exercise, you tested a macro by entering field values to see if the macro worked correctly for orders of more than $500. However, if the macro does not perform as expected, entering field values doesn't really provide you with a way to debug the macro. **Debugging** refers to procedures that you can use to find and fix an error in a macro.

> ## tip
> It's easier to write a long macro one step at a time instead of trying to write all of the steps at once. If you are creating a complicated macro, write a few steps, save your work, and then run the macro. When the first part of the macro runs correctly, you can add more steps.

Single Step

If the macro does not run correctly, you might not be able to find the error by examining the macro in the Macro window. To check the macro step by step and view the results of each step, you can use the **Single Step** button on the Macro Design toolbar. If you run the macro after clicking the Single Step button, the Macro Single Step dialog box appears.

You can also use the Macro Single Step dialog box to test a macro because the dialog box allows you to examine the results of each step to be sure that the macro works correctly.

Macro Single Step	? X
Macro Name:	Step
AdvanceTenRecords	Halt
Condition:	Continue
True	
Action Name:	
GoToRecord	
Arguments:	
2, FrmAllOrders, Next, 10	

The Macro Single Step dialog box shows four elements of the macro:

■ *Macro Name* is the name of the macro file or the entry in the Macro Name column for the macro that you are testing. Check this box to verify that Access is running the correct macro.

■ *Condition* indicates whether the statement in the Condition column is evaluated as true or false for this step. Check the contents of this box to verify that you typed the condition correctly. Common errors include switching greater than (>) and less than (<) signs or defining a condition for the contents of the wrong field.

■ *Action Name* is the next action in the macro. If the macro isn't running properly, you might have selected the wrong action from the menu. Check this box to verify that the next action is the one that you wanted to occur next.

■ *Arguments* displays the contents of the Action Arguments section of the Macro window for the action in the Action Name box. Check the arguments to verify that the macro is running with the correct information.

There are also three command buttons in the Macro Single Step dialog box:

■ *Step* performs the action in the Action Name box and advances to the next step in the macro.

■ *Halt* stops the macro without performing the current action.

■ *Continue* performs the remaining steps in the macro without halting after each action.

The macro OpenApprovedToOrder was designed to open, maximize (if necessary), and then close frmApprovedToOrder, but the form does not close at the end of the macro. In this exercise, you use the Single Step dialog box to find and correct the error.

1   Open the OpenApprovedToOrder macro in Design view.

2   On the Macro Design toolbar, click the Single Step button, and click the Run button.

The Macro Single Step dialog box appears.

> If you want to test a macro that runs on the contents of a database object—like the records in a table—but does not open the object, you must open the object before testing the macro. Access will display an error message if the object isn't open.

Single Step

Run

> This step in the macro will open frmApprovedToOrder.

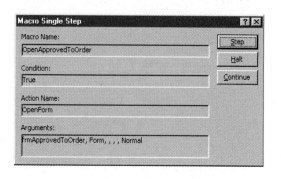

3   In the Macro Single Step dialog box, click Step.

frmApprovedToOrder opens in the background, and the Macro Single Step dialog box displays the next step in the macro.

This step in the macro will maximize the open window, in this case, frmApprovedToOrder. Note that the form is not specifically named and does not need to be named for this step to work correctly.

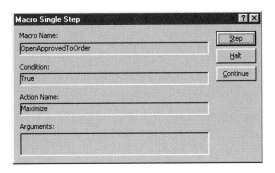

4   Click Step.

Access maximizes the frmApprovedToOrder window, and the Macro Single Step dialog box displays the next step in the macro.

This step in the macro should close frmApprovedToOrder.

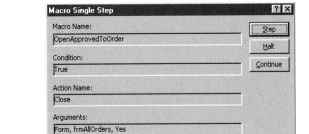

5   Click Step.

The Macro Single Step dialog box closes, indicating that the macro is finished, but frmApprovedToOrder does not close as it should.

6   Close frmApprovedToOrder.

The OpenApprovedToOrder macro is still open, and the Single Step button is still selected.

Run

7   On the Macro Design toolbar, click the Run button.

The Macro Single Step dialog box appears.

8   Click Step.

frmApprovedToOrder opens in the background, and the Macro Single Step dialog box displays the next step in the macro.

Forms will not run normally until you deselect the Single Step button.

9   Click Step.

The form is already maximized, and the Macro Single Step dialog box displays the next step in the macro—the step that should close frmApprovedToOrder

The form is already maximized because frmApprovedToOrder was not minimized again after you ran the macro previously.

10   Examine the Macro Single Step dialog box to find the error.

The Arguments box shows that the macro is attempting to close frmAllOrders, not frmApprovedToOrder.

11   Click Halt.

The Macro Single Step dialog box closes.

12   Close frmApprovedToOrder.

13   In the Macro window, click in the Close cell in the Action column.

The arguments for the Close action appear in the Action Arguments section.

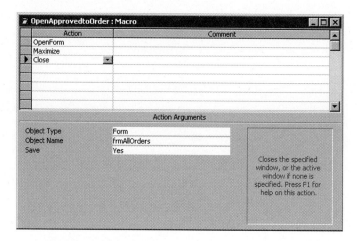

14   In the Action Arguments section, click in the Object Name box, click the down arrow that appears, and then click frmApprovedToOrder.

15   Save the macro.

Run

16   On the Macro Design toolbar, click the Run button.

The Macro Single Step dialog box appears.

17   Click Step.

frmApprovedToOrder opens in the background, and the Macro Single Step dialog box displays the next step in the macro.

18   Click Step.

The form is already maximized, and the Macro Single Step dialog box displays the next step in the macro.

19   Click Step.

The macro runs correctly: frmApprovedToOrder closes, the Macro Single Step dialog box closes, and the Macro Window appears.

Single Step

20   On the Macro Design toolbar, click the Single Step button.

The Single Step button is deselected; macros will now run normally.

21   Close the OpenApprovedToOrder macro.

Lesson Wrap-Up

This lesson covered how to create and modify AutoKeys, event, and conditional macros in Access 2000. You also learned how to run macros using command buttons and how to debug macros by using the Macro Single Step dialog box.

If you are continuing to the next lesson:

Close

● Click the Close button in the top-right corner of the Database window.
The Lakewood Mountains 06 database closes.

If you are not continuing to other lessons:

Close

● To quit Access for now, click the Close button in the top-right corner of the Access window.
Access and the Lakewood Mountains 06 database close.

Lesson Glossary

action An instruction in a macro that causes the macro to do something.

arguments Information that a macro needs to run.

AutoKeys macro A macro run by pressing an assigned sequence of keys.

conditional macro A macro that runs only if the field or control values meet the criteria specified by the user.

debugging Following procedures used to find and correct errors in a macro.

event An action performed within a database, such as clicking the mouse button, opening a form, or printing a report. Events can be used to trigger macros.

event macro A macro that runs whenever a specific event occurs, such as double-clicking a control.

macro A sequence of predefined actions that can be used to automate many activities within Microsoft Access.

Macro Builder Another name for the Macro window, which is used to create and modify macros.

macro group A file that contains more than one macro.

Macro window The window in which you create and modify macros.

Single Step A button that, when pressed, causes Access to display the details of each step in a macro, making it easier to find and correct errors.

Quick Quiz

1 How do you make a macro action conditional?

2 What is an AutoKeys macro?

3 What does attaching a macro to a command button do?

4 What happens when the condition for a conditional macro action is false?

5 How do you locate and correct errors in a macro?

6 In the Macro Single Step dialog box, how do you run the rest of the steps in a macro without stopping for each step?

7 How do you create an AutoKeys macro?

8 What is an event macro?

9 What is a conditional macro?

Putting It All Together

Exercise 1: Create two AutoKeys macros: one to open qrySalaryByTitle, which starts by pressing Ctrl+5, and another to close qrySalaryByTitle, which starts by pressing Ctrl+6.

Exercise 2: Create a conditional macro that tests whether the VendorID field equals "EN" (the vendor code for Party Eternal). If the condition is true, the macro will display the message *Party Eternal is no longer an approved vendor*. Save the macro as **Vendor_Notice**. Add the macro to frmMarchOrders so that the message appears if the user enters EN in the VendorID field and tries to exit the field. Test the macro by opening a blank record in frmMarchOrders, typing **EN** in the VendorID text box, and then pressing Tab. Delete EN, and save the form.

Exercise 3: Add a command button to frmMarchOrders that prints the current record whenever the button is clicked. (Hint: Use the PrintCurrentRecord macro.) Make the text on the button read *Print This Record* and name the button PrintButton. Test the button. Save and close the form.

Exercise 4: The AdvanceFiveRecords macro is supposed to open frmFebruaryOrders, advance five records, and close the form. Figure out why the macro skips the sixth record and goes straight to the eleventh record. Fix the problem, and run the macro again.

LESSON 7

Using Database Tools

After completing this lesson, you will be able to:

✔ *Set a database password.*

✔ *Modify and delete a database password.*

✔ *Encrypt and decrypt a database.*

✔ *Replicate a database.*

✔ *Split a database.*

✔ *Convert a database to the Access 97 file format.*

✔ *Set startup options.*

So far, this book has focused on how to customize database objects like tables, queries, forms, reports, macros, and data access pages. With Microsoft Access, however, you can also customize the database itself.

To restrict access to a database, you can set a **password** so that only users who know the password can open the database. You can also **encrypt** the database, which prevents it from being opened in applications other than Access.

Access lets you customize the database for the needs of the people who will use it. You can allow many users to work with a database over a network by splitting the database into separate files. If some database users travel a lot, you can create a **replica** of the database for them to use, which makes it easy to incorporate their changes into the main database when they return. If you work with users who don't have Access 2000, you can convert an Access 2000 database to an Access 97 database with a few clicks of the mouse. You also can determine how much control users have over the database by setting specific **startup options** for the database.

For additional information about opening the practice files for this lesson, see the "Using the CD-ROM" section at the beginning of this book.

Sample files for the lesson

To complete the procedures in this lesson, you will need to use files named Lakewood Mountains 07, Lakewood Mountains 07a, Lakewood Mountains 07b, and Lakewood Mountains 07c in the Access Expert Practice folder that is located on your hard disk.

AC2000E.7.1

Setting a Database Password

Databases often contain sensitive information that should be handled only by certain employees. For example, tblMarketingDepartment in the Lakewood Mountains 07 database contains salary information for the resort's marketing employees, which is information that should be available only to the general manager and the resort's administrative assistants. When you set a password for a database containing sensitive information, you restrict access to authorized users.

When setting a database password, you should remember that the more complex the password, the more secure the database. The best passwords are long sequences of random characters because those are more difficult to guess, even if the person trying to enter the database tries every possible combination on a fast computer. However, it's difficult to remember long strings of random characters, so many users set their pet's name, child's birthday, or mother's maiden name as their password. Passwords based on any of these sources, or similar ones, are much easier to guess than random character sequences. Here are some guidelines for creating a secure password:

- Make the password at least eight characters long.

- Don't use dictionary words, even if you replace letters with numbers (for example, "3" for "e"). There are "cracking dictionaries" (computer files with dictionary words and common variations) that contain any combination of words that you can create. Someone trying to break into a database can write a computer program that tries every password in the cracking dictionary.

- Use both uppercase and lowercase letters; Access passwords are case-sensitive.

- Use numbers and special characters like #, &, and *.

- Combine parts of dictionary words (like "ele" and "digan") with characters and numbers (for example, "ElE*6dIgAn").

- Vary the method that you use to create passwords, such as changing the special characters that you use or placing them in different places within the password.

Passwords are set on a database-by-database basis; every database can, and should, have a unique password. To set a database password, you need to open the database in **Exclusive mode,** meaning that while you have the database open, you are the only person who can modify it.

Create some passwords using the partial word, number, and special character combinations described in this lesson.

important

Under no circumstances should you give the same password to more than one database or other secured item, like an e-mail account.

Microsoft Windows and Access do not provide a way to identify a password if you've forgotten it. You should keep a record of your passwords in a safe place, such as a safe deposit box or a safe, but you can leave hints for yourself in less secure locations, such as a locked desk drawer. Make sure that the hints are vague enough so that you are the only person who can guess the password from the hints.

In this exercise, you open the Lakewood Mountains 07 database in Exclusive mode and give it the password *CaV*6pHaNt*.

Open

1   With Access open, click the Open button on the Database toolbar.

The Open dialog box appears.

2   Navigate to the Access Expert Practice folder on your hard disk, and click Lakewood Mountains 07.

3   Click the Open down arrow, and click Open Exclusive.

The database opens in Exclusive mode.

4   On the Tools menu, point to Security, and click Set Database Password.

The Set Database Password dialog box appears.

> **You will not be able to see the actual password when you type it into the Set Database Password dialog box; Access displays an asterisk for each letter that you type so that no one can see the password.**

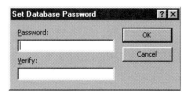

5   In the Password box, type **CaV*6pHaNt**, and press Tab.

The insertion point moves to the Verify box.

6   Type **CaV*6pHaNt**, and click OK.

Access sets CaV*6pHaNt as the password for the database, and the Set Database Password dialog box closes.

7   Close Lakewood Mountains 07.

8   Open Lakewood Mountains 07 in Exclusive mode.

The Password Required dialog box appears.

9   In the Enter Database Password box, type **CaV*6pHaNt**, and click OK.

Lakewood Mountains 07 opens.

AC2000E.7.1

Modifying and Deleting a Database Password

Setting database passwords is one way to restrict access to sensitive data. Given enough time, however, a determined individual might be able to either guess or discover the password for your database. To make this scenario less likely, you should change database passwords frequently. For databases containing very sensitive information, you should change the password at least once every month. For less critical databases, you should still change the password at least once every three months.

To change a database password, you remove the old password and set a new one, following the steps in the previous exercise for setting a password. When you change a database password, make sure that the new password is truly new. Avoid the temptation to recycle passwords, and don't use simple numerical progression in the password, such as changing the password from *pir&phant03* to *pir&phant04*.

You can remove a password from a database by opening the database in Exclusive mode, removing the current password, and not setting a new one. In this exercise, you remove·the password for Lakewood Mountains 07.

> If you speak a foreign language, you might try using parts of words in that language as the basis for passwords. You still shouldn't use common words from *any* language, though.

1   On the Tools menu, point to Security, and click Unset Database Password.

   The Unset Database Password dialog box appears.

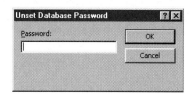

> Access requires users to enter the password for a database before removing it to ensure the user has permission to remove the password. In other words, anyone who knows the password for a database can remove it.

2   In the Unset Database Password dialog box, type **CaV*6pHaNt**, and click OK.

   The Unset Database Password dialog box closes, and Access removes the password from Lakewood Mountains 07.

3   Close Lakewood Mountains 07.

AC2000E.7.4

Open

Encrypting and Decrypting a Database

One of the strengths of Access 2000 is the ability to transfer data to and from other applications, particularly other programs in Microsoft Office. This strength is also a disadvantage because users can open, view, and modify Access databases with applications other than Access, even if the database is protected by a password. For example, you can open a password-protected Access database using Microsoft Word 2000 by clicking the Open button on the Database toolbar, clicking the database that you want to open, and setting the file type to Recover Text From Any File in the Open dialog box. The database contents appear in a Word document, and you do not need to use a password to see them. The following illustration shows what part of a database looks like when it is opened in Word.

> You will not be able to see the actual password when you type it into the Set Database Password dialog box; Access displays an asterisk for each letter that you type so that no one can see the password.

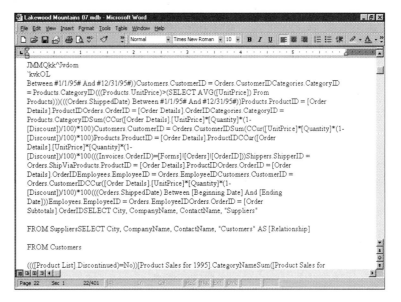

Although some of the contents are incomprehensible, an unauthorized user still might gain enough information from the text file to learn about your company's business practices.

You can prevent users from opening a database in another Microsoft Office program and circumventing password protection by encrypting the database. Encrypting a database makes the database files indecipherable to all applications except Access. The illustration on the next page shows what the encrypted version of the database looks like when it is opened in Word.

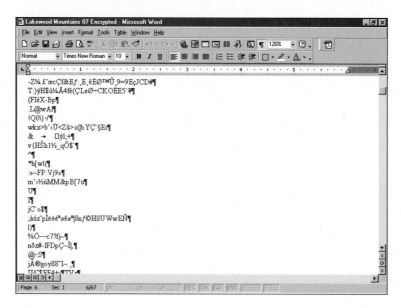

When you encrypt a database, you create a new copy of the database, which you save with a new name in a different location than the original. The original, unencrypted database remains on your computer in its original location. If possible, you should store the unencrypted copy of the database on a removable hard disk, different computer, floppy disk, or CD-ROM in a secure location.

If you combine encryption with password protection, the database cannot be opened in Access without a password and won't make sense if opened in any other Office application. If you **decrypt** a database, you reverse the encryption, making the database readable by other applications.

To encrypt or decrypt a database, the database must be closed.

In this exercise, you encrypt and decrypt Lakewood Mountains 07.

1   On the Tools menu, point to Security, and click Encrypt/Decrypt Database.

The Encrypt/Decrypt Database dialog box appears.

Depending on whether or not you have completed the Putting It All Together exercises in the previous lessons, the contents of your Access Expert Practice folder might look different from the illustration shown here.

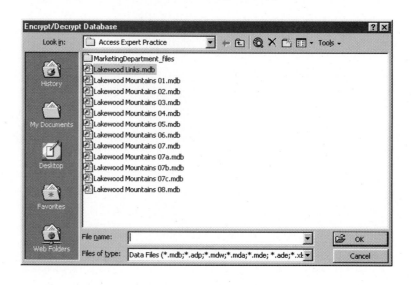

If you select an unencrypted database in the Encrypt/Decrypt Database dialog box, the Encrypt Database As dialog box appears when you click OK.

2 Click Lakewood Mountains 07, and click OK.

The Encrypt Database As dialog box appears.

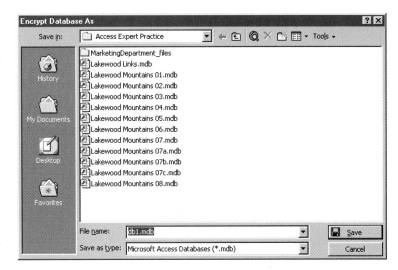

If you use the same file name as the original database, the encrypted version of the database will replace the original.

3 In the File Name box, type **Lakewood Encrypted**, and click Save.

The Encrypt As dialog box closes, and Access saves the encrypted version of the database in the Access Expert Practice folder.

4 On the Tools menu, point to Security, and click Encrypt/Decrypt Database.

The Encrypt/Decrypt Database dialog box appears, with Lakewood Encrypted already selected.

Note that Lakewood Mountains 07 and Lakewood Encrypted are listed as separate databases; the encrypted database does not replace the original.

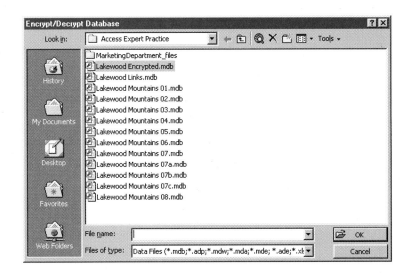

5   Click OK.

The Decrypt Database As dialog box appears.

If you select an encrypted data-base in the Encrypt/Decrypt Database dialog box, the Decrypt Database As dialog box appears when you click OK.

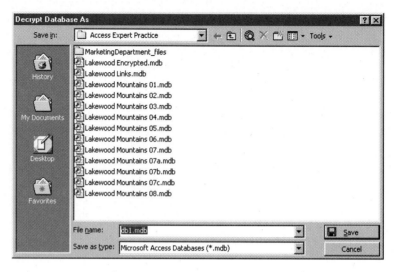

6   In the File Name box, type **Lakewood Unencrypted**, and click Save.

The Decrypt Database As dialog box closes, and Access saves the decrypted version of the database in the Access Expert Practice folder.

AC2000E.7.5

Replicating a Database

Databases, especially large ones, are kept on the same computer or network so that many users can enter, view, or manipulate the data in the database. However, some users might need to enter new records into the database while they're out of the office.

With Access 2000, you can create a special copy of a database, called a replica, for users to take with them when they leave the office. When you **replicate** a database, or create a replica of the database, the original database can be updated easily with any changes made to the replica. The original database is referred to as the **Design Master**, which reflects the fact that its design has been imposed on the replica.

It might seem easier to use the Copy command to create a new version of the database, but this command creates a separate copy of the database; the original and the copy are related only in the sense that they tempo-rarily contain identical data. For example, assume that you made a copy of Lakewood Mountains 07. If you added records to tblFebruaryOrders in both the original file and the copy, the changes could not be combined without manually examining the tables to determine what records were new, importing the new records from the copy into the original database, and then running an append query to add the new records to the original version of tblFebruaryOrders.

Append queries are discussed in Lesson 2, "Creating Custom Queries."

You can also compact a database so that it will use less space on your hard disk and store data more efficiently. To compact a database, open the database, point to Database Utilities on the Tools menu, and click Compact And Repair Database.

You must remove a database's password before creating a replica.

You can make as many replicas of a database as you like.

When you replicate a database, you do more than copy the original file. Access compares the replica with the original database so that the changes in the replica are detected and incorporated into the original database—a process called **synchronization**. In the example in the previous paragraph, Access would detect the new records in the replicated version of tblFebruary-Orders and then add them to the Design Master.

There is one limitation to working with replicas: you can't change the structure of the replica database by adding or deleting tables, adding or deleting table fields, or changing relationships. By freezing the design of the replica, it becomes easy for Access to identify changes.

important

You can modify a Design Master, although those modifications might make it impossible to synchronize the Design Master with any replicas.

In this exercise, you create a replica of Lakewood Mountains 07, add a record to frmApprovedToOrder in the replica, and then synchronize the Design Master and the replica so that the Design Master is updated with the new record.

1 Open Lakewood Mountains 07.

2 On the Tools menu, point to Replication, and click Create Replica.

   An alert box appears, warning that the database must be closed before it can be replicated.

3 Click Yes.

   A message box appears, asking if you want to create a backup copy of Lakewood Mountains 07 named Lakewood Mountains 07.bak before converting the original database to a Design Master.

Access assigns the .bak extension when you create a backup copy of a database.

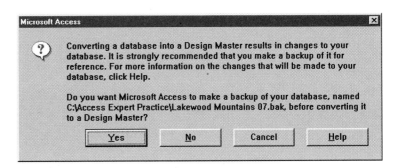

4   Click Yes.

The Location Of New Replica dialog box appears with *Replica of Lakewood Mountains 07* already inserted in the File Name box.

To save the replica in a different location than the original, click the Save In down arrow and navigate to the location where you want to save the replica.

New!

If you select the Prevent Deletes check box, users cannot delete records in the replica.

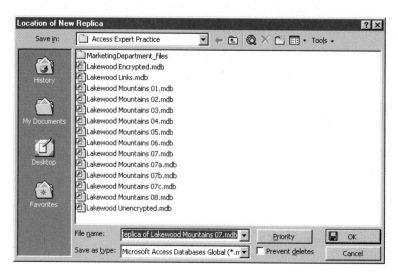

5   Click OK.

A message box appears, indicating that Access has created a replica of Lakewood Mountains 07 and changed the original to the Design Master.

6   Click OK.

Replica Symbol

The Database window for Lakewood Mountains 07: Design Master appears. The words *Design Master* appear on the title bar of the Database window, and the replica symbol appears next to the object icon for each database object.

The replica symbol indicates that these objects have replicas, not that these *are* the replicas.

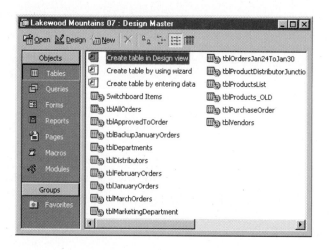

7 Close Lakewood Mountains 07: Design Master.

8 Open Replica Of Lakewood Mountains 07.

9 Display the list of forms in the Database window, and open frmApprovedToOrder.

Note that you cannot change the form to Design view. You cannot modify the design of a form stored in a replica database.

On your computer, dates might appear with four-digit years (2000), instead of two-digit years (00). For additional information on setting the years to two digits or four digits, see the "Using the CD-ROM" section at the beginning of this book.

New Record

10 Click the New Record button, and create a new record with the following information, using the Tab key to move from control to control.

Employee ID: **H140**

Last Name: **Lang**

First Name : **Eric**

Title field: **Assistant Manager**

Department Name: **Housekeeping**

Office #: **104**

Ext: **205**

Date Hired: **2/28/00**

Salary: **36000**

11 Close frmApprovedToOrder, and close Replica Of Lakewood Mountains 07.

12 Open Lakewood Mountains 07.

13 On the Tools menu, point to Replication, and click Synchronize Now.

The Synchronize Database dialog box appears.

You can make the replica into the Design Master by selecting the Design Master in the Directly With Replica box, selecting the Make 'Filename' The Design Master check box, and then clicking OK.

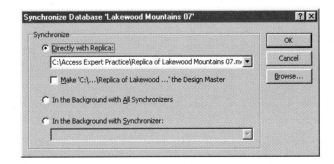

14 Verify that the Replica Of Lakewood Mountains 07 appears in the Directly With Replica box, and click OK.

An alert box appears, warning that the database must be closed before synchronization.

15   Click Yes to close the database.

Access displays a message box, indicating that the synchronization was successful.

16   Click OK.

The Lakewood Mountains 07 Database window appears

Next Record

17   Open frmApprovedToOrder in Form View, and click the Next Record button until you see the record for employee H140. (The records are in order by employee ID.)

18   Close frmApprovedToOrder.

19   Close Lakewood Mountains 07.

AC2000E.7.3

Splitting a Database

If many people need to use the data in a database simultaneously, creating and later synchronizing multiple replicas can be time-consuming and difficult. If the database is on a network, network and server performance might also slow down as a result of the constant changes to the database.

Fortunately, there is an easier way to allow multiple users to work with a database on a network: you can **split** the database. When you split a database, all the tables in the database are placed in one database, and all the other database objects (queries, forms, reports, macros, and data access pages) are stored in another. The database file containing the tables is called the **back-end file**, because it is the base for the rest of the database objects. Rather than attempting to share the same objects, which can result in slow network and server service, users can create their own objects using the tables in the back-end file. The database file containing the database objects created from the tables is called the **front-end file**. The front-end file itself does not contain any tables. You can create as many front-end files as you want from the tables in one back-end file. For example, at the Lakewood Mountains Resort, the marketing department, reservations desk, and human resources department could each have separate front-end files containing queries, reports, and forms suited to that particular department.

In this exercise, you use the Database Splitter Wizard to split Lakewood Mountains 07a into two files—one containing the database's tables, and the other containing the rest of the database objects.

1   Open Lakewood Mountains 07a.

You should always back up a database before splitting it. Lakewood Mountains 07a is a duplicate of the original Lakewood Mountains 07, so you do not need to make a backup copy before working through this exercise.

2   On the Tools menu, point to Database Utilities, and click Database Splitter.

The Database Splitter Wizard dialog box appears.

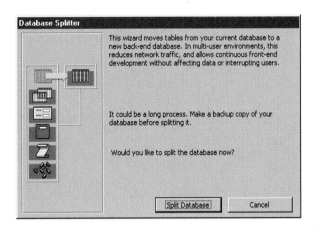

3   Click Split Database.

The Create Back-End Database dialog box appears with the name Lakewood Mountains 07a_be already inserted in the File Name box.

The *_be* portion of the name indicates that the file is a back-end file, although this portion of the name is not essential. You can change the name if you like.

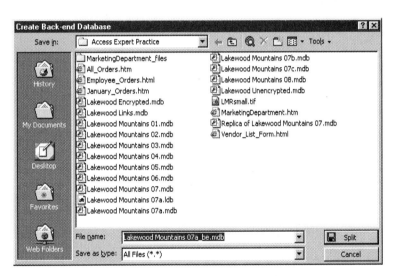

4   Click Split.

Access splits the database, and a message box appears, indicating that the database split was successful.

5   Click OK.

The Database window for the front-end file appears.

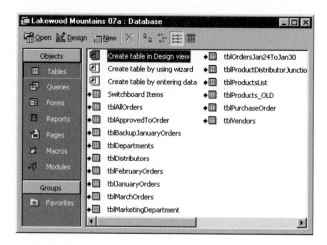

> The arrows next to the table icons indicate that the tables are linked and not part of the file itself.

6   Close Lakewood Mountains 07a.

AC2000E.7.8

Converting a Database to the Access 97 File Format

It's possible that some of the users who need the data in your database might not have upgraded to Access 2000. Fortunately, saving an Access 2000 database in the Access 97 file format is a straightforward process in Access 2000.

When you convert a database to the Access 97 file format, you lose any functions that are new to Access 2000 and didn't exist in Access 97. For example, you will lose links to data access pages. Also, if you have a field with the Number data type, you must change the Field Size property to a value besides Decimal or you must change the data type to Currency before you can successfully convert the database.

In this exercise, you save Lakewood Mountains 07b in the Access 97 file format.

> You can save an Access 2000 database in the Access 97 file format.

> To change individual database objects to other file formats, you export the database objects by clicking the object to export and clicking Export on the File menu. Exporting forms to HTML is discussed in Lesson 5, "Using Databases on the Internet."

1   Open Lakewood Mountains 07b.

2   On the Tools menu, point to Database Utilities, point to Convert Database, and then click To Prior Access Database Version.

The Convert Database Into dialog box appears, as shown on the next page.

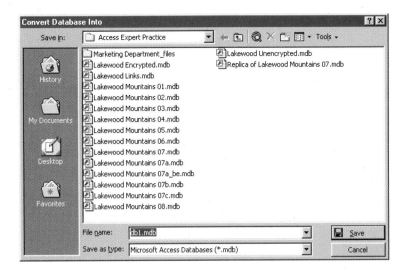

You do not choose which earlier version of Access to use because Access 2000 can convert a database to only the Access 97 file format.

3 In the File Name box, type **Lakewood Mountains 07_97**, and click Save.

Access saves Lakewood Mountains 07_97 in the Access 97 file format.

4 Close Lakewood Mountains 07b.

important

When you convert an Access 2000 database to Access 97, you might get an alert box telling you that your computer is missing one or more Access 97 project libraries. When you first open the new database in Access 97, you might also get an alert box warning about the missing libraries. To get the new Access 97 database to work correctly, you will need to open the new database in Access 97 and press Ctrl+G. On the Tools menu, click References. In the list that appears, clear the check box for the Microsoft DAO 3.6 Object Library, and select the check box for the Microsoft DAO 3.5 Object Library.

AC2000E.7.2

Setting Startup Options

So far in this lesson, you have learned how to use built-in Access features to change how a database handles data for individual users, for multiple users, and over networks. You can also change the startup options for the database to specify how much flexibility users have when using the database.

The following table describes the startup options that you can set for the database.

Option	Description
Application Title	Use to set the text that appears on the Database title bar.
Application Icon	Use to choose a custom icon for the database. The default selection is the standard Access icon.

Standard Access Icon

(continued)

continued

Option	Description
Menu Bar	Use to select the menu bar that appears at the top of the database window. If you created a custom menu bar, you can select it as the default menu bar.
Allow Full Menus	Use to restrict the menu commands available to the user. If this check box is selected, the user can use all the commands on all the menus.
Allow Default Shortcut Menus	Use to select whether shortcut menus appear when you right-click a database object. If this check box is selected, the default shortcut menus will appear.
Display Form/Page	Use to specify the form or data access page that Access displays when you open the database. The default choice is (None).
Display Database Window	Use to specify whether the Database window appears when you open the database. If this check box is selected, the Database window will appear.
Display Status Bar	Use to specify whether the **status bar** (the bar at the bottom of the Access window, which shows the progress of actions like saving and copying) appears in the Access window. If this check box is selected, the status bar will appear.
Shortcut Menu Bar	Use to specify which shortcut menu appears when you right-click an object. If you created a custom shortcut menu, you set it as the default shortcut menu.
Allow Built-In Toolbars	Use to specify whether you can view and use the default Access toolbars. If this check box is selected, the toolbars will appear.
Allow Toolbar/Menu Changes	Use to specify whether you can modify toolbars and menu bars. If this check box is selected, changes will be allowed.

You should back up your database before you change the startup options.

You set startup options in the Startup dialog box, which you open by clicking Startup on the Tools menu.

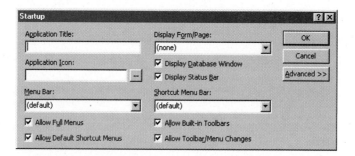

If you want users to have the ability to change a database whenever they want, you can leave all the options in the Startup dialog box selected. The more options that you clear or leave blank, the harder it is for users to modify (and make mistakes in) the database.

Switchboards are discussed in Lesson 3, "Customizing Forms."

For example, if you cleared all the check boxes in the Startup dialog box for Lakewood Mountains 07c and set switchboard as the default form, only the switchboard would be available to users when the database is opened. With these startup options, it would be impossible for users to modify the database or do anything except use the items on the switchboard.

important

To bypass the startup options, hold down the Shift key when you open the database.

In this exercise, you change the startup options of Lakewood Mountains 07c so that *Lakewood Mountains Resort* appears on the title bar of the database and the switchboard is already open when you open the database.

1 Open Lakewood Mountains 07c.

2 On the Tools menu, click Startup.

The Startup dialog box appears.

To learn more about each option in the Startup dialog box, click the question mark (?) in the top-right corner and click the property about which you want to learn more.

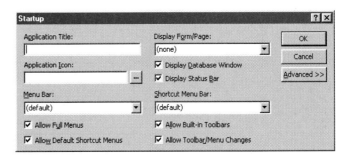

3 In the Application Title box, type **Lakewood Mountains Resort**.

4 Click the Display Form/Page down arrow, click Switchboard, and then click OK.

The Startup dialog box closes.

5 Close Lakewood Mountains 07c.

6   Open Lakewood Mountains 07c.

The Switchboard is already open, and *Lakewood Mountains Resort* appears on the title bar of the Access window.

Title bar

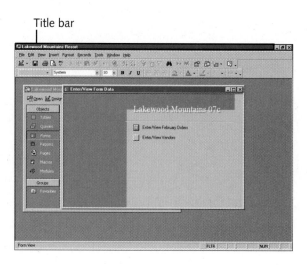

7   Close Lakewood Mountains 07c.

Lesson Wrap-Up

This lesson covered how to create and remove database passwords, encrypt and decrypt databases, replicate databases, split databases, convert databases to the Access 97 file format, and set startup options for the databases in Access 2000.

If you are continuing to the next lesson:

Close

● Click the Close button in the top-right corner of the Database window.

The Lakewood Mountains 07 database closes.

If you are not continuing to the next lesson:

Close

● To quit Access for now, click the Close button in the top-right corner of the Access window.

Access and the Lakewood Mountains 07 database close.

Lesson Glossary

back-end file   In a split database, the file that contains the tables from the database.

decrypt   To remove the encryption from an Access database to make it readable by applications other than Access.

Design Master   A database that has one or more replica databases.

encrypt   To make an Access database indecipherable when opened using an application other than Access.

Exclusive mode   A database setting in which only one user can have a database open at a time.

front-end file In a split database, the file that contains the forms, queries, and other non-table objects from the database.

password A sequence of characters that a user must type to open a database.

replica A special copy of a database in which Access can detect changes and automatically update the Design Master with those changes.

replicate To create a replica of a database. After you create a replica, the original database becomes a Design Master.

split A process to place database tables and other database objects into separate files.

startup options Properties that limit or expand how much flexibility users have to change a database.

status bar The bar at the bottom of the Access window that shows the progress of actions like saving and copying.

synchronization The process of updating the Design Master with changes made in the replica.

Quick Quiz

1   What is Exclusive mode?

2   What does encrypting a database do?

3   What happens when you change the startup options for a database?

4   What are some advantages to splitting a database?

5   What is a Design Master?

6   How do you remove a database password?

7   How do you convert an Access 2000 database to an Access 97 database?

8   What is synchronization?

9   What is the difference between setting a password for a database and encrypting a database?

10   How do you open a database in Exclusive mode?

Putting It All Together

Exercise 1: Encrypt Lakewood Mountains 07c as a database named Mountains Encrypted and require users to enter the password *uMb9^VoRe* to open it. Change the database's startup options so that frmAllOrders appears (instead of the switchboard) when the database is opened.

Exercise 2: Remove the password from Mountains Encrypted, and replicate the database. Enter the following record into the replica's version of frmAllOrders:

> Order#: **1092**
>
> OrderDate: **2/14/00**
>
> Code: **HK-SOP**
>
> Description: **Bar Soap (500)**
>
> #ofUnits: **1**
>
> Price: **$34.95**
>
> Shipping: **$5.00**
>
> EmployeeID: **H102**

Close frmAllOrders, and close the replica database. Open Mountains Encrypted, and then synchronize the databases. Check to see if order 1092 is in frmAllOrders. Close the database.

Exercise 3: Split the Lakewood Unencrypted database, convert the back-end file to the Access 97 file format, and then save it as **Lakewood Unencrypted Back-End_97**. Close the database.

LESSON 8

Integrating Access with Other Office Applications

After completing this lesson, you will be able to:

✔ *Create a graph.*

✔ *Export data to Excel.*

✔ *Drag tables and queries to an Excel worksheet.*

✔ *Create a link.*

Microsoft Access allows you to store, organize, and summarize data in many ways, but you can also integrate Access data with other Microsoft Office 2000 applications. In Lesson 5, "Using Databases on the Internet," you learned how to display table and query data as data access pages in Microsoft Internet Explorer. In this lesson, you'll learn how to move table and query data to Microsoft Excel, a program designed to analyze numerical data in ways that Access cannot. You'll also learn how to establish a connection, or **link**, to data in other databases or programs, even database programs such as dBASE and FoxPro.

This lesson also introduces Microsoft Graph, an application installed with Office. You use Microsoft Graph to create a pictorial representation of data, or a **graph**, based on the data in a database. When you create graphs based on Access data, you can show trends and relative values that can be difficult to see when looking at lists of numbers in a table or query.

To complete the procedures in this lesson, you will need to use files named Lakewood Mountains 08 and Lakewood Links in the Access Expert Practice folder that is located on your hard disk. You will also need to have Microsoft Excel 95 or later installed on your computer.

For additional information about opening the practice file for this lesson, see the "Using the CD-ROM" section at the beginning of this book.

Sample files for the lesson

AC2000E.8.3

Creating a Graph

Large tables of data can be hard to read, especially if the tables don't fit on a computer screen or a single printed page. If you create a report from a large table or query, the amount of data might make it difficult for your audience to read and understand the data. Numerical data can often be difficult to understand, even in small quantities.

Access uses the terms *graph* and *chart* interchangeably, but Microsoft Graph refers to all visual representations as charts.

One way to display table or query data effectively is to create a graph or **chart** based on the data. Graphs and charts are types of form controls that summarize data visually. For example, if you are in charge of the budget for the Housekeeping department, you could create a **pie chart** to display the percentage of orders placed by each Housekeeping employee. Pie charts show how much each entry in the chart contributes to the whole. Compare the data in Dataseet view for a query with the same data in a pie chart.

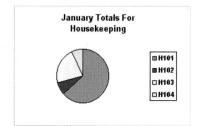

The pie chart in the illustration above has two main parts—the **body** and the **legend**. The body of the chart is the area that displays the data in the chart. The chart's legend explains the colors, shading patterns, and shapes used to represent and describe the entities in the chart. In the pie chart above, the legend shows that employees H101, H102, H103, and H104 are represented in the chart.

To create a chart or graph in Access, you use the Chart Wizard. The Chart Wizard allows you to select the type of chart that you want to create, the table or query that will provide values for the body of the chart, and the name of the chart. You can use the Chart Wizard to make 20 chart types, many of which are variations on a few basic types: the **column chart**, the **bar chart**, the **area chart**, the **line chart**, the **xy (scatter) chart**, the pie chart, and the **doughnut chart**. The table on the next page describes the basic chart types and their variations.

Some of the chart types in this table are typically referred to as "charts," while other types are commonly called "graphs." For example, a line chart is typically called a line graph, while a bar chart is typically called a bar chart.

The X-axis is the horizontal axis, and the Y-axis is the vertical axis on a chart.

Button	Chart Type	Variations	Description/Use
	Column	3-D, cylinder, cone, pyramid	Displays categories on the X-axis and values on the Y-axis and emphasizes comparisons over time.
	Bar	3-D bar, 3-D cylinder, 3-D cone, 3-D pyramid	Displays values on the X-axis and categories on the Y-axis and emphasizes comparisons over time.
	Area	3-D	Displays the sum of the values in the chart and emphasizes change over time.
	Line	3-D	Displays time on the X-axis, values on the Y-axis, and data from a single series in the body of the chart. Data is represented as a series of points connected by a line.
	Scatter	Bubble, 3-D bubble	Displays one set of values on the X-axis and another set of values on the Y-axis and marks intersections with points or bubbles. For bubble charts, the size of a bubble corresponds to its value. Especially useful for scientific and financial data.
	Pie	3-D	Displays the percentages of the different categories that make up one value.
	Doughnut	N/A	Displays the relationships of parts to the whole. Can contain more than one series of values.

It is possible to create charts using Microsoft Graph, but those skills are outside the scope of this course. Rather than attempt to create charts using Microsoft Graph, you should create the charts with the Chart Wizard and then edit them using Microsoft Graph.

After you create a chart, you can make changes to the chart by using Microsoft Graph. With Microsoft Graph, you can add explanatory text to a chart, change the colors used in the chart, and even change the chart type.

In this exercise, you open the Lakewood Mountains 08 database and use qrySalaryByTitle to create a pie chart that shows how salaries are divided among different types of markerting employees.

Open

1   On the Database toolbar, click the Open button, navigate to the Access Expert Practice folder on your hard disk, and then open the Lakewood Mountains 08 database.

2   Display the list of forms in the Database window, and click New on the Database window toolbar.

The New Form dialog box appears.

> The capabilities of the Chart Wizard in Access are fairly rudimentary. You can create more complex charts by inserting a Microsoft Excel chart into a form as an object and then using Excel's capabilities to modify the chart.

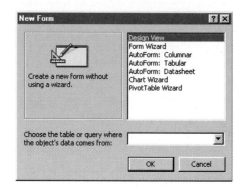

3   In the New Form dialog box, click Chart Wizard.

4   Click the Choose The Table Or Query Where The Object's Data Comes From down arrow, click qrySalaryByTitle, and then click OK.

The first Chart Wizard dialog box appears.

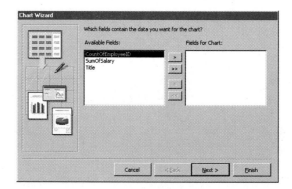

5   Add the SumOfSalary and Title fields to the Fields For Chart list, and click Next.

The next Chart Wizard dialog box appears.

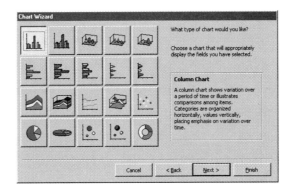

When you select a type of chart, the box on the right side of the Chart Wizard dialog box changes to show details about that type of chart.

Pie Chart

If you click the Preview Chart button in the top-left corner of the Chart Wizard dialog box, you can see what your chart will look like using the current settings.

The name below the sample chart (in this case, SumOfSumOfSalary) combines the name of the field providing data for chart and the summary operation performed on the data in the chart (in this case, Sum). The value set to the side of the chart (in this case, the Title field) is used to label each section of the pie chart.

The default settings for the final Chart Wizard dialog box create a legend and cause the chart and the form that it is on to be displayed in Form view. If you don't want a legend or you want to display the form containing the chart in Design view, you can click the appropriate options in this Chart Wizard dialog box. If you want to open Access Help for more information about charts, select the Display Help On Working With My Chart check box.

6   Click the Pie Chart button (the first button in the fourth row), and click Next.

The next Chart Wizard dialog box appears.

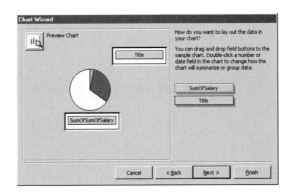

7   Click Next to accept the default layout for the pie chart.

The next Chart Wizard dialog box appears.

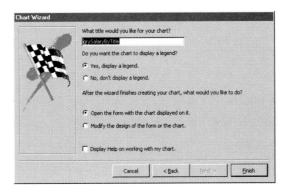

When you name a chart, you do not need to follow the Leszynski naming convention. You can use spaces in chart names.

8   In the What Title Would You Like For Your Chart? box, type **Salary By Title**, and click Finish.

Access names the chart Salary By Title, and the form containing the chart appears in Form view.

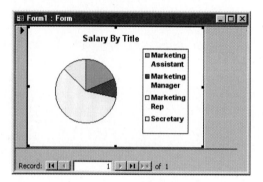

9   On the Form View toolbar, click the View button.

The form appears in Design view.

View

You can move the chart on the form in the same way that you move any other form control.

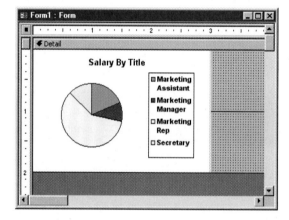

10   Click anywhere in the chart to select it.

11   On the Edit menu, point to Chart Object, and click Edit.

Microsoft Graph starts, and a form appears that shows the pie chart data in Datasheet view.

In this form, you can change the numbers and titles displayed on the form by clicking the item that you want to change and typing the new value. You can add or remove rows from the chart by double-clicking to the left of the record in the box containing a number and a color slice.

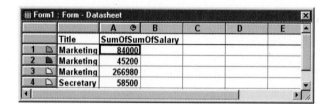

12 On the Chart menu, click Chart Options.

The Chart Options dialog box appears.

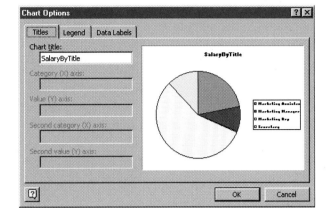

The picture on the right side of the Chart Options dialog box shows what the chart will look like with the new settings applied.

13 Click the Data Labels tab, click the Show Percent option, and then click OK.

The Chart Options dialog box closes, and Access adds percentages to the pie chart.

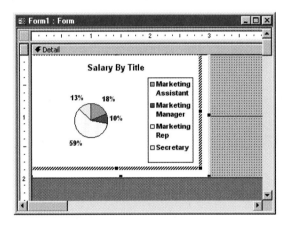

14 Close the form that shows the pie chart data in Datasheet view.

15 Save the form containing the chart as **frmSalaryChart**, and close it.

Exporting Data to Excel

AC2000E.8.1

Access works well if you want to store and retrieve large collections of information about people, places, and things, but it is less effective at processing financial, scientific, and other numeric data. You can use totals and crosstab queries with numeric data, but Excel offers even more tools for processing numbers. When your Access database contains financial data, you can use some of Excel's capabilities to process the data. You can use Excel when you have a lot of financial data and need to use advanced data analysis techniques not easily accomplished in Access, such as creating scenarios based on alternative data sets or calculating running subtotals for a data series.

Totals and crosstab queries are discussed in Lesson 2, "Creating Custom Queries."

You can export financial data to Excel, analyze the data using Excel, and then import the data back into Access when you're finished. Exporting data to Excel makes it easier to collaborate with others who do not have Access but do have Excel. When you export a table or query to Excel, people within your organization who use Excel regularly will be better equipped to understand and analyze the data.

A file in Excel is called a **workbook**, and each Excel workbook is made up of one or more **worksheets**, which display data in rows and columns, similar to tables in Access.

In this exercise, you export qryTotalByVendorCrosstab to an Excel workbook.

> You can always create a new query if none of the existing tables or queries contains the data that you want to export to Excel.

1   Display the list of queries in the Database window, and click qryTotalByVendorCrosstab.

2   On the File menu, click Export.

The Export Query To dialog box appears.

> The Export Query To dialog box displays the contents of the My Documents folder on your computer by default. Depending on the contents of this folder on your computer, your screen might not match the illustration here.

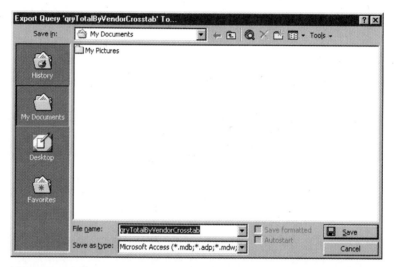

3   Navigate to the Access Expert Practice folder on your hard disk.

4   Click in the File Name box, delete the existing text, and then type **Total By Vendor**.

> You do not need to use the Leszynski naming convention with files exported to Excel.

5   Click the Save As Type down arrow, click Microsoft Excel 97-2000 (*.xls), and then click Save.

The Export Query dialog box closes, and Access exports the query to an Excel workbook named Total By Vendor.

6   On the Windows taskbar, click the Start button, point to Programs, and then click Microsoft Excel.

Excel starts.

Open

7   In Excel, click the Open button on the Standard toolbar.

The Open dialog box appears.

8   Navigate to the Access Expert Practice folder on your hard disk, and click Total By Vendor.

9   Click Open.

Total By Vendor opens, and the data from the qryTotalByVendorCrosstab appears on an Excel worksheet.

	A	B	C	D	E	F	G	H	I	J
1	VendorID	H102	H103	R221	R234	R455	S504	S505	S606	S607
2	CH	$13.90		$5.00	$29.90					
3	EN								$99.95	
4	HK						$199.50	$20.95	$41.90	
5	KC						$99.00			
6	KS									$9.90
7	PP								$29.95	$101.80
8	RC	$129.90		$39.95		$25.90				
9	RS		$100.00							
10										
11										

There are two Close buttons in the top-right corner of the Excel window. You click the bottom Close button to close the Total By Vendor workbook. The top Close button closes Excel and all open workbooks.

10   Close the Total By Vendor workbook, but do not close Excel.

AC2000E.8.2

Dragging Tables and Queries to an Excel Worksheet

You can export queries and tables to Excel worksheets, but it is also possible to drag a table or query directly into an existing Excel worksheet. You should consider dragging a table or query to Excel when you want to use the entire contents of the table or query in Excel. This method of moving data to Excel is faster and easier than exporting a table or query.

You can also select and copy a few Access datasheet cells into an Excel worksheet. To do so, you select the datasheet cells that you want to move, click the Copy button, click the cell in the Excel worksheet where you want the pasted cells to begin, and then click the Paste button to paste the cells into the worksheet.

In this exercise, you drag tblJanuaryOrders to an Excel worksheet and then paste the first three records from tblFebruaryOrders into the same worksheet.

New

1   With Excel open, click the New button on the Standard toolbar.

A new workbook appears.

2   Right-click the Windows taskbar, and click Tile Windows Horizontally on the shortcut menu that appears.

The Excel and Access windows both appear on your screen, which should appear similar to the illustration on the following page.

In the illustration, the Excel window is on the top half of the screen and the Access window is on the bottom half. You can scroll up or down in the individual windows by using the scroll bars at the right side of the windows.

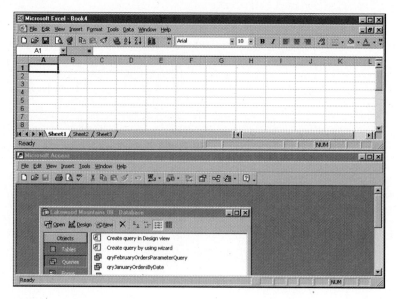

3 Click in the Access window, display the list of tables in the Database window, scroll down, and then drag tblJanuaryOrders to cell A1 of the Excel worksheet.

The data from tblJanuaryOrders appears on the Excel worksheet.

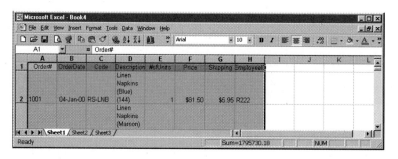

4 Click in the Access window, and open tblFebruaryOrders in Datasheet view.

5 Hold down the Shift key, and select the first three records in tblFebruaryOrders.

Copy

6 In Access, click the Copy button on the Table Datasheet toolbar.

7 Click in the Excel window, scroll down to the end of the file, and then click in the first blank cell in the A column.

Paste

8 In Excel, click the Paste button on the Standard toolbar.

The first three records from tblFebruaryOrders appear on the Excel worksheet. Note that the pasted records include the field names from tblFebruaryOrders, as shown on the following page.

You can also copy selected items by pressing Ctrl+C and then paste them by pressing Ctrl+V.

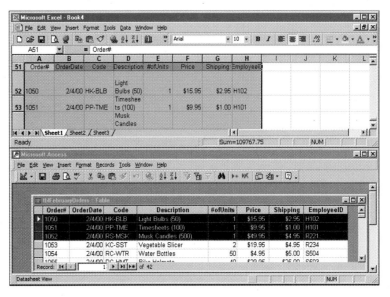

To delete the extra field names, click the numbered box to the left of the row that you want to delete, and click Delete on the Edit menu.

9 Save the Excel worksheet in the Access Expert Practice folder as **Orders**, and quit Excel.

10 In the Access window, close tblFebruaryOrders.

Maximize

11 Click the Maximize button in the top-right corner of the Access window.

The Access window expands to fill the entire screen.

AC2000E.7.3
AC2000E.8.4

Creating a Link

Despite the advantages of exporting or dragging tables to Excel, these procedures do have one important limitation: exporting a table or query makes a copy of the table or query data, but the original table and the copy are not connected in any way. As a result, if you modify the original table, the changes won't appear in the copy, meaning that the copy might quickly become outdated. The reverse is also true; changes made to the copy won't appear in the original.

Hyperlinks are discussed in Lesson 5, "Using Databases on the Internet."

Fortunately, you can easily create a link from an Access database to data in other programs, such as Excel, or other database programs, such as dBase and FoxPro. On the surface, links appear to be the same as hyperlinks, but there is an important difference. A hyperlink to a table in another database allows users to open the table for viewing and editing, but it does not make the data in the table available for use in queries and other database objects. By contrast, a link to a table in another database makes the data in the table available for other database objects.

You can create a new database from data in another program.

tip

You can use links to convert a database created in another program, such as dBASE, FoxPro, or Paradox, to Access. You start Access, and click the Open button on the Database toolbar. In the Open dialog box, you click the Files Of Type down arrow and select the program used to create the database that you want to convert. When you open the database, Access creates a blank database and establishes links to every object in the other database.

In this exercise, you create a link to tblPriorities in the Lakewood Links database and test it by creating a query in the Lakewood Mountains 08 database that uses information from tblPriorities.

1   On the File menu, point to Get External Data, and click Link Tables.

The Link dialog box appears with the Access Expert Practice folder already open.

The contents of the Access Expert Practice folder on your computer might not match the illustration here.

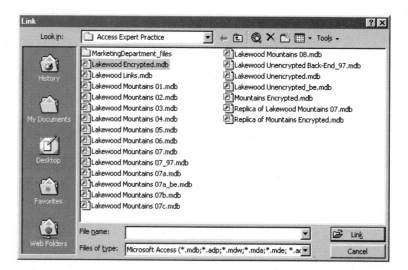

2   Click the Lakewood Links database, and click Link.

The Link Tables dialog box appears, showing one table in the Lakewood Links database.

If you want to create links to more than one table, you can select multiple tables or you can link to every table by clicking Select All.

3 Click tblPriorities, and click OK.

tblPriorities appears in the list of tables in Lakewood Mountains 08.

The arrow next to the icon for tblPriorities indicates that the database is linked to the tables and the table is not physically in the database.

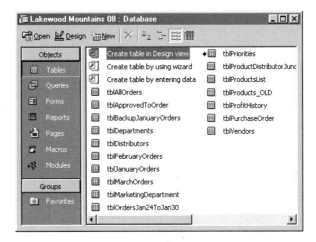

4 Display the list of queries in the database, and double-click Create Query By Using Wizard.

The first Simple Query Wizard dialog box appears.

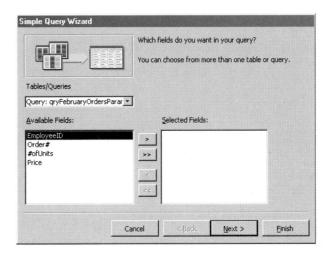

5 Click the Tables/Queries down arrow, scroll up, and then click Table: tblPriorities.

The fields in tblPriorities appear in the Available Fields list.

6 Click the >> (Add All) button.

All the fields in tblPriorities move to the Selected Fields list.

7   Click Finish.

The query results appear.

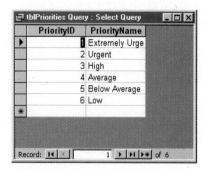

The data that appear in the query is actually stored in tblPriorities in the Lakewood Links database.

8   Close the query.

Lesson Wrap-Up

This lesson covered how to create and modify a graph, export data to Excel, drag tables and queries directly to Excel, and create links in Access 2000.

If you are continuing to another lesson:

Close

●   Click the Close button in the top-right corner of the Database window.

The current database closes.

If you are not continuing to another lesson:

Close

●   To quit Access for now, click the Close button in the top-right corner of the Access window.

Access and the current database close.

Lesson Glossary

area chart   A chart that displays the sum of the values in the chart.

bar chart   A chart that displays categories (like months in a year, employee ID numbers, or products) on the Y-axis, and values (like the amount of sales, salaries, or product costs) on the X-axis. Values appear as relatively sized bars.

body   The area of a chart that displays the data in the chart.

chart   A pictorial representation of data. Same as *graph*.

column chart   A chart that displays categories (like months in a year, employee ID numbers, or products) on the X-axis, and values (like the amount of sales, salaries, or product costs) on the Y-axis.

doughnut chart   A chart that displays the relationship of parts to the whole. This chart can contain more than one series of data.

graph   A pictorial representation of data. Same as *chart*.

legend A list of the categories or values represented in a chart.

line chart A chart that displays time on the X-axis, values on the Y-axis, and data from a single series in the body of the chart.

link A connection from an Access database to a table in another database or database program.

pie chart A chart that shows how each value in the chart contributes to the whole.

workbook A file in Excel, which contains worksheets.

worksheets Pages in Excel consisting of horizontal and vertical gridlines where you enter and analyze data. One or more worksheets make up a workbook.

xy (scatter) chart A chart that displays one set of value on the X-axis and another set of values on the Y-axis and marks intersections with points on the chart.

Quick Quiz

1   How do you export data from Access to Excel?

2   What does a link do?

3   What is a chart legend?

4   How do you create a chart?

5   Why would you link to a table instead of exporting it?

6   How do you drag a table or query from Access to Excel?

7   What is a workbook?

8   What is the difference between the Chart Wizard and Microsoft Graph?

9   Why would you drag a table or query from Access into Excel instead of exporting the same data to Excel?

10   What is the body of a chart?

Putting It All Together

Exercise 1: Create a line chart based on tblProfitHistory with the title *Profit History* and without a legend. Remove the gridlines from the chart. Save the chart as **frmProfitChart**, and close it.

Exercise 2: Export tblJanuaryOrders to an Excel workbook named Orders. Drag tblFebruaryOrders to the end of the file.

Exercise 3: Create a link in the Lakewood Links database to tblAllOrders in the Lakewood Mountains 08 database.

Quick Reference

Core Skills

Lesson 1: Understanding Databases

To start Access

1 On the Windows taskbar, click the Start button.

2 On the Start menu, point to Programs, and click Microsoft Access.

To open an existing database

1 If Access is not already open, start Access, and in the Microsoft Access dialog box that appears, verify that the Open An Existing File option is selected, and click OK.

Or

If Access is already open, click the Open button on the Database toolbar.

Open

2 Click the Look In down arrow, and navigate to the location of the database that you want to open.

3 Click the database that you want to open, and click Open.

To display the Office Assistant

● On the Help menu, click Show The Office Assistant.

To hide the Office Assistant

● Right-click the Office Assistant, and click Hide on the shortcut menu that appears.

To move around the Database window

● On the Objects bar, click the type of object for which you want to view a list of available objects.

To open an object in Datasheet view

1 On the Objects bar, click the type of object that you want to open.

2 Click the name of the object that you want to open.

3 On the Database window toolbar, click Open.

Or

Double-click the name of the object that you want to open.

To open an object in Design view

1   On the Objects bar, click the type of object that you want to open.

2   Click the name of the object that you want to open.

3   On the Database window toolbar, click Design.

To switch between Datasheet view and Design view for a table

 Or

View   *View*

●   On the Table Datasheet or Table Design toolbar, click the View button.

To navigate in Datasheet view

●   Use the mouse to click in the cell that you want to select.
    Or
    Use the navigation buttons in the bottom-left corner of the table.
    Or
    Use the shortcut keys.

To close an object

Close

●   Click the Close button in the top-right corner of the object.
    Or
    On the File menu, click Close.

Lesson 2: Creating Tables

To create a database

1   If Access is not already open, point to Programs on the Windows taskbar, and click Microsoft Access. In the Microsoft Access dialog box that appears, click the Blank Access Database option, and click OK.
    Or

New

   If Access is already open, click the New button on the Database toolbar. In the New dialog box that appears, click the Database icon, and click OK.

2   In the File New Database dialog box, click the Save In down arrow to navigate to the location where you want to save the new database.

3   In the File Name box, type the name of the new database, and click Create.

To create a table using the Table Wizard

1   On the Objects bar, click Tables.

2   Double-click Create Table By Using Wizard.

3   Select the Business or Personal option.

4   Click a sample table, click the fields that you want to add to the table, and then click the > (Add) button for each.

5   Click Next.

6 Enter a name for the table, and click Next.

7 Click Finish.

To create a table in Design view

1 On the Objects bar, click Tables.

2 Double-click Create Table In Design View.

3 In the Field Name column, click in the first empty cell, type the new field name, and then press Tab.

4 In the Data Type column, click the down arrow, and click the data type for the field.

5 Repeat steps 3 and 4 for each new field.

To add a hyperlink to a table

1 With the table open in Design view, click in the Data Type cell for the field where you want the hyperlink, click the down arrow that appears, and then click Hyperlink.

View

2 On the Table Design toolbar, click the View button. When you are prompted to save changes, click Yes.

3 Click in the first record for the field set to Hyperlink.

4 Type the Web or intranet address.

To add a field to a table

1 Display the table in Design view.

2 In the Field Name column, click in the first empty cell, type the new field name, and then press Tab.

3 In the Data Type column, click the down arrow, and click the data type for the field.

To add a record to a table

1 Display the table in Datasheet view.

2 Click in the first empty record.

3 Enter data, using the Tab key to move from field to field.

To edit records in a table

1 Click in the field that you want to edit.

2 Using the mouse pointer or keyboard keys, delete the old data.

3 Type the new data.

To print a table

1 Open a table in Datasheet view.

Print

2 On the Table Datasheet toolbar, click the Print button.

Or

On the File menu, click Print.

To move a field

1 Display the table in Design view.

Row selector

2 Click in the row for the field that you want to move, and click the row selector to the left of the row.

3 Drag the row to its new location.

To delete a field

1 Display the table in Design view.

2 Click in the row that you want to delete.

Delete Rows

3 On the Table Design toolbar, click the Delete Rows button, and click Yes in the alert box that appears.

4 Save the table.

To delete a record

1 Display the table in Datasheet view.

2 Click in the record that you want to delete.

Delete Record

3 On the Table Datasheet toolbar, click the Delete Record button, and click Yes in the alert box that appears.

Lesson 3: Working with Tables

To change the format of a table

1 Display the table in Datasheet view.

2 On the View menu, point to Toolbars, and click Formatting (Datasheet), if necessary

3 On the Formatting toolbar, use the buttons for Font, Font Size, Bold, Italic, Underline, and Font/Fore Color to modify the font.

4 To resize the columns, double-click the line between the field names of the columns that you want to change.

To save a table as a Web page

1 In the Database window, select the table to be saved as a Web page.

2 On the File menu, click Export.

3 Click the Save In down arrow, and navigate to the place where you want to save the new file.

4 Click the Save As Type down arrow, and click HTML (*.htm; *.html).

5 In the File Name box, type the new name of the file, and click Save.

To modify field properties

1 Display the table in Design view.

2 In the Field Name column, click in the cell for the field for which you want to change the properties.

3 In the Field Properties section, click the box next to the property that you want to change.

4 Click the down arrow that appears, and select the new property setting.

Or

Type the new property in the box.

To use the Input Mask Wizard

1 Display the table in Design view, and click in the cell for the field that you want to contain the input mask.

2 In the Field Properties section, click in the Input Mask box.

Build

3 Click the Build button that appears.

4 Follow the wizard's instructions.

To use the Lookup Wizard

1 In Design view, click in the Data Type cell for the field that you want to contain the Lookup field, click the down arrow that appears, and then click Lookup Wizard.

2 Follow the wizard's instructions.

To sort records in a table

1 Display the table in Datasheet view.

2 Click in the field by which you want to sort the records.

Sort Ascending   *Or*   *Sort Descending*

3 Click the Sort Ascending or Sort Descending button.

To find records in a table

1 Display the table in Datasheet view.

2 In the field that you want to search, click any cell.

Find

3 On the Table Datasheet toolbar, click the Find button.

4 In the Find And Replace dialog box, type the text that you want to find, and click Find Next.

To apply a filter to a table

1 Display the table in Datasheet view.

Filter By Selection

2 Click in any cell in the table that contains the value that you want to use to filter, and click the Filter By Selection button.

Or

1 Display the table in Datasheet view.

Filter By Form

2 On the Table Datasheet toolbar, click the Filter By Form button.

3 Click in the first record of the field to which you want to apply a filter, click the down arrow that appears, and then click the item that you want to use to filter.

Apply Filter

4 On the Filter/Sort toolbar, click the Apply Filter button.

To remove a filter

Remove Filter

● On the Table Datasheet toolbar, click the Remove Filter button.

To establish a relationship

Relationships

Show Table

1 On the Database toolbar, click the Relationships button.
2 On the Relationship toolbar, click the Show Table button, if necessary.
3 Add the tables that you want to use in the relationship to the Relationships window, and click Close.
4 Drag the field that you want to use to create the relationship from one field list to its location in the other field list.
5 In the Edit Relationships dialog box, click Create.
6 Save the Relationships window.

To enforce referential integrity

Relationships

1 On the Database toolbar, click the Relationships button.
2 Double-click the relationship to which you want to apply referential integrity.
3 In the Edit Relationships dialog box, select the Enforce Referential Integrity check box, and click OK.
4 Save the Relationships window.

To create a subdatasheet

1 Verify that the two tables you want to use have a relationship.
2 Display the table on the *one* side of the relationship in Datasheet view.
3 On the Insert menu, click Subdatasheet.
4 Verify that the table on the *many* side of the relationship is selected, and click OK.
5 Click the plus sign (+) to the left of the record for which you want to see the subdatasheet.

To import records from an external source

1 On the File menu, point to Get External Data, and click Import.
2 Click the Files Of Type down arrow, and click the type of file that you want to import.
3 In the Look In box, navigate to the location of the file that you want to import.
4 Click the name of the file that you want to import, and click Import.
5 Follow the instructions in the Import Wizard. The steps will vary depending on the type of file you are importing.

To copy records into a table

Copy

Paste

1   Select the records that you want to copy.

2   On the Table Datasheet toolbar, click the Copy button.

3   Open the table to which you want to add the records, and select the first record where the new records should go.

4   On the Table Datasheet toolbar, click the Paste button.

5   In the alert box that appears, click Yes.

Lesson 4: Creating and Using Queries

To create a query using the Simple Query Wizard

1   On the Objects bar, click Queries.

2   Double-click Create Query By Using Wizard.

3   Click the Tables/Queries down arrow, and click the table or query on which you want to base the query.

4   In the Available Fields list, click the field that you want to add to the query, and click the > (Add) button. Repeat to add all the fields that you want to your query.

5   Click Next.

6   Type the name of your query, and click Finish.

To run a query

Run

●   On the Query Design toolbar, click the Run button.

To specify criteria in a query

1   Display the query in Design view.

2   In the Criteria row, type the criteria in the column for the field that you want to restrict.

To create a query in Design view

1   On the Objects bar, click Queries.

2   Double-click Create Query In Design View.

3   In the Show Table dialog box, click the table(s) on which you want to base your query, and click Add.

4   Click Close.

5   In the field list, double-click the fields that you want to add to your query.

To use comparison operators in a query

1   Display the query in Design view.

2   In the Criteria row, type the criterion containing the comparison operator in the column for the field that you want to restrict.

To create a calculated field in a query

1   Display the query in Design view.

2   In the Field row, click in the first blank cell, and type the field name and the expression for the calculation.

To create a multiple-table query

1   On the Objects bar, click Queries.

2   Double-click Create Query In Design View.

3   In the Show Table dialog box, click the table on which you want to base the query, and click Add. Repeat for any additional tables with related fields, and click Close.

4   If necessary, drag the field that you want to join from the first field list to the corresponding field in the second field list to create the join line.

5   In the field lists, double-click the fields that you want to add to your query.

To print a query

1   Display the query in Datasheet view.

Print

2   On the Query Datasheet toolbar, click the Print button.

Or

On the File menu, click Print.

Lesson 5: Designing a Form

To create a form using AutoForm

1   On the Objects bar, click Forms

2   On the Database window toolbar, click New.

3   In the New Form dialog box, click AutoForm: Columnar, AutoForm: Tabular, or AutoForm: Datasheet.

4   In the New Form dialog box, click the Choose The Table Or Query Where The Object's Data Comes From down arrow, click the name of the table on which you want to base the form, and then click OK.

To create a form using the Form Wizard

1   On the Objects bar, click Forms.

2   Double-click Create Form By Using Wizard.

3   In the first Form Wizard dialog list, click the Tables/Queries down arrow, and click the table on which you want to base the form.

4   In the Available Fields list, click the field(s) that you want to add to the form, and click the > (Add) button.

5   Click Next.

6   In the next Form Wizard dialog box, select the layout that you want to use for your form, and click Next.

7 In the next Form Wizard dialog box, select the style that you want to use for your form, and click Next.

8 In the next Form Wizard dialog box, type the name that you want your form to have, and click Finish.

To add controls to a form

1 Display the form in Design view.

Toolbox

2 On the Form Design toolbar, click the Toolbox button, if necessary.

3 In the toolbox, click the tool for the type of control that you want to add.

4 Click in the form where you want the control to go.

To print a form

1 Open the form.

Print

2 On the Form View toolbar, click the Print button.

Or

On the Form Design toolbar, click the Print button.

Or

On the File menu, click Print.

To modify control properties using the property sheet

1 Display the form in Design view.

2 Double-click the edges of the control that you want to change.

3 In the property sheet for the control, click the tab that contains the property that you want to change.

4 Scroll down, if necessary, to find the property that you want to change.

5 Click in the box for the property that you want to change.

6 Click the down arrow that appears, and click the new setting.

Or

Type the new setting.

Close

7 Click the Close button in the top-right corner of the property sheet.

To modify control properties using the toolbar

1 Display the form in Design view.

2 Click the control that you want to change.

3 On the Formatting toolbar, click the button for the property that you want to change.

To resize a control in a form

1 Display the form in Design view.

2 Click the control that you want to resize.

3   Move the mouse pointer over the handles of the control until the pointer turns into a horizontal, vertical, or diagonal double-headed arrow.

4   Drag the edge(s) of the control in the direction that you want to resize the control.

To move a control in a form

1   Display the form in Design view.

2   Click the control that you want to move.

3   To move a control with its accompanying text box or label (if applicable), move the mouse pointer over the edge of the control until the pointer turns into a hand.

Or

To move a control without also moving its accompanying text box or label, move the mouse pointer over the top-right handle until the pointer turns into a pointing hand.

4   Drag the control to the location in the form where you want the control to go.

To create a form in Design view

1   On the Objects bar, click Forms, if necessary.

2   Double-click Create Form In Design View.

3   On the View menu, click Properties.

4   In the Form property sheet, click the Data tab, click in the Record Source box, click the down arrow that appears, and then click the table that you want to use as the source for the form.

Close

5   Click the Close button in the top-right corner of the Form property sheet.

6   Drag the fields that you want to use from the field list to the form.

7   Use the toolbox to create unbound or calculated controls.

To navigate in a form

●   Use the mouse to click the control that you want to select.

Or

Use the navigation buttons in the button-left corner of the form window.

Or

Use the shortcut keys.

To enter records into a form

1   Display the form in Form view.

New Record

2   Click the New Record button.

3   Type the new information, navigating from control to control.

To create a calculated control

Toolbox

Text Box

1 Display the form in Design view.

2 On the Form Design toolbar, click the Toolbox button, if necessary.

3 In the toolbox, click the Text Box tool.

4 Click the area of the form where you want the calculated control to go.

5 Click the label for the calculated control, move the mouse pointer over the label until the pointer turns into an insertion point, click the mouse, delete the existing text, and then type the name of the calculated control.

6 Click the text box for the calculated control, move the mouse pointer over the label until the pointer turns into an insertion point, click the mouse, and then type an expression into the text box.

To back up a database

1 Make sure that the database is closed.

2 Navigate to the location where the database is stored.

3 Copy the database.

4 Navigate to the location where you want to store the backup database.

5 Paste the database, creating a backup copy of the original database.

To restore the database from the backup

1 Navigate to the place where the backup database is stored.

2 Copy the backup database.

3 Navigate to the place where you want the restored database.

4 Paste the database, creating a new copy of the backup database.

Lesson 6: Designing a Report

To create a report using AutoReport

1 On the Objects bar, click Reports.

2 On the Database window toolbar, click New.

3 In the New Report dialog box, click either AutoReport: Columnar or AutoReport: Tabular.

4 In the New Report dialog box, click the Choose The Table Or Query Where The Object's Data Comes From down arrow, click the name of the table on which you want to base the report, and then click OK.

To create a report using the Report Wizard

1 On the Objects bar, click Reports.

2 Double-click Create Report By Using Wizard.

3 In the first Report Wizard dialog box, click the Tables/Queries down arrow, and click the table on which you want to base the report.

4   In the Available Fields box, click the field(s) that you want to add to the report, and click the > (Add) button.

5   Click Next.

6   In the next Report Wizard dialog box, select the field(s), if any, that you want to use as grouping levels, and click Next.

7   In the next Report Wizard dialog box, select the field by which you want to sort the data in each group, click the Sort button to change the sort order of the data, if necessary, and then click Next.

8   In the next Report Wizard dialog box, select the layout that you want to use for your report, and click Next.

9   In the next Report Wizard dialog box, select the style that you want to use for your report, and click Next.

10   In the next Report Wizard dialog box, type the name that you that want your report to have, and click Finish.

To add a control to a report

1   Display the report in Design view.

Toolbox

2   On the Report Design toolbar, click the Toolbox button, if necessary.

3   In the toolbox, click the tool for the type of control that you want to add.

4   Click in the report where you want the control to go.

To create a report in Design view

1   On the Objects bar, click Reports.

2   On the Database window toolbar, click New.

3   In the New Report dialog box, click Design View, if necessary.

4   Click the Choose The Table Or Query Where The Object's Data Comes From down arrow, click the name of the table on which you want to base the report, and then click OK.

5   To add bound controls, drag the field names that you want to add from the field list to the report.

Or

To add unbound controls, click the tool in the toolbox for the type of control that you want to add, and click in the report where you want the control to go.

To format a report using the property sheet

1   Display the report in Design view.

2   Double-click the part of the report that you want to change.

3   In the property sheet, click the tab that contains the property you want to change.

4   Scroll down, if necessary, to find the property that you want to change.

5   Click in the box for the property that you want to change.

6 Click the down arrow that appears, and click the new setting.

Or

Type the new setting.

Close

7 Click the Close button in the top-right corner of the property sheet.

To format a report using the toolbar

1 Display the report in Design view.

2 Select the part of the report that you want to change.

3 On the Formatting toolbar, click the button(s) for the format(s) that you want to apply to the report.

To resize a control in a report

1 Display the report in Design view.

2 Click the control that you want to resize.

3 Move the mouse pointer over the handles of the control until the pointer turns into a horizontal, vertical, or diagonal double-headed arrow.

4 Drag the edge(s) of the control in the direction that you want to resize the control.

To move a control in a report

1 Display the report in Design view.

2 Click the control that you want to move.

3 To move a control with its accompanying text box or label (if applicable), move the mouse pointer over the edge of the control until the pointer turns into a hand.

Or

To move a control without also moving its accompanying text box or label (if applicable), move the mouse pointer over the top-left handle until the pointer turns into a pointing hand.

4 Drag the control to the location in the report where you want the control to go.

To create a calculated control

1 Display the report in Design view.

Toolbox

2 On the Report Design toolbar, click the Toolbox button, if necessary.

3 In the toolbox, click the Text Box tool.

4 Click the area of the report where you want the calculated control to go.

Text Box

5 Click the label for the calculated control, move the mouse pointer over the label until the pointer turns into an insertion point, click the mouse, delete the existing text, and then type the name of the calculated control.

6 Click the text box for the calculated control, move the mouse pointer over the text box until the pointer turns into an insertion point, click the mouse, and then type the expression for the calculated control.

To preview a report

1   Display the report in Design view.

2   On the Report Design toolbar, click the Print Preview button.

Or

On the Report Design toolbar, click the View button.

Print Preview · *Or* · *View*

To print a report

1   Display the report in the view that you want to print.

2   On the Report Design toolbar, click the Print button.

Or

On the Print Preview toolbar, click the Print button.

Or

On the File menu, click Print.

Print

To compact a database

1   If the database is a multiuser database located on a server or shared folder, verify that the database is not open.

2   Open the database that you want to compact.

3   On the Tools menu, point to Database Utilities, and click Compact And Repair Database.

To automatically compact a database every time you close it (unless another user is using the database)

1   Open the database that you want to compact automatically.

2   On the Tools menu, click Options.

3   In the Options dialog box, click the General tab, select the Compact On Close check box, and then click OK.

Expert Skills

Lesson 1: Customizing Tables

To create an index

1   In the Table Design view window, click in the row for the field to which you want to assign an index.

2   In the Field Properties section, click in the Indexed box, click the down arrow that appears, and then click Yes (No Duplicates) or Yes (Duplicates OK).

To normalize a table

1   On the Tools menu, point to Analyze, and click Table.

2   In the first two Table Analyzer Wizard dialog boxes, click Next.

3   In the next Table Analyzer Wizard dialog box, select the table to normalize, and click Next.

4   In the next Table Analyzer Wizard dialog box, click Next to allow the wizard to set the break.

5   In the next Table Analyzer Wizard dialog box, rename the tables that the wizard creates, and click Next.

6   In the next Table Analyzer Wizard dialog box, select a primary key, and click Next.

7   In the next Table Analyzer Wizard dialog box, decide if you want to create a query that will look like your original table, and click Finish.

To set a default data entry value

1   In the Table Design view window, click in the row for the field to which you want to assign the default value.

2   In the Field Properties section, click in the Default Value box, and type the rule.

To create and modify an input mask

1   In the Table Design view window, click in the row for the field to which you want to assign an input mask.

2   In the Field Properties section, click in the Input Mask box, and click the Build button that appears.

3   Use the Input Mask Wizard to create or modify the input mask, and click Finish.

To define a data validation rule

1   In the Table Design view window, click in the row for the field to which you want to assign the rule.

2   In the Field Properties section, click in the Validation Rule box, and type the validation rule.

3   If desired, click in the Validation Text box, and type the message that you want to appear if the user enters a value that does not meet the data validation rule.

To create a Lookup field

1   In the Table Design view window, click in the Data Type column for the field to which you want to assign the Lookup field, click the down arrow that appears, and then click Lookup Wizard.

2   In the first Lookup Wizard dialog box, click Next to draw the values for the Lookup field from an existing table or query.

3   In the next Lookup Wizard dialog box, select the table or query from which to draw the values, and click Next.

4   In the next Lookup Wizard dialog box, select the field to supply the values for the Lookup field, and click Next.

5   In the next Lookup Wizard dialog box, resize the column, if necessary, and click Next.

6   In the next Lookup Wizard dialog box, name the Lookup field, and click Finish.

To modify a Lookup field

●   Add new values to the field on which the list is based.

Or

Run the Lookup Wizard again.

Or

If the Lookup Wizard is still open, click the Back button until you reach the dialog box where you type the values in the list or choose the table or query from which to draw the values.

To create a relationship

Relationships

Show Table

1   On the Database toolbar, click the Relationships button.

2   On the Relationships toolbar, click the Show Table button, if necessary.

3   Add the tables that you want to use in the relationship to the Relation-ships window, and click Close.

4   Drag the field that you want to use to create the relationship from one field list to its location in the other field list.

5   In the Edit Relationships dialog box, click Create.

6   Save the Relationships window.

To enforce referential integrity in a relationship

Relationships

1   On the Database toolbar, click the Relationships button.

2   If the relationship already exists, double-click the relationship, select the Enforce Referential Integrity check box in the Edit Relationships dialog box, and click OK.

Or

If the relationship does not already exist, create the relationship, and select the Enforce Referential Integrity check box before you click Create in the Edit Relationships dialog box.

3   Save the Relationships window.

To set cascade options in a relationship

Relationships

1   On the Database toolbar, click the Relationships button.

2   If the relationship already exists, double-click the relationship, select the Enforce Referential Integrity check box in the Edit Relationships dialog box, select one or both of the Cascade Update Related Fields and Cascade Delete Related Records check boxes, and then click OK.

Or

If the relationship does not already exist, create the relationship, and select the Enforce Referential Integrity check box and one or both of the Cascade Update Related Fields and Cascade Delete Related Records check boxes before you click Create in the Edit Relationships dialog box.

3   Save the Relationships window.

Lesson 2: Creating Custom Queries

To specify criteria in multiple fields

1   Display the query in Design view.

2   Click in the Criteria row of the first field for which you want to set a criterion, and type the criterion.

3   Click in the Criteria row of the second field for which you want to set a criterion, and type the criterion (to find results for the first criterion *and* the second criterion).

Or

Click in the Or row of the second field for which you want to set a criterion, and type the criterion (to find results for the first criterion *or* the second criterion).

To modify query properties

1   Display the query in Design view.

2   Click in the column for the field that you want to change.

Properties

3   On the Query Design toolbar, click the Properties button.

4   In the Field Properties dialog box, change the query properties.

5   Close the Field Properties dialog box.

To apply a filter to a query

1   Display the query in Datasheet view.

Filter By Form

2   On the Query Datasheet toolbar, click the Filter By Form button.

3   Click in the field that you want to filter, click the down arrow that appears, and then click the item by which you want to filter.

Apply Filter

4   On the Query Datasheet toolbar, click the Apply Filter button.

Or

1   Display the query in Datasheet view.

Filter By Selection

2   Click in any cell in the query that contains the value that you want to use to filter, and click the Filter By Selection button.

To calculate totals in a query

1   Display the query in Design view.

Totals

2   On the Query Design toolbar, click the Totals button.

3   In the column for the field in which you want the aggregate function, click in the Total row, click the down arrow that appears, and then click the aggregate function that you want to use.

4   Run the query.

To specify criteria in a totals query

1   Display the query in Design view.

2   Click in the Criteria row for the field for which you want to set a criterion.

3   Type the criterion.

To create an action query

1   Display the query in Design view.

2   On the Query menu, click the type of action query that you want to create.

3   The steps that you follow vary depending on the type of query that you choose.

To create a parameter query

1   Display the query in Design view.

2   Click in the Criteria row for the field in which you want the user to enter a parameter.

3   Type the expression.

To create a crosstab query

1   Display the query in Design view.

2   On the Query menu, click Crosstab Query.

3   Click in the Crosstab row for the field that you want to use as a row heading, click the down arrow that appears, and then click Row Heading.

4 Click in the Crosstab row for the field that you want to use as a column heading, click the down arrow that appears, and then click Column Heading.

5 In the first empty cell in the Field row, type an expression for the calculation that you want to create.

6 Click in the Crosstab row for the field that you created in step 5, click the down arrow that appears, and then click Value.

To create a PivotTable

1 Display the list of forms in the Database Window, and click New on the Database Window toolbar.

2 In the New Form dialog box, click PivotTable Wizard, and click OK.

3 In the first PivotTable Wizard dialog box, click Next.

4 In the next PivotTable Wizard dialog box, click the Tables/Queries down arrow, and click the table that has the fields that you want to use in the PivotTable.

5 Add the fields to the Fields Chosen For Pivoting list, and click Next.

6 In the next PivotTable Wizard dialog box, click Layout.

7 Drag the fields to the appropriate areas of the Layout window, and click OK.

8 In the next PivotTable Wizard dialog box, click Finish.

To join tables to create a query

1 Display the query, which contains the tables that you want to join, in Design view.

2 Add the desired fields to the Field row.

3 On the View menu, click Join Properties.

4 Click the option that you want to use to display records when the query runs, and click OK.

To use other data formats

1 Display the table in Design view.

2 Click in the row for the field that you want to change.

3 In the Field Properties section, click in the Field Size box, click the down arrow that appears, and then select the data type that you want.

To create a many-to-many relationship

1 Create a junction table that contains the primary key fields from both of the tables that will be in the many-to-many relationship.

2 Open the Relationships window, and add the two tables and their junction table to the window.

3 Create a one-to-many relationship between the first table and the junction table by dragging the primary key field that they share from the table to the junction table.

4   In the Edit Relationships dialog box, select the Enforce Referential Integrity check box, and click Create.

5   Create a one-to-many relationship between the second table and the junction table by dragging the primary key field that they share from the table to the junction table.

6   In the Edit Relationships dialog box, select the Enforce Referential Integrity check box, and click Create.

7   Save and close the Relationships window.

Lesson 3: Customizing Forms

To create a form in Design view

1   Display the list of forms in the Database window, and click New on the Database window toolbar.

2   In the New Form dialog box, verify that Design View is selected.

3   Click the Choose the Table Or Query Where This Object's Data Comes From down arrow, click the table or query on which you want to base the form, and then click OK.

Toolbox

4   On the Form Design toolbar, click the Toolbox button, if necessary.

5   In the toolbox, verify that the Control Wizards tool is deslected, if necessary.

Control Wizards

6   Add bound controls to the form by dragging field names from the field list for the table or query that you selected to the form.

And/Or

Add unbound or calculated controls to the form by using the tools in the toolbox.

To add a list box to a form

1   Display the form to which you want to add the list box in Design view..

2   On the Form Design toolbar, click the Toolbox button, if necessary.

Toolbox

3   In the toolbox, verify that the Control Wizards tools is deslected, if necessary.

Control Wizards

4   In the toolbox, click the List Box tool, and click in the form where you want the list box to go.

List Box

To add a combo box to a form

1   Display the form to which you want to add the combo box in Design view.

Toolbox

2   On the Form Design toolbar, click the Toolbox button, if necessary.

3   In the toolbox, verify that the Control Wizards tool is deselected, if necessary.

Control Wizards

4   In the toolbox, click the Combo Box tool, and click in the form where you want the combo box to appear.

Combo Box

To define the list of values for a list box or combo box control

1 Double-click the edge of the control.

2 In the property sheet for the control, click the Data tab.

3 In the Row Source box, type the values for the list, separated by semicolons.

Or

Set the Control Source property to the field to which you want the list values to be related, set the Row Source Type property to Table/Query, and then set the Row Source property to the table or query from which you want to pull the values.

4 Close the property sheet.

To add sections to a form

1 Display the form in Design view.

2 On the View menu, click Page Header/Footer or Form Header/Footer.

To open the property sheet for a form section

● Double-click the section bar.

Or

Double-click any blank area in the form section.

Or

Double-click the section selector.

To insert a graphic in a form

1 Display the form in Design view.

2 On the Insert menu, click Picture.

3 Navigate to the directory containing the graphic that you want to add.

4 Click the file name, and click OK.

To modify control properties

1 Display the form in Design view.

2 Double-click the edge of the control that you want to change.

3 In the property sheet for the control, click the tab that contains the property that you want to change.

4 Click in the box for the property that you want to change.

5 Click the down arrow that appears, and click the new setting.

Or

Type the new setting.

6 Close the property sheet.

To modify form properties

1   Display the form in Design view.

2   Double-click the form selector.

3   In the property sheet, click the tab for the property that you want to change.

4   Click in the box for the property that you want to change.

5   Click the down arrow that appears, and click the new setting.

Or

Type the new setting.

6   Close the property sheet.

To create a subform

Relationships

1   On the Database toolbar, click the Relationships button.

2   Verify that the tables underlying the main form and subform are in a one-to-many relationship, and close the Relationships window.

3   Display the main form in Design view.

Toolbox

4   On the Form Design toolbar, click the Toolbox button, if necessary.

5   In the toolbox, click the Subform/Subreport tool, and click in the form where you want the subform to go.

Subform/Subreport

6   Double-click the edge of the subform.

7   In the Subform/Subreport property sheet, click the Data tab, if necessary.

8   Click in the Source Object box, click the down arrow that appears, and then click the name of the table on the *many* side of the one-to-many relationship.

9   Close the Subform/Subreport property sheet.

To synchronize form data

Relationships

1   On the Database toolbar, click the Relationships button.

2   On the Relationship toolbar, click the Show Table button, and add the tables between which you want to create a relationship, if necessary.

Show Table

3   Drag the primary key field from the table on the *one* side of the relationship to the identical field in the table on the *many* side of the relationship.

4   In the Edit Relationships dialog box, select the Enforce Referential Integrity check box, and click Create.

5   Save and close the Relationships window.

To create a switchboard

1   On the Tools menu, point to Database Utilities, and click Switchboard Manager.

2   Click Yes to create a new switchboard.

3   To add a new page to the switchboard, click New in the Switchboard Manager, type the name of the new switchboard page in the Create New dialog box, and then click OK.

4   To edit an existing page in the switchboard, click the page that you
     want to edit in the Switchboard Manager, and click Edit.

5   In the Edit Switchboard Page dialog box, click New.

6   In the Edit Switchboard Item dialog box, type the name of the new
     button in the Text box.

7   In the Edit Switchboard Item dialog box, click the Command down
     arrow, and select the action that the button will perform.

8   In the Edit Switchboard Item dialog box, click the last down arrow (the
     name of the box varies depending on the action that you chose in the
     previous step), and click the database object on which the action will
     be performed.

9   In the Edit Switchboard Item dialog box, click OK.

10   Close the Edit Switchboard Page dialog box and the Switchboard
     Manager dialog box.

Lesson 4: Customizing Reports

To create a report in Design view

1   Display the list of reports in the Database window, and click New on
     the Database window toolbar.

2   In the New Report dialog box, verify that Design View is selected.

3   Click the Choose The Table Or Query Where The Object's Data
     Comes From down arrow, and click the table or query that you want to
     use as the basis for the report.

4   Click OK.

5   Add bound controls to the report by dragging the fields that you want
     to add from the field list for the table or query that you selected.

     Or

     Add unbound or calculated controls to the report by using the tools in
     the toolbox.

To add sections to a report

1   Display the report in Design view.

2   On the View menu, click Report Header/Footer.

     Or

     On the View menu, click Page Header/Footer.

To adjust the size of a section

1   Move the mouse pointer over the bottom edge of the section until the
     pointer turns into a resizing double-headed arrow.

2   Drag the edge of the section up or down to change the size of the
     section.

To sort and group data in a report

Sorting And Grouping

1   On the Report Design toolbar, click the Sorting And Grouping button.

2   In the Sorting And Grouping dialog box, click in the first blank cell in the Field/Expression column, click the down arrow that appears, and then click the field by which you want to sort the data in the report. Repeat for additional grouping levels.

3   To change the order of the data in the groups, click in the Sort Order column for the group that you want to organize, click the down arrow that appears, and then click Ascending or Descending.

To add group header and footer sections

1   Sort and group the data in the report.

2   Click in the row for the group to which you want to add a group header or footer.

3   In the Group Properties section, click in the Group Header box, click the down arrow that appears, and then click Yes.

And/Or

In the Group Properties section, click in the Group Footer box, click the down arrow that appears, and then click Yes.

To modify report properties

1   Display the report in Design view.

2   Double-click the report selector.

3   In the property sheet, click the desired tab.

4   Click in the box for the desired property.

5   Type the new value for the property.

Or

Click the down arrow that appears, and click the new value for the property.

6   Close the property sheet.

To add report controls

1   Display the report in Design view.

Toolbox

2   On the Report Design toolbar, click the Toolbox button, if necessary.

3   In the toolbox, click the tool for the type of control that you want to add.

4   Click in the report where you want the control to go.

To modify report controls

1   Double-click the edge of the control.

2   In the property sheet, click the desired tab.

3   Click in the box for the desired property.

4 Type the new value for the property.

Or

Click the down arrow that appears, and click the new value for the property.

5 Close the property sheet.

To create a subreport

1 Display the report that you want to use as the main report in Design view.

Toolbox

2 On the Report Design toolbar, click the Toolbox button, if necessary.

3 In the toolbox, click the Subform/Subreport tool, and click in the report where you want the subreport to go.

Subform/Subreport

4 Double-click the edge of the subreport.

5 In the Subform/Subreport property sheet, click the Data tab, if necessary.

6 Click in the Source Object box, click the down arrow that appears, and then click the name of the report that you want to use as the subreport.

7 Close the Subform/Subreport property sheet.

To synchronize report data

Relationships

1 On the Database toolbar, click the Relationships button.

2 On the Relationship toolbar, click the Show Table button, and add the tables between which you want to create a relationship, if necessary.

Show Table

3 Drag the primary key field from the table on the *one* side of the relationship to the identical field in the table on the *many* side of the relationship.

4 In the Edit Relationships dialog box, select the Enforce Referential Integrity check box, and click Create.

5 Save and close the Relationships window.

Lesson 5: Using Databases on the Internet

To create a hyperlink to a Web page

1 Open the object where you want the hyperlink in Design view.

2 Click in the field where you want the hyperlink.

3 On the Insert menu, click Hyperlink.

4 In the Link To box, click Existing File Or Web Page icon.

5 In the Text To Display box, enter the text that you want displayed in the hyperlink.

6 In the Type The File Or Web Page Name box, enter the Web address for the Web page.

7 Click OK.

To create a hyperlink to another object within the current database

1   Open the object where you want the hyperlink in Design view.

2   Click in the field where you want the hyperlink.

3   On the Insert menu, click Hyperlink.

4   In the Link To box, click the Object In This Database icon.

5   Navigate to the object to which you want to make a hyperlink.

6   Click OK.

To export an object to HTML

1   In the Database window, click the name of the object that you want to export.

2   On the File menu, click Export.

3   Click the Save In down arrow, and navigate to the location where you want to export the folder.

4   Click the Save As Type down arrow, and click HTML Documents (*.html; *htm).

5   Click OK.

To create a data access page using AutoPage

1   Display the list of pages in the Database window, and click New on the Database window toolbar.

2   In the New Data Access Page dialog box, click AutoPage: Columnar.

3   Click the Choose The Table Or Query Where The Object's Data Comes From down arrow, click the table or query that you want to use as the source for the data access page, and then click OK.

To create a data access page using the Page Wizard

1   Display the list of pages in the Database window.

2   Double-click Create Data Access Page By Using The Wizard.

3   In the first Page Wizard dialog box, click the Tables/Queries down arrow, and click the table or query that you want to use as the source for the data access page.

4   In the Available Fields list, click the field that you want to include on the page, and click the > (Add) button.

5   Repeat step 4 for all the fields that you want to include on the data access page, and click Next.

6   In the next Page Wizard dialog box, click the fields to use as grouping levels, use the Priority buttons to assign the fields levels, and then click Next.

7   In the next Page Wizard dialog box, click the down arrow in the first sorting box, click the field that you want to use to sort the records in the page, click the Sort Order button to choose ascending or descending order, and then click Next.

8   In the next Page Wizard dialog box, type a name for the page in the What Title Do You Want For Your Page? box, and click Finish.

To create a data access page in Design view

1   Display the list of pages in the Database window.

2   Double-click Create Data Access Page In Design View.

Field List

3   On the Page Design toolbar, click the Field List button to display the tables and queries in the database, select the table or query from which you want to add fields to the data access page, and then drag the fields to the page.

And/Or

Toolbox

On the Page Design toolbar, click the Toolbox button, and use the tools in the toolbox to add unbound controls to the data access page.

To change the grouping levels for a data access page

1   Display the page in Design view.

Promote

2   To demote a grouping level, click the Demote button on the Page Design toolbar.

Or

Demote

To promote a grouping level, click the box for the field that you want to add as a grouping level, and click the Promote button on the Page Design toolbar.

To change the sort order for the data in a data access page

Sorting And Grouping

1   On the Page Design toolbar, click the Sorting and Grouping button.

2   In the Sorting And Grouping dialog box, click in the row for the field that you want to change.

3   In the Group Properties section, click in the Default Sort box, and type the new sort criterion.

4   Close the Sorting And Grouping dialog box.

Lesson 6: Automating Tasks

To create an AutoKeys macro

1   Display the list of macros in the Database window, and click New on the Database window toolbar.

Macro Names

2   On the Macro Design toolbar, click the Macro Names button.

3   In the Macro Names column, type the key combination that you want to use for the macro, and press Tab.

4   In the Action column, click the down arrow that appears, and select the action that you want the macro to perform.

5   In the Action Arguments section, set the arguments for the action that you have chosen, if necessary.

6   Save the macro as AutoKeys.

To use a control to run a macro

1   Open the form or report to which you want to add a control in Design view.

2   Display the toolbox, if necessary.

Control Wizards

3   In the toolbox, select the Control Wizards tool.

4   In the toolbox, click the Command tool.

Command

5   Click the place on the form where you want the command button to appear.

6   In the first Command Button Wizard dialog box, click Miscellaneous in the Categories section, click Run Macro in the Actions section, and then click Next.

7   In the next Command Button Wizard dialog box, click the macro that you want to assign to the command button, and click Next.

8   In the next Command Button Wizard dialog box, create text for the button, select a graphic for the button face or create your own graphic, and then click Next.

9   In the next Command Button Wizard dialog box, type a name for the command button, and click Finish.

To assign a macro to an event

1   Open the form to which you want to assign the event macro in Design view.

2   Double-click the form selector, and click the Event tab in the Form property sheet.

3   Click in the box for the event that you want to use, click the down arrow that appears, and then click the macro to which you want to apply the event.

4   Close the Form property sheet, and save the form.

To assign a macro to a condition

1   Open the macro in Design view.

Conditions

2   On the Macro Design toolbar, click the Conditions button.

3   Click the Condition cell next to the action that you want to make conditional, and type the condition.

4   Close the macro.

5   Open the form or report in Design view.

6   Double-click the form or report selector, and click the Event tab.

7   Click in the box next to the action that you want to use, click the down arrow that appears, and then click the macro to which you want to attach the action.

8   Close the Form or Report property sheet, and save the form or report.

To test and debug a macro

Single Step

1   Open the macro in Design view.

2   On the Macro Design toolbar, click the Single Step button.

3   On the Macro Design toolbar, click the Run button.

4   In the Macro Single Step dialog box, click Step.

5   Examine the information in the Macro Single Step dialog box to locate potential errors.

Run

6   Repeat steps 4 and 5 until you find the error.

Or

Click Halt to stop the macro, and fix the error.

Or

Click Continue to run the entire macro without pausing at each step.

Lesson 7: Using Database Tools

To open a database in Exclusive mode

Open

1   With Access open, click the Open button on the Database toolbar.

2   In the Open dialog box, navigate to the location of the database that you want to open.

3   Click the Open down arrow, and click Open Exclusive.

To set a database password

1   Open the database in Exclusive mode.

2   On the Tools menu, point to Security, and click Set Database Password.

3   In the Password box, type the password, and press Tab.

4   In the Verify box, type the password, and click OK.

To delete a database password

1   Open the database in Exclusive mode.

2   On the Tools menu, point to Security, and click Unset Database Password.

3   In the Password box, type the password, and click OK.

To encrypt a database

1   On the Tools menu, point to Security, and click Encrypt/Decrypt Database.

2   In the Encrypt/Decrypt dialog box, navigate to the location of the database you want to encrypt, click the database, and then click OK.

3   In the Encrypt Database As dialog box, type the name for the encrypted database in the File Name box, and click Save.

To decrypt a database

1   On the Tools menu, point to Security, and click Encrypt/Decrypt Database.

2   In the Encrypt/Decrypt dialog box, navigate to the location of the database that you want to decrypt, click the database, and then click OK.

3   In the Decrypt Database As dialog box, type the name for the decrypted file in the File Name box, and click Save.

To replicate a database

1   Open the database that you want to replicate.

2   On the Tools menu, point to Replication, and click Create Replica.

3   Click Yes to close the database.

4   Click Yes to create a backup copy of the database.

5   In the Location Of New Replica dialog box, navigate to the location where you want to store the replica, and click OK.

To synchronize a Design Master and replica

1   Open the Design Master database.

2   On the Tools menu, point to Replication, and click Synchronize Now.

3   In the Synchronize Replica dialog box, select the replica in the Directly With Replica box, and click OK.

4   Click Yes to close the database.

To split a database

1   Open the database that you want to split.

2   On the Tools menu, point to Database Utilities, and click Database Splitter.

3   In the Database Splitter Wizard dialog box, click Split Database.

4   In the Create Back-End Database dialog box, navigate to the location where you want to store the back-end file, and click Split.

5   In the message box that appears, click OK.

To convert a database to the Access 97 file format

1   In Access 2000, open the database that you want to convert.

2   On the Tools menu, point to Database Utilities, point to Convert Database, and then click To Prior Access Database Version.

3   In the Convert Database Into dialog box, type a name for the new database in the File Name box, and click Save.

To set startup options

1   Open the database that you want to modify.

2   On the Tools menu, click Startup.

3   In the Startup dialog box, use the boxes and check boxes to set the desired options, and click OK.

Lesson 8: Integrating Access with Other Office Applications

To create a graph

1   Display the list of forms in the Database window, and click New on the Database window toolbar.

2   In the New Form dialog box, click Chart Wizard,

3   In the New Form dialog box, click the Choose the Table Or Query Where The Object's Data Comes From down arrow, click the table or query that you want to use as the basis for the chart, and then click OK.

4   In the first Chart Wizard dialog box, add the fields that you want to use to the Fields For Chart list, and click Next.

5   In the next Chart Wizard dialog box, click the button for the type of chart that you want to create, and click Next.

6   In the next Chart Wizard dialog box, configure the fields on the chart, and click Next.

7   In the last Chart Wizard dialog box, type the title of the chart in the What Title Would You Like For Your Chart? box, select whether the chart will have a legend, select whether the chart will display in Form or Design view, and then click Finish.

To modify a graph

1   Display the form containing the chart in Design view, and click the chart.

2   On the Edit menu, point to Chart Object, and click Edit.

3   Use Microsoft Graph to modify the chart.

To export data to Excel

1   In the Database window, click the table or query that you want to export.

2   On the File menu, click Export.

3   In the Export Query dialog box, navigate to the directory where you want to save the exported file.

4   In the File Name, type a name for the exported file.

5   Click the Save As Type down arrow, click Microsoft Excel 97-2000 (*.xls), and then click Save.

To drag tables and queries to an Excel workbook

1   In Access, open the database that contains the data that you want to move to Excel.

2   Start Excel, and click the New button on the Standard toolbar.

New

3   Right-click the Windows taskbar, and click Tile Windows Horizontally.

4   Drag the table or query that you want to move from Access to the cell in the Excel worksheet where you want the new data to start.

To copy and paste records into Excel from Access

1   In Access, open the table or query that contains the records that you want to copy.

2   In Excel, open the worksheet where you want the records to go.

3   In Access, select the records that you want to move.

Copy

4   In Access, click the Copy button on the Table Datasheet toolbar.

5   In Excel, click in the cell where you want the records to start.

6   In Excel, click the Paste button on the Standard toolbar.

Paste

To create a link

1   Open the Access database where you want to put the link.

2   On the File menu, point to Get External Data, and click Link Tables.

3   In the Link dialog box, click the Files Of Type down arrow, and click the type of application used to create the other database, if necessary.

4   Navigate to the folder where the other database is stored, click the file, and then click Link.

5   In the Link Tables dialog box, click the table to which you want to link, and click OK.

Index

Special Characters

A

ActiveEducation and Microsoft Press

Microsoft Access 2000 Step by Step Courseware has been created by the professional trainers and writers at ActiveEducation, Inc., to the exacting standards you've come to expect from Microsoft Press. Together, we are pleased to present this training guide.

ActiveEducation creates top-quality information technology training content that teaches essential computer skills for today's workplace. ActiveEducation courses are designed to provide the most effective training available and to help people become more productive computer users. Each ActiveEducation course, including this book, undergoes rigorous quality control, instructional design, and technical review procedures to ensure that the course is instructionally and technically superior in content and approach.

ActiveEducation (*www.activeeducation.com*) courses are available in book form and on the Internet.

Microsoft Press is the book publishing division of Microsoft Corporation, the leading publisher of information about Microsoft products and services. Microsoft Press is dedicated to providing the highest quality computer books and multimedia training and reference tools that make using Microsoft software easier, more enjoyable, and more productive.

About the Author

Curtis Frye is a freelance writer from Portland, Oregon. He is the author of three online courses (two on Microsoft Excel 2000 and one on advanced database design techniques) and *Master Access 2000 Visually* (IDG/Maran). He was also a major contributor to Deborah and Eric Ray's *Microsoft Access 2000 for Windows: Visual QuickStart* (PeachPit Press).

His academic and policy writing ventures include sole authorship of *Privacy-Enhanced Marketing* (Quorum Books), lead authorship of *The State of Web Commerce* (a 1997 market research report from O'Reilly & Associates), a chapter on Internet commerce in Osborne's *Internet: The Complete Reference, Millennium Edition*, and writing "Regulated Privacy," an article on cryptography policy in the premier issue of *Infobahn* magazine.

Frye is the editor and lead reviewer for *Technology & Society Book Reviews* (*www.techsoc.com*). He is also a member of the Society of Competitive Intelligence Professionals and the Electronic Commerce SIG for the Association for Computing Machinery.

MICROSOFT LICENSE AGREEMENT
Book Companion CD

IMPORTANT—READ CAREFULLY: This Microsoft End-User License Agreement ("EULA") is a legal agreement between you (either an individual or an entity) and Microsoft Corporation for the Microsoft product identified above, which includes computer software and may include associated media, printed materials, and "online" or electronic documentation ("SOFTWARE PRODUCT"). Any component included within the SOFTWARE PRODUCT that is accompanied by a separate End-User License Agreement shall be governed by such agreement and not the terms set forth below. By installing, copying, or otherwise using the SOFTWARE PRODUCT, you agree to be bound by the terms of this EULA. If you do not agree to the terms of this EULA, you are not authorized to install, copy, or otherwise use the SOFTWARE PRODUCT; you may, however, return the SOFTWARE PRODUCT, along with all printed materials and other items that form a part of the Microsoft product that includes the SOFTWARE PRODUCT, to the place you obtained them for a full refund.

SOFTWARE PRODUCT LICENSE

The SOFTWARE PRODUCT is protected by United States copyright laws and international copyright treaties, as well as other intellectual property laws and treaties. The SOFTWARE PRODUCT is licensed, not sold.

1. **GRANT OF LICENSE.** This EULA grants you the following rights:

   a. **Software Product.** You may install and use one copy of the SOFTWARE PRODUCT on a single computer. The primary user of the computer on which the SOFTWARE PRODUCT is installed may make a second copy for his or her exclusive use on a portable computer.

   b. **Storage/Network Use.** You may also store or install a copy of the SOFTWARE PRODUCT on a storage device, such as a network server, used only to install or run the SOFTWARE PRODUCT on your other computers over an internal network; however, you must acquire and dedicate a license for each separate computer on which the SOFTWARE PRODUCT is installed or run from the storage device. A license for the SOFTWARE PRODUCT may not be shared or used concurrently on different computers.

   c. **License Pak.** If you have acquired this EULA in a Microsoft License Pak, you may make the number of additional copies of the computer software portion of the SOFTWARE PRODUCT authorized on the printed copy of this EULA, and you may use each copy in the manner specified above. You are also entitled to make a corresponding number of secondary copies for portable computer use as specified above.

   d. **Sample Code.** Solely with respect to portions, if any, of the SOFTWARE PRODUCT that are identified within the SOFTWARE PRODUCT as sample code (the "SAMPLE CODE"):

      i. **Use and Modification.** Microsoft grants you the right to use and modify the source code version of the SAMPLE CODE, *provided* you comply with subsection (d)(iii) below. You may not distribute the SAMPLE CODE, or any modified version of the SAMPLE CODE, in source code form.

      ii. **Redistributable Files.** Provided you comply with subsection (d)(iii) below, Microsoft grants you a nonexclusive, royalty-free right to reproduce and distribute the object code version of the SAMPLE CODE and of any modified SAMPLE CODE, other than SAMPLE CODE, or any modified version thereof, designated as not redistributable in the Readme file that forms a part of the SOFTWARE PRODUCT (the "Non-Redistributable Sample Code"). All SAMPLE CODE other than the Non-Redistributable Sample Code is collectively referred to as the "REDISTRIBUTABLES."

      iii. **Redistribution Requirements.** If you redistribute the REDISTRIBUTABLES, you agree to: (i) distribute the REDISTRIBUTABLES in object code form only in conjunction with and as a part of your software application product; (ii) not use Microsoft's name, logo, or trademarks to market your software application product; (iii) include a valid copyright notice on your software application product; (iv) indemnify, hold harmless, and defend Microsoft from and against any claims or lawsuits, including attorney's fees, that arise or result from the use or distribution of your software application product; and (v) not permit further distribution of the REDISTRIBUTABLES by your end user. Contact Microsoft for the applicable royalties due and other licensing terms for all other uses and/or distribution of the REDISTRIBUTABLES.

2. **DESCRIPTION OF OTHER RIGHTS AND LIMITATIONS.**

   - **Limitations on Reverse Engineering, Decompilation, and Disassembly.** You may not reverse engineer, decompile, or disassemble the SOFTWARE PRODUCT, except and only to the extent that such activity is expressly permitted by applicable law notwithstanding this limitation.

   - **Separation of Components.** The SOFTWARE PRODUCT is licensed as a single product. Its component parts may not be separated for use on more than one computer.

   - **Rental.** You may not rent, lease, or lend the SOFTWARE PRODUCT.

   - **Support Services.** Microsoft may, but is not obligated to, provide you with support services related to the SOFTWARE PRODUCT ("Support Services"). Use of Support Services is governed by the Microsoft policies and programs described in the user manual, in "online" documentation, and/or in other Microsoft-provided materials. Any supplemental software code provided to you as part of the Support Services shall be considered part of the SOFTWARE PRODUCT and subject to the terms and conditions of this EULA. With respect to technical information you provide to Microsoft as part of the Support Services, Microsoft may use such information for its business purposes, including for product support and development. Microsoft will not utilize such technical information in a form that personally identifies you.

   - **Software Transfer.** You may permanently transfer all of your rights under this EULA, provided you retain no copies, you transfer all of the SOFTWARE PRODUCT (including all component parts, the media and printed materials, any upgrades, this EULA, and, if applicable, the Certificate of Authenticity), **and** the recipient agrees to the terms of this EULA.

   - **Termination.** Without prejudice to any other rights, Microsoft may terminate this EULA if you fail to comply with the terms and conditions of this EULA. In such event, you must destroy all copies of the SOFTWARE PRODUCT and all of its component parts.

3. **COPYRIGHT.** All title and copyrights in and to the SOFTWARE PRODUCT (including but not limited to any images, photographs, animations, video, audio, music, text, SAMPLE CODE, REDISTRIBUTABLES, and "applets" incorporated into the SOFTWARE PRODUCT) and any copies of the SOFTWARE PRODUCT are owned by Microsoft or its suppliers. The SOFTWARE PRODUCT is protected by copyright laws and international treaty provisions. Therefore, you must treat the SOFTWARE PRODUCT like any other copyrighted material **except** that you may install the SOFTWARE PRODUCT on a single computer provided you keep the original solely for backup or archival purposes. You may not copy the printed materials accompanying the SOFTWARE PRODUCT.

4. **U.S. GOVERNMENT RESTRICTED RIGHTS.** The SOFTWARE PRODUCT and documentation are provided with RESTRICTED RIGHTS. Use, duplication, or disclosure by the Government is subject to restrictions as set forth in subparagraph (c)(1)(ii) of the Rights in Technical Data and Computer Software clause at DFARS 252.227-7013 or subparagraphs (c)(1) and (2) of the Commercial Computer Software—Restricted Rights at 48 CFR 52.227-19, as applicable. Manufacturer is Microsoft Corporation/One Microsoft Way/Redmond, WA 98052-6399.

5. **EXPORT RESTRICTIONS.** You agree that you will not export or re-export the SOFTWARE PRODUCT, any part thereof, or any process or service that is the direct product of the SOFTWARE PRODUCT (the foregoing collectively referred to as the "Restricted Components"), to any country, person, entity, or end user subject to U.S. export restrictions. You specifically agree not to export or re-export any of the Restricted Components (i) to any country to which the U.S. has embargoed or restricted the export of goods or services, which currently include, but are not necessarily limited to, Cuba, Iran, Iraq, Libya, North Korea, Sudan, and Syria, or to any national of any such country, wherever located, who intends to transmit or transport the Restricted Components back to such country; (ii) to any end user who you know or have reason to know will utilize the Restricted Components in the design, development, or production of nuclear, chemical, or biological weapons; or (iii) to any end user who has been prohibited from participating in U.S. export transactions by any federal agency of the U.S. government. You warrant and represent that neither the BXA nor any other U.S. federal agency has suspended, revoked, or denied your export privileges.

DISCLAIMER OF WARRANTY

NO WARRANTIES OR CONDITIONS. MICROSOFT EXPRESSLY DISCLAIMS ANY WARRANTY OR CONDITION FOR THE SOFT-WARE PRODUCT. THE SOFTWARE PRODUCT AND ANY RELATED DOCUMENTATION ARE PROVIDED "AS IS" WITHOUT WARRANTY OR CONDITION OF ANY KIND, EITHER EXPRESS OR IMPLIED, INCLUDING, WITHOUT LIMITATION, THE IMPLIED WARRANTIES OF MERCHANTABILITY, FITNESS FOR A PARTICULAR PURPOSE, OR NONINFRINGEMENT. THE ENTIRE RISK ARISING OUT OF USE OR PERFORMANCE OF THE SOFTWARE PRODUCT REMAINS WITH YOU.

LIMITATION OF LIABILITY. TO THE MAXIMUM EXTENT PERMITTED BY APPLICABLE LAW, IN NO EVENT SHALL MICROSOFT OR ITS SUPPLIERS BE LIABLE FOR ANY SPECIAL, INCIDENTAL, INDIRECT, OR CONSEQUENTIAL DAMAGES WHATSOEVER (INCLUDING, WITHOUT LIMITATION, DAMAGES FOR LOSS OF BUSINESS PROFITS, BUSINESS INTERRUPTION, LOSS OF BUSINESS INFORMATION, OR ANY OTHER PECUNIARY LOSS) ARISING OUT OF THE USE OF OR INABILITY TO USE THE SOFTWARE PRODUCT OR THE PROVISION OF OR FAILURE TO PROVIDE SUPPORT SERVICES, EVEN IF MICROSOFT HAS BEEN ADVISED OF THE POSSIBILITY OF SUCH DAMAGES. IN ANY CASE, MICROSOFT'S ENTIRE LIABILITY UNDER ANY PROVISION OF THIS EULA SHALL BE LIMITED TO THE GREATER OF THE AMOUNT ACTUALLY PAID BY YOU FOR THE SOFTWARE PRODUCT OR US$5.00; PROVIDED, HOWEVER, IF YOU HAVE ENTERED INTO A MICROSOFT SUPPORT SERVICES AGREEMENT, MICROSOFT'S ENTIRE LIABILITY REGARDING SUPPORT SERVICES SHALL BE GOVERNED BY THE TERMS OF THAT AGREE-MENT. BECAUSE SOME STATES AND JURISDICTIONS DO NOT ALLOW THE EXCLUSION OR LIMITATION OF LIABILITY, THE ABOVE LIMITATION MAY NOT APPLY TO YOU.

MISCELLANEOUS

This EULA is governed by the laws of the State of Washington USA, except and only to the extent that applicable law mandates governing law of a different jurisdiction.

Should you have any questions concerning this EULA, or if you desire to contact Microsoft for any reason, please contact the Microsoft subsidiary serving your country, or write: Microsoft Sales Information Center/One Microsoft Way/Redmond, WA 98052-6399.

OWNER REGISTRATION CARD   *Register Today!*   0-7356-0707-9

Return the bottom portion of this card to register today.

Microsoft® Access 2000 Step by Step Courseware Expert Skills Student Guide

---

FIRST NAME   MIDDLE INITIAL   LAST NAME

INSTITUTION OR COMPANY NAME

ADDRESS

CITY   STATE   ZIP

( )

E-MAIL ADDRESS   PHONE NUMBER

U.S. and Canada addresses only. Fill in information above and mail postage-free.
Please mail only the bottom half of this page.

For information about Microsoft Press® products, visit our Web site at **mspress.microsoft.com**